This new examination of the First World War pulls together often untold stories and includes famous names such as Sir Douglas Haig, John Buchan and Lord Kinnaird, known as football's first superstar. These three were all linked with Scottish organisations in London which had to rise to the challenge of the war. Churches and clubs which looked after Scots who had moved south to work in the capital played an important role on the Home Front. The book, drawing on unpublished articles at the time, describes how St Columba's Church of Scotland in Knightsbridge fed and entertained nearly 50,000 Scottish troops heading home on leave or returning to the trenches. This immense effort was largely driven by women in the congregation. Moving letters from grateful families are quoted. John Buchan was an elder of the church, so too Sir Douglas Haig after the war. The other Scottish Kirk in London, Crown Court numbered Lord Kinnaird among its elders – he lost two sons during the conflict.

Rugby players from London Scottish were quick to join up. Three quarters of the 60 who turned out for the club in the last matches before the war never returned. There was a heavy toll amongst Scots in London who were members of the Caledonian Club. The Club's substantial art collection immortalises its connection to the Great War, some of which is reproduced in the book. Many members and associates of Scottish churches and clubs were quick to join the London Scottish Regiment on the outbreak of war. They became the first Territorials to see action after being rushed to the frontline close to Ypres in October 1914. The Scots Guards, too, had longstanding links with the capital. Scottish exiles in Canada joining their local regiments were pleased to remember their roots and traditions as they moved through wartime London.

Charities founded by Scottish benefactors in London, which have since evolved into ScotsCare and the Royal Caledonian Education Trust, supported the troops and families and their role is covered.

One hundred years on from the final year of conflict this book examines the close links between these organisations and their shared hopes, fears and tragic losses. Scotland's casualties in the First World War were disproportionately higher than those from other parts of the UK. The book reflects on the London through which so many Scottish soldiers would have passed on their way to and from the horrors of war.

Paul McFarland has a personal interest in First World War history: one grandfather served on the Western Front with the Canadian Army, the other was a Canadian padre awarded an MC. In 1912 the poet John McCrae proposed to his grandmother. Paul is secretary at his rugby club, London Scottish FC, where he has served in various capacities on Board and Committee since 1996. He graduated MA in History from Edinburgh University in 1976 and trained and worked as a journalist and then spent 12 years in the then very new electronic media industry, while freelancing as a weekend sports reporter for the national press, BBC and commercial radio. In 1990, Paul became marketing director at the Press Association, and later managing director of its main commercial subsidiary, before striking out on his own. From 1997, he was a consultant and then investor in the new media sector, before selling a sports web business to ESPN and focusing on his current enterprise, a specialist sports team wear provider he started in 2001. When not watching sport or reading history he goes to the theatre and concerts with his theatrical/musical family. He previously edited *Zelia Raye and the Development of Modern Theatre Dance* (London 2002). He is married with two grown-up sons.

Scots in Great War London

A Community at Home and on the Front Line 1914–1919

Edited by Paul McFarland
with Hugh Pym

 Helion & Company Limited

Helion & Company Limited
Unit 8 Amherst Business Centre
Budbrooke Road
Warwick
CV34 5WE
England
Tel. 01926 499 619
Fax 0121 711 4075
Email: info@helion.co.uk
Website: www.helion.co.uk
Twitter: @helionbooks
Visit our blog http://blog.helion.co.uk/

Published by Helion & Company 2018
Designed and typeset by Mach 3 Solutions Ltd (www.mach3solutions.co.uk)
Cover designed by Paul Hewitt, Battlefield Design (www.battlefield-design.co.uk)
Printed by Gutenberg Press Limited, Tarxien, Malta

Text © individual contributors 2018
Images © as individually credited

Front cover: Photograph of the women who led the hospitality effort at St Columba's Church of Scotland in Knightsbridge. (Courtesy of St Columba's); Painting of the London Scottish Regiment boarding a London Omnibus outside the Cloth Hall in Ypres: painted in 1936 by George Duncan Macdougald 1880-1945 from an original photo, commissioned and presented to the Regiment by Lieutenant Colonel James Patterson MC. Fife-born sculptor Macdougald had enlisted in the London Scottish Regiment in November 1914, a few days after the scene he depicts here. (London Scottish Regiment). Rear cover: The Return to the Front: Victoria Railway Station - Richard Jack (1866–1952). British-born, Jack became Canada's official war artist, and would have known first-hand London's main departure point for the Western Front. (York Museums Trust (York Art Gallery), UK / Bridgeman Images)

Every reasonable effort has been made to trace copyright holders and to obtain their permission for the use of copyright material. The authors and publisher apologise for any errors or omissions in this work, and would be grateful if notified of any corrections that should be incorporated in future reprints or editions of this book.

ISBN 978-1-912390-78-6

British Library Cataloguing-in-Publication Data.
A catalogue record for this book is available from the British Library.

For details of other military history titles published by Helion & Company Limited contact the above address, or visit our website: http://www.helion.co.uk.

We always welcome receiving book proposals from prospective authors.

Contents

List of Contributors

David Coughtrie, chartered architect, educated at Ayr Academy and Strathclyde University, with an international career in public transport and urban integration, is vice-president and former chairman of The Caledonian Club.

Hugh Cowan is a retired Royal Engineers officer and a past president and former honorary historian of The Caledonian Society of London.

Jim Henderson, retired lecturer in statistics, was educated at Perth Academy and universities of St Andrews and London, and is honorary life president of The Burns Club of London.

Paul McFarland read history at Edinburgh University. A former journalist who now owns his own business, he is London Scottish FC's honorary secretary. This is his second book as editor.

Reverend Angus MacLeod is the Minister of St Columba's, Pont Street, London, and a former Army chaplain. His great-grandfather was minister of both Crown Court and St Columba's pre-1914.

Randall Nicol read history at Cambridge, spent 10 years in the Scots Guards, and is the author of *Till the Trumpet Sounds Again: The Scots Guards 1914–19 In Their Own Words*.

Malcolm Noble, educated at Peebles High School and the University of London, was a London secondary school headmaster for 19 years and is now chairman of the Royal Caledonian Education Trust.

Andrew D. Parsons studied military history in Newfoundland and London. He is a piper and reservist with the London Scottish, and is the curator and archivist at the Regimental Museum.

Hugh Pym is Health Editor, BBC News, formerly chief economics correspondent and author of books on banking and politics. An Oxford graduate, he is an elder at St Columba's.

Canon Professor Michael Snape is Durham University's inaugural Michael Ramsey Professor of Anglican Studies. He is an ecumenical lay canon of Durham Cathedral, and official historian of the Royal Army Chaplains' Department.

Sheena Tait, a former civil servant, is now a professional genealogist with a master's degree in local and family history. She is an elder and trustee at Crown Court Church.

Justine Taylor, with degrees from St Andrews and University College London, is archivist for two London institutions, consultant to ScotsCare and the Scots Guards, and has published several history books.

Foreword by HRH The Princess Royal

BUCKINGHAM PALACE

I was delighted to accept the invitation to be Patron of the Scots in Great War London Group. The Group comprises the leading Scottish organisations based in London and is co-ordinating a series of events in 2018 to commemorate the centenary of the end of World War I.

The role that all these organisations played in the Great War is a story that needs to be told, and this book does exactly that. Their members made important contributions to Britain's war effort. Tens, perhaps hundreds, of thousands of Scots came through London during 1914–19 on their way to and from the Front, and were fed, watered, housed, counselled and succoured by their exiled countrymen in London, more often than not at St Columba's, Pont Street. Equally, members of these organisations, not just of the regiments, served at the Front and, in many cases, did not return. Evocative war memorials remain, a testimony to sacrifice.

These are not just dry-as-dust tales of the long-forgotten. Their stories didn't end with the cessation of hostilities: their humanity and sacrifice strike chords with us today, and a century later these organisations remain shaped by the Great War.

This book synthesises their efforts and contributions, and is central to the commemorative events and activities of the Scots in Great War London Group. New light is cast on one of the most notable Scots in London, Field Marshal Earl Haig; but rather more of these pages tell stories of largely unknown Scots, their contributions to the war effort and the legacy for future generations including our own.

Anne

Preface

Scots In Great War London was conceived at a meeting convened at St Columba's Church of Scotland, in London's Knightsbridge in early 2017. The minister, Rev. Angus MacLeod, was looking ahead at plans to commemorate the Armistice in November 2018 and realised all the various Scottish organisations in London would be doing the same. Many of the Scots who live and/or work in London belong to several of these, and would likely be attending many events. To obviate diary clashes, after discussing with David Coughtrie at the Caledonian Club, Angus called us all in.

Over a few cups of tea and coffee, it emerged that all of these organisations – churches, charities, regiments, sports and social clubs – had fascinating tales to tell of what they and their members actually did a century ago, not just at the various fronts but at home in London. *Scots in Great War London* would not have happened without Angus MacLeod's initiative and drive to bring us together. Two people particularly encouraged Angus to expand the scope of *Scots in Great War London*. Canon Professor Michael Snape, the leading authority on faith in the First World War, recognised the importance of the *St Columba's Magazine* archive and Scots artist Gael Robertson identified the potential of a significant and unrepeatable moment, combining anniversary, place and people.

We hope you, the reader, will share not just our interest in these stories of the Scots in Great War London, but be inspired by some of their deeds.

Paul McFarland
Hugh Pym
London June 2018
www.scotsingreatwar.london

"A Flight of Scotchmen" by Richard Newton, 1796; this hand-coloured etching shows Scotsmen "raining" onto London, Ireland, the West Indies, America and Germany, with the signpost towards London stating, "The best road for a Scot". (© Trustees of the British Museum)

Introduction: "Don't Worry Padre, We're in Good Company"

The Rev. Angus MacLeod

Shortly before Remembrance Sunday 2012, two reservist soldiers of the London Scottish Regiment came to St Columba's, one of London's two existing Church of Scotland congregations. The two servicemen had just completed a six-month operational tour in Afghanistan. While deployed they had made a pact – if they were to get home safely they would meet up in London for a big day out. They also agreed that their rendezvous would begin at St Columba's Church of Scotland – or more specifically, in its London Scottish Regimental Chapel. There, in their own way, they would be grateful for coming through the tour and mindful of those who had not.

The minister was made aware of their visit that day and joined them for a little. Together they spoke about the chapel, recalling how on Remembrance Sunday it is the tradition of serving members of the London Scottish Regiment to leave at the end of the church service, via their regimental chapel – walking in silence past its memorial pillars; a simple mark of acknowledgement and respect. The soldiers also talked a little of their tour. After a while the minister thought to give them the chapel to themselves. "Do you mind if I leave you in peace now?" The most recent generation of returning servicemen, looking round at their surrounds – the laid up regimental colours, the books of remembrance and battle honours etched into the pillars – replied: "Don't worry Padre, I think we're in good company."

This book is about "good company." As the nation marks the hundredth anniversary of the Armistice, which brought an end to hostilities (the formal end to the war was yet some months away), it is timely to recount the stories, experiences and achievements of a previous generation. Yet worthy as they may be, the good company is not restricted to the soldiers' regimental ancestors. We have grown accustomed to the images and accounts of the First World War's battles; less well known are the sights and sounds of the Home Front – the often-unheralded contribution of civilians, family members, charitable organisations and congregations.

Throughout the First World War there were Scots in London – those who already lived and continued to work in the metropolis; those who enlisted and left to serve, and those who transited through the capital in vast numbers, bound by the demands of duty or the desire for home. The following commemorative record is a small honouring of their organisations and wartime contributions by the present-day members and inheritors. The First World War profoundly affected these organisations; their subsequent histories would be shaped, perhaps haunted, by the conflict. At work, play and contributing to the community, the Scottish diaspora's story is a fascinating one. It can be told through the activities of churches, charities, regiments, clubs and societies.

Skimming the pages of the *St Columba's Church Magazines* of the era, there is reference to a Crown Court church member:

> ... a true comrade of the war ... A member of the Crown Court Mothers' Union for over forty years, Mrs ___, joined a War Work Committee and paid 2d monthly. All members were supplied with material to make sand and other bags for the Soldiers; and in June last Mrs Parker, Lord Kitchener's sister, presented her and one other member with a medal for having made 1000 bags. She is eighty-two years old.
>
> *St Columba's Church Magazine*, October 1918

A month later, there was tribute to the late Miss Amy Fairfax:

> Her special care were children and the lonely soldiers of her beloved Australia. All she did was quiet, unnoticed, self-effacing; in the places where the most strident voices are the most regarded, she will not be missed at all. But many Australian mothers whose boys she kept from harm, and in whose hearts she kept alive the dear lights of home, name her today in their orisons.
>
> *St Columba's Church Magazine*, December 1918

The October 1918 magazine reported:

> Lady Marjory Dalrymple's Temporary Artificial Leg Depot has now removed to larger premises, 2, Eaton Square. Voluntary workers are urgently needed for this interesting work, which is very easily learnt.

Earlier, volunteers who deserted their commitments in favour of accepting more pleasant social engagements, were trenchantly rebuked in the same pages. In December 1917 a letter addressed to St Columba's expressed the wish that the munitions girls could be included in the prayers of intercession – and admitted "that the courage of the nation is not confined to its fighting men."

This communal response to the demands of war found rich expression in the hospitality offered to soldiers passing through London. Between 1915 and 1919 St Columba's offered hospitality to nearly 50,000 troops. Identified at the weekend train stations, Scottish soldiers were invited back to Pont Street, where they were welcomed and looked after. Often, they were piped back to the station the next day for their onward journeys – leave in Scotland or return to the Front. From modest beginnings, this Home Front response grew to something widely known and greatly appreciated. By 1916 a mother replied to an enquiry from St Columba's about her injured son:

"Boys like mine, brought up in a country place, have very little idea of London, and I am sure it must be a relief to many a mother besides myself to know that there are kindly folks to look after their boys."

This looking out for Scots in London, by Scots in London, was not restricted to one congregation of the Church of Scotland. As early as 1914 the Federated Council of Scottish Associations in London drew together a collective response from the organisations that constituted it. In December 1915 the Council reported a balance sheet on a year's work completed, a record of good work well done. "There is an almost bewildering list of miscellaneous articles distributed, from 10,314 pairs of socks to smaller items such as six copies of Burns' Poems and one concertina." (*St Columba's Church Magazine*, December 1915)

Scots had been drawn to London since James VI of Scotland had moved south in 1603 as James I of England, bringing a retinue, and followed by many more Scots, uninvited but hopeful of work or other advancement. By 1911, the Census was recording around 90,000 Scots living in London and the immediately surrounding counties of Middlesex, Surrey, Kent and Essex. Many were invisible then as now, but exiled Scots in London also convened in Scottish clubs and societies, raised money to support compatriots less well off, trained as soldiers, played sport, and went to church.

By 1914 the Royal Scottish Corporation, with its tradition of assisting Scots who had fallen on hard times, was already 300 years old. Crown Court was the oldest of London's Kirk congregations, the first church being dedicated in 1719. The Royal Caledonian Education Trust – in its original guise as the Royal Caledonian Asylum – had been looking after the orphans of Scottish soldiers since the days of Napoleon. London's Scots had their own clubs, sporting and social, and their own regiment. Founded in 1859, originally as part of the Volunteer Force, sponsored by the Highland Society of London and the Caledonian Society of London, a group of individual Scots raised the London Scottish Rifle Volunteers under the command of Lieutenant Colonel Lord Elcho, later the Earl of Wemyss.

In July 1914, a month before the outbreak of war, a memorial service was held at St Columba's for the Regiment's founder and first colonel. In the address, the minister, Dr Archibald Fleming, referred to three prominent members of the Regiment who had recently died, Colonel Eustace Balfour, the Duke of Argyll and the Earl of Wemyss.

> For each of these officers, though an intense and fervid and patriotic Scot, never for a moment allowed a narrow local patriotism to blur the larger outlines of race and Empire. A true and a great Scot never forgets that if he owes himself to Scotland, yet in her turn Scotland owes herself and her sons to the world; and it was into this larger service that these officers delighted to enter, and that they taught their countrymen to follow them. To be a good Scot is to be the better citizen of the world, and to be a good citizen of the world is to be the better Scot.
> *St Columba's Church Magazine*, August 1914

At the outbreak of war, Scots held prominent positions in the professions, the Civil Service, business, politics and the military. In 1883, the year before St Columba's was dedicated, its first session clerk, Mr Macvicar Anderson, addressed the General Assembly of the Church of Scotland:

> Do you never reflect that there are probably more Scotchmen in London, than in any city of Scotland? Is not London the heart of the Empire, from which the slightest pulsation vibrates throughout the length and breadth of the land to its remotest corner? Is she not the magnetic centre that attracts to herself the highest intelligence and the accumulated wealth of the kingdom? And is it not there, of all other places that the Church of Scotland should strive to maintain a strong and influential Representative Church?
>
> *St Columba's Church Magazine*, August 1913

Advertisements, such as those for the Dundee, Perth & London Shipping Company, carried in the church magazines of the era, cajoled readers with: "If you must live in London: Take your Holiday in Scotland and keep fit." For Scots who had prospered south of the border, there appeared to be no contradiction between pride in the home-land of birth and loyalty to both Crown and Empire. When the call to arms came, Scots in London were swift to respond. Of the four rugby-playing XVs of the London Scottish Football Club selected to play on the opening day of the 1914 season, we believe all 60 players may have enlisted. The London Scottish Regiment, the first Territorial Army regiment into action in Belgium, gained its famous Hallowe'en battle honour at Messines Ridge, barely three months after war was declared. At home there were already appeals in September 1914 for "garments for our Scottish soldiers and sailors:"

> We shall be deeply grateful for large quantities of Socks (these should be roomy, hand-knitted, and made from Alloa wool. Best 3-ply wheeling, two cuts for a pair. Each pair should be fastened together, and provided with a darning needle and some wool.) Flannel Undervests and men's Shirts will be in great demand.
>
> *St Columba's Church Magazine*, September 1914

By January 1915, reporting on a dinner of the Royal Scottish Corporation, two attendees were commended for their presence, despite the loss of their sons.

By 1916 Dr Fleming would preach on the text of Isaiah 60: 4, "Thy sons shall come from afar." His sermon recalls hearing the news of the outbreak of war in August 1914:

> When this storm broke upon our Empire, I was in a remote part of the Highlands of Scotland … there I saw a solitary horseman in full war array riding down by the shores of Loch Assynt. He had come from one of those rude and scattered hamlets near Cape Wrath to join his brothers in the great congress of races that

so soon gathered around our motherland. That single warrior was to me a symbol not only of that unity which our trials are going to deepen and secure; he was a symbol of that rich stream of life which then began to flow and flows now for our succour from every city, strath and hamlet, every colony, every island of the sea where our Scottish kinfolk have found a home. For we are a far-travelled and persistent race. And though we claim no special excellence, no exceptional virtue in patriotism or fidelity, of no constituent of our Empire can it be said today with more truth and pride, 'Thy sons shall come from afar.'

St Columba's Church Magazine, January 1916

In time, the Scots who would seek shelter at St Columba's were not only from the homeland. They came from Canada, South Africa, Australia, New Zealand and the USA. That Scots diaspora is illustrated by the *Far-Travelled Magazine,* referred to in the November 1917 issue of the *St Columba's Church Magazine.* A Canadian, professionally occupied in London since the beginning of the war, admired the magazine "for its truly British and Imperial spirit." He goes on to record:

After reading it more than once myself, I forward it on to a little group of Scots Kirk people in a little town in Nova Scotia which has lost many of its sons lately in the War; and from there it goes to members of my family in Ottawa, Toronto, and

The hall at St Columba's full of serving soldiers benefitting from the church's generous hospitality during their respite from battle. (St Columba's Church of Scotland)

Saskatchewan, and finally ends up on a farm in Alberta near Edmonton, where they are growing No 1 wheat for London. So you have a wide circle of readers.
St Columba's Church Magazine, November 1917

The chapters that follow tell the stories of some of these London–Scottish organisations, their characters and contributions. Though reference will be made to certain individuals who achieved wider fame, it is primarily the story of ordinary men and women in time of national emergency. It acknowledges and salutes their conviction and common purpose, humour and humanity, pride of nation and tenacity of faith. This is the tale of the Scots in Great War London.

1

Feeding the Fifty Thousand: St Columba's Church

Hugh Pym

There is no sign now of the church building which stood on the corner of Pont Street and Lennox Gardens in the smart Knightsbridge district of west London at the outbreak of war in 1914. It was severely bombed in the Second World War and rebuilt in the distinctive white stone as the St Columba's Church which stands there to this day. Many artefacts and documents were destroyed because of the enemy action but the church magazines from 1914–1918 survived. They paint a vivid and fascinating picture of a church making extraordinary efforts to support Scottish troops, a church mourning the fallen from its own ranks, and a church playing a full part in life on the Home Front.

The story of the work of St Columba's during the First World War has not been told before in any great detail. It is a story of dedication and compassion as members reached out to Scottish soldiers either coming through London on leave from the Front or heading back after a period of rest on "furlough." Nearly 50,000 Scots were fed and accommodated during the course of the Great War. No charge was made and the costs were covered by donations. Their hosts were volunteers, often elderly, who willingly "did their bit."

There are records of Scots' Kirks in London as far back as the late 16th Century. The first reference to a Church of Scotland kirk in Covent Garden was in 1711. There has been continuous worship at Crown Court there ever since (see the chapter on Crown Court in this book). By the 1880s as kirk leaders reviewed the needs of far-flung Scottish members across the capital it was decided to build a new church. George Cameron in *The Scots Kirk in London* notes that "Covent Garden was no longer a focal point of Scottish life in London. The 'Scotch Corner' had moved westward." Land was leased in Pont Street and in March 1884 what was subsequently named St Columba's was dedicated. Cameron notes that "its simple dignity was emphasised by the enriched arcade of stone and granite with marble mosaic which decorated the end wall of the chancel." Under the church was a hall with room for 400 people, a facility which was put to an unanticipated use three decades later.

By 1914 St Columba's had a prominent position in London society and was seen as a magnet for exiled Scots in the capital. The minister, Rev. Dr Archibald Fleming was a gifted writer as well as having a strong reputation as a preacher and theological student. He was involved in the founding of *The National Observer*, later edited by the poet W.E. Henley. Fleming's literary talents helped establish the *St Columba's Church Magazine* as a popular and highly regarded journal. This ensured that the tumultuous experiences of the church in the Great War were recorded in more detail and with more colour than at most other churches of the time.

The roll call of church elders at St Columba's in July 1914 is in effect a list of the great and the good of Scottish society in London. Lord Balfour of Burleigh was one. He had held office in Lord Salisbury's government in the late 19th Century, was Governor of the Bank of Scotland and was seen as a leading figure in Scottish church and academic life.

There were Members of Parliament amongst the elders sitting on the St Columba's ruling body, the Kirk Session. Arthur Steel-Maitland was in due course to join the wartime coalition Government. William Mitchell-Thomson was to hold a senior Whitehall role during the war, a ministerial post in the 1920s and then play a prominent part in the development of BBC Television. The Marquess of Tullibardine had fought under Lord Kitchener at Omdurman and again in the Boer War. During the Great War years he managed to serve both as an MP and command troops at Gallipoli.

The name of John Buchan on the church eldership list seems almost like an also-ran alongside the eminent politicians and aristocrats with long lists of honours after their names. Born in Perth and the son of a minister, he had deep roots in church life. In his biography *John Buchan, the Presbyterian Cavalier*, Andrew Lownie notes that after moving south he "kept up his ties with the Church of Scotland and regularly worshipped at St Columba's in Pont Street and in April 1912 he joined his old Oxford friend Arthur Steel-Maitland, now an MP, as an elder of the church."

On the outbreak of war, he was well known as an author with *Prester John* published in 1910. *The Thirty-Nine Steps* followed in 1915. After writing for the War Propaganda Department and a stint as a correspondent for *The Times* in France, in 1917 he became the government's Director of Information. All this would have left little time for church business but Buchan was known for his commitment to the kirk in the decades after the war.

In his 1932 biography of Archibald Fleming, A.A. Gammie writes that while the list of office-bearers may have been imposing, "it had gathered within its borders and among its elders representatives of almost every class in the community. To many it may come as a revelation that this aristocratic congregation has on its roll of members over 500 domestic servants." Added to that were hundreds of "business lads and girls, civil servants and many others."

There was no shortage of experience and influence, then, amongst the leading figures of St Columba's and Rev. Fleming could rely on wise counsel and firmly held opinion during Kirk Session meetings. There were no female elders then (women were not allowed to become elders in the Church of Scotland until the 1960s). Church activities appear to have been thriving. Alongside information about the Choral Society, Sunday School, Woman's Guild and Bible Class for Young Men, the magazine listed contact details for the Cricket, Miniature Rifle, Lawn Tennis and Football Clubs.

From Peacetime to War

With such a cast of characters and spread of influence, it was not surprising that St Columba's was quick to face up to the challenge of war. Never mind their lack of representation on the Kirk Session, women were to play prominent roles in the opening of the church to feed and accommodate Scottish soldiers passing through London and efforts to supply comforting items to the troops at the Front. The early optimism of the first months of war and the assumption it would be "all over by Christmas," mirrored that of society beyond the church doors. The St Columba's congregation would have had family all over Scotland and throughout the regiments. The tone of the magazine, as casualty lists mounted, reflects the changing mood while never deviating from patriotic support of "King and Country."

The first sad news for St Columba's arrived barely a fortnight after war was declared. Lieutenant General Sir James Grierson, a church regular, had died after a heart attack in France on his way to take command of the Second British Army Corps. Sir James had been seen as one of the brightest military thinkers and most accomplished generals in the British Army before the war. He was hurriedly succeeded by Sir Horace Smith-Dorrien who within days was caught up in the rushed retreat from Mons, and then opted to fight the crucial rear-guard action at Le Cateau.

The magazine carried four pages of tributes to Grierson. It noted that on the previous Sunday he had been in his usual seat at St Columba's in full uniform. Sir James, according to the magazine, had been invited to be an elder just a few months earlier but had declined "for professional reasons." He had clearly been a close associate of the minister. Rev. Fleming's tribute to the general referred to a "biting loss" and "our dear friend, our loyal fellow-Scot." It ended thus: "His passage to Victory and Peace has been swifter and surer than he thought. Good soldier of the Cross and of the King – your rest is won."

The September 1914 edition of the magazine, the first since the outbreak of war, is full of appeals to readers to rally to the cause. There was no time wasted as the church swung into action. Gifts for the "Sick and Wounded" were encouraged, either via St Columba's or the Red Cross Society. There are references to organising the "workers" at the church and requests are made for large quantities of socks ("roomy, hand knitted, and made from Alloa Wool … fastened together and provided with a darning needle and some wool"), flannel undervests and old clothes and boots.

The appeals for donations, gifts and clothing were made by signatories to the article in the magazine. Three of them were women, one of whom was Mary Blackwood who was to be the driving force behind the church's *Soldiers on Furlough* project. Cameron says she was known as "The High Heid Yin" by the soldiers.

The magazine also records the names of members of the congregation who had joined up with their units ready for war service, many with the London Scottish Regiment "of which we are all so proud." Noted with obvious approval is the fact that two sons of an elder Mr Jas. E. Scott have come forward to "serve and defend their country."

There is a charming paragraph recording that some members have "suffered inconvenience" on foreign travel because of the outbreak of hostilities. A Mr and Mrs H.S. Ellis departed on their unfortunately timed honeymoon after their wedding at St Columba's on 30 July. After what are described as some "anxious days" they had made their way home from Switzerland via Genoa and the Bay of Biscay. There is a sense of minor turbulence in a normally ordered world which could be expected to ease in due course.

The October 1914 edition contains an appeal for sweaters for members of the Scottish Horse and one for comforts for the troops launched by Mrs Malcolm, wife of the Colonel of the London Scottish Regiment. It is reported that the 1st Battalion of the regiment has departed for the Front under Colonel G.A. Malcolm and pride is expressed that the regiment is being called upon so soon, "the highest honour" which could be paid to a Territorial battalion.

Written just a few weeks before the London Scottish were hurled into the heat of battle at Ypres, little of the horror of war had found a way into the pages of the St Columba's magazine. But the first casualties of war known to St Columba's folk were reported in this October edition. The death of Lord Arthur Hay was marked with deep regret though noted to be "gallant and glorious." Sympathies are extended to two members of the congregation, his mother the Dowager Marchioness of Tweeddale and his younger brother Lord Edward Hay. The magazine reports that Lord Arthur was a grandson of a Waterloo veteran known as the "Fighting Marquess."

The loss of Lieutenant James Fergusson of the Highland Light Infantry is also reported, the son of Sir James Fergusson, "a frequent worshipper." Leslie Richmond was another of those known to St Columba's who had "given their young lives for their country and the cause of civilised mankind." The Master of Burleigh, son of Lord and Lady Balfour of Burleigh, was said to be wounded and missing.

The response to the appeal to the congregation to get knitting and donate clothing was said to have been "encouraging and helpful." Recipients included the Seaforth Highlanders at Aldershot and the Naval Base at Cromarty. In a reminder of the socially stratified nature of St Columba's at the outbreak of war, it was said to be "very gratifying to know that several of our working-class women have had coats and skirts etc which their children had outgrown, cleaned and sent to the poor Belgians" in the shape of the Belgian Relief Committee. Thanks are given for donations towards materials which had "given work to unemployed women.'"

Any sense that a church like St Columba's and its magazine might keep at arm's length from the patriotic fervour of the recruitment drive is dispelled in a detailed description of who is expected to join up immediately and where they should go. Ex-non-commissioned officers and warrant officers are required, says the church magazine, to enlist for the duration of the war. The article ends "God Save the King." Lists of those who have answered the call to the colours are set out in this and subsequent months. In one such section of the magazine, 42 names from the church branch of the Young Men's Guild are listed.

As November's edition was published and a line of trenches had spread from the Belgian coast down towards the Swiss border, the magazine continues in its quaint juxtaposition of routine church notices with sometimes tragic news from the Front. Reports of a new Sunday School teacher and social evenings for young women are followed by the sad announcement of the loss of Major Alexander MacLean, described as a "gallant soldier and loyal churchman." Members of the congregation "mentioned in dispatches" are noted.

A charming story is revealed in a letter to St Columba's from the Rev. J.M. Vallance, a chaplain serving in France with the London Scottish Regiment. He describes his encounter with a British tommy stranded in a French hospital. He was the only patient and was being looked after by five French nurses and medical staff. He had apparently fallen out of a train and hurt his back. His main trouble was said to be hunger and he was eating local food every three hours. A sore throat was being treated with "oxygenated gargle," otherwise known as champagne, and the nurses revealed the soldier had had the champagne three times a day for four days. Rev. Vallance notes that "if I had a pain in my back I would try to make it last for a little longer to get our friend's privileges."

The same chaplain, on a later visit to London, tells the magazine of a "remarkable communion service" held near the Front in a Roman Catholic church, whose priest had been shot by the Germans, with 300 men from different denominations. A soldier who was present notes that "it was conducted by a Presbyterian minister and attended by members of both Scottish and English churches. The building was a Roman Catholic church in a foreign land; the wine was the wine of the country; the bread ration bread; and the cup and plate those used in everyday life." The soldier says he is certain that "it was a more sincere congregation than is generally found in any church with all the usual paraphernalia."

The seasonal edition contains the first reference to the work which would in due course develop into the extensive hospitality for troops coming through London. Mary Blackwood, who would become the leader and driving force, had organised an entertainment in the Church Hall on New Year's Day for Scottish wounded from various hospitals. Members of the congregation had volunteered to "lend their motors" to pick up the soldiers. The next edition describes the exercise as a great success: "Wounded Belgians and soldiers from many Scottish regiments were entertained and thanks were extended to those church members who had helped with song, violin, food, money and good company."

The magazine's influence, meanwhile, had spread beyond its home readership to soldiers in the front line. A Seaforth Highlander expressed his thanks for receiving it and added that about 50 men had read it, including the text of a sermon, which had "given comfort in a cheerless hour to men who do not get much to read."

In February 1915, the St Columba's Roll of Honour was set out for the first time, spreading to two pages and containing the names of those serving, wounded and killed in action. There is a poignant tribute to Sergeant Norman Mcleod Brown who had served the church as a sidesman and as president of the Literary Branch of the Young Men's Guild: "The war could have exacted no severer a toll on the young manhood of our congregation than that of taking from us this beloved young soldier." Dr Fleming had paid his respects in the pulpit during a service: "his manly bearing, his cheerful kindliness, his beautiful smile, the quiet honest ring of his religion … we had hoped one day soon he might have borne office among us as an elder." Fleming and his flock could hardly have imagined then the future scale of losses of such young men in the congregation.

The energetic and enterprising Mary Blackwood was soon extending the scope of the church's outreach to Scottish soldiers. An offer, through the pages of the magazine, is made to anyone in Scotland who knows of wounded soldiers in London needing a visit. Reference is made to a Gordon Highlander found in a London hospital who was "very lonely" and visitors from his own town were organised to cheer him up. It was pointed out that "Gaelic speaking men, who are specially lonely, can always have visitors who can talk to them in their mother tongue." One such soldier was said by a nurse to have recovered quickly when he found someone from his home who could understand what he wanted to say.

The Birth of Soldiers on Furlough

By August 1915 the first evidence of what became known as the *Soldiers on Furlough* scheme appears. A lengthy piece in the magazine by an anonymous writer describes how the work began. An elder and assistant are said to have gone to Victoria Station early one Sunday morning in July. Word had gone round that Scottish soldiers from France would arrive by train to find a whole day of their leave used up because there were no rail services to Scotland till the evening.

"Must the door of St Columba's remain closed," asks the anonymous writer, "when Scotsmen were wandering the streets?" The two church emissaries waited at Victoria and picked out "a band of Scotties" before marching them to Pont Street. Hot water and a good breakfast was provided.

An idea was born and the author continues: "That day showed that there was work here that St Columba's could do, and plans were made on a larger scale for the following Sunday." What had begun with "a band of Scotties" would develop into feeding 50,000 over the wartime years.

Leave trains arrived two hours earlier the following Sunday and the magazine notes wryly that the authorities might have organised this deliberately to shake off the "suspicious characters" from St Columba's loitering at the station. By 4:00 a.m., 18 soldiers from the Gordons and Camerons, Argylls and Royal Scots "tanned by the sun of Flanders and France, coated with foreign mud" have arrived in the church hall and are telling the volunteers they have "struck a good billet."

A detailed and evocative description of this first full day of *Soldiers on Furlough* follows. The visitors wash and brush up. A sergeant says he has not seen a piano since going to the Front and asks to play with the help of a hymn book. "Even the policeman on his beat lingered by the windows to listen to his playing." Some go for a stroll in Hyde Park while others lie down for a snooze on one side of the hall. "By half past six the ladies had breakfast ready, and it was judged "bon, très bon." The soldiers are taken to a post office, open it seems early on a Sunday morning, to send telegrams home. A drive round London follows and at 12:30 p.m. they are back at the church for lunch.

The energetic volunteers of St Columba's are determined not to allow their guests to go hungry. At 5:00 p.m. there is a "very bright and happy tea-party." An impromptu sing-song develops with the sergeant at the piano – "the men chose the hymns and sang them lustily." Prayers are said. A sergeant major makes a speech of thanks with words which are said to be deeply moving: "The lads that wear the tartan have made a deep resolve that they will sell their lives dearly before they allow to happen here the things that we have seen in France and Belgium."

The soldiers begin their onward travel to Scotland with half a dozen having to wait till 11:30 p.m. for the train to the far north and so staying for the evening service. More food is served and packs of sandwiches are provided for the long journey ahead. The doors of the church are finally closed at 10:00 p.m. It has been an astonishing effort by church members, almost non-stop from the early hours of the morning. What had begun with a tentative visit to Victoria Station had evolved within a week

Scottish soldiers enjoying a refreshing shave at St Columba's during their short break while on leave from the Front and on their way home to Scotland. (St Columba's Church of Scotland)

to a very full day of hospitality. "All were tired but all were happy. Not one had helped without realising that it was a privilege, and it would really be boring to recount the times one heard the remark, 'What a fine lot of fellows they are!'"

So enthusiastic were the St Columba's volunteers that one Sunday when no leave trains bringing troops back from France were found at Victoria, "any lonely Scotsman going back to the Front" was invited to the church. Breakfast and dinner are laid on as well as a drive round the sights of London. Some of the guests, though, discover that their train will not depart that night and there are difficulties finding accommodation. Undaunted, the church opens its doors and "a very grateful set of men spent the night in sound sleep in the hall." The St Columba's hospitality now extends into Monday with breakfast, dinner and tea provided. "Then came once more the good-byes to the brave fellows going back to defend those of us who had been privileged to do something for them." A Gordon Highlander tells his hosts he has been at the Front for nearly a year and there are only 23 left of those who went out with him.

The project grew and expanded rapidly. Scottish troops arriving at Victoria Station in the early hours of a Sunday morning started looking out for a St Columba's host. Thomas Moncrieff, Secretary of the Royal Scottish Corporation, was said to be unfailing in his attendance at the station in the early morning. The hospitality flourished: "invitations for mid-day dinners have been most numerous and kind; motor runs, visits to the park, and sometimes to their comrades lying in hospitals, are the order of the afternoon, and then back for a real Scotch tea." Visits to the Chelsea Public Baths were organised. A churchwarden from a neighbouring church asked to accompany the St Columba's representatives on the early morning station run to see if the Church of England could do something similar for English troops facing long rail journeys home.

With increasing numbers of guests, the workload for St Columba's folk was growing. But the demand each Sunday was unpredictable with some weekends very quiet during heavy fighting when not much leave was granted.

The organisers appealed for understanding that help might be needed at very short notice or not at all. Help from members ready to provide dinner in their own homes was requested. "The week," notes the magazine "holds no more pleasant hours than those spent in the bustle at Victoria, or in making cocoa, lighting fires, writing telegrams or washing dishes, or in discussing the latest news from the Front with those straight from the spot."

Letters of thanks to St Columba's started arriving and some of the more poignant were quoted in the magazine. The brother of a Seaforth Highlander who was grieving after the loss of his sister and who had been looked after in Pont Street expressed his appreciation: "After all the horrors of France it was so lovely he said to be taken in hand and cared for. God bless and keep you in your good work in helping the brave men who return to our shores on leave." One soldier told his hosts: "We didn't know there were such people in London."

Thanks were also received from the recipients of parcels and church magazines. A former Sunday School boy was especially grateful for socks: "The socks I was wearing just reached my ankles and I can tell you it was very uncomfortable on the march. Now I feel as if I could march to Berlin or, better still, to Scotland." Much effort by church members was put into supplying the London Scottish. A member of the regiment home on leave told them that a parcel of socks "simply saved our men." They had come in drenched and exhausted and a parcel from St Columba's had arrived – "ten men and twelve pairs of socks."

Mementos were left behind by some of the visitors, presumably as tokens to reflect their gratitude. These included a piece of shrapnel, a bullet and a sprig of white heather which had been kept in the pocket book of a Gordon Highlander during every battle since the start of the war and which was exchanged with the Deaconess for purple heather fresh from the moors. Sometimes the soldiers left money and one day there was a collection which they asked to be sent to the Belgian Relief Fund.

An anonymous visitor records an appreciation of the hospitality work and the desire of the volunteers to be doing their bit, something "to assist in this titanic struggle of Right with Wrong." The writer notes how depressing it must be for Scottish soldiers back from the Front to wait so long for the trains north:

> Can you imagine how the heart of a Scotsman sinks to his boots when, joyful at the thought of getting home for five short days, he alights at Victoria at 2 am on a Sunday only to find that there is no chance of going on to Bonnie Scotland before 10 or 11 that night? Eighteen or 20 hours of his precious leave cancelled! A railway station is not the most cheerful place in the world in which to fill an hour at the best of times, but to idle away a round and a half of the clock when you are in a fever of anxiety to get home …! It is almost beyond the powers of human endurance.

One letter touches on the fact that the church's outreach at Victoria Station is providing a wholesome alternative to the sort of activities a soldier with hours to kill might pursue: "I have mentioned all about the Church and how it cares for all Scottish soldiers that are in London and have nowhere to go. It keeps one from getting into bad company." Another praises the kindness shown to "a soldier practically stranded in a strange city."

A future controller of BBC Scotland wrote to the church in similar vein. Captain Melville Dinwiddie, son of the minister of Ruthwell near Dumfries, was awarded the MC and DSO during his service with the Gordon Highlanders on the Western Front. He would later be ordained, and served as minister at St Machar's Cathedral, Aberdeen, before being recruited to the BBC.

He recalled a conversation with a private who had told him what a fine time he had enjoyed at St Columba's on his way home on leave. He was, he said

> delighted to hear that you are doing such splendid work among these lads from Scotland stranded in London for a day with nothing in particular to do and nowhere to go. Without such an organisation as yours, these fellows, through no

fault of their own, would probably get into mischief and tend to drag down the present good reputation of the Scotsman in London.

By the autumn of 1915, what was now branded officially in the magazine as *Soldiers on Furlough* encompassed nearly 100 guests on some Sundays. Word about the welcome to be had at St Columba's had spread among Scottish regiments. A tribute is paid to "the unflagging zeal of a multitude of helpers" allowing the church to look after so many guests. Appeals are made for "personal, material and financial" assistance. It is noted "with pleasure" that the king is receiving some of the men at the Royal Mews at Buckingham Palace early on Sundays after they have arrived at St Columba's.

Ministering to soldiers returning from leave and heading back to the Front was organised on a different basis to the Victoria Station run. Church volunteers would meet trains coming down from Scotland on Sunday mornings. These included members of the Caledonian Church in Holloway and boy scouts who would act as guides to St Columba's. Returning to the horrors of trench warfare would have dampened the mood of these guests and the welcome at St Columba's lifted their spirit. The magazine notes that "many who had come sadly away from the homes they love in Scotland have appreciated a kindly welcome."

One letter of thanks probably spoke for many: "On the day I spent at your Church on my way back I felt very down-hearted and homesick, but I feel all right now. You might remember me to all your Church folk and tell them that I can never forget the kindness they showed to me." A wife in Scotland writes to thank the church for the welcome given to her husband: "My wee girl has nearly broken her heart since he left

Soldiers enjoying the washing facilities on their arrival at St Columba's; boy scouts volunteered to help. (St Columba's Church of Scotland)

on Saturday, crying for her daddy, but I hope and pray it will soon be all over and my husband safe to me again."

The efforts of St Columba's to support Scottish soldiers were not restricted to central London. The Rev. Joseph Moffett, born in Donegal, had been a popular assistant to Dr Fleming at St Columba's. He was later to become minister at Crown Court. When war broke out he joined up as an army chaplain. He wrote to his former colleagues at St Columba's reporting that at the base depot of the Highland Division in France each of the churches represented had a "Hut" in which communion services could be celebrated. He wanted to create one for St Columba's but needed funds to make this happen. Within 24 hours the required money was raised by members of the congregation. Moffett wrote back expressing his gratitude: "The tent will be a sort of little Bethel, consecrated to the Faith of their fathers, to remind the boys that the Church at home has not altogether left them to fight in this war without the comfort and succour of their Faith."

There are later references to a St Columba's Hut under the wing of the YMCA. The writer advances the thought that the YMCA had in the past been regarded as a "preserve of prigs" but now represented "all that is virile, progressive and clean in the young manhood of our country." One hundred and fifty YMCA huts had sprung up in France, proving highly popular with soldiers wanting to write letters home. A St Columba's hut was sited near the firing line and on ground used for the first wave of attacks in the Battle of the Somme.

As the war progressed, St Columba's funded at least 10 huts, some run by the YMCA and others by the Scottish Churches Organisation. Each cost about £500 to build and each, apparently, provided 10,000 sheets of notepaper free every week to soldiers. Raising the money to construct and run these huts was quite an achievement by St Columba's. An appeal was made nationally by the Church of Scotland and the United Free Church for £20,000 to build more. This was said to be the "first great united enterprise on which the two Churches have embarked together," helping pave the way perhaps for the reunion of both Churches in 1929.

The *Soldiers on Furlough* system changed by the end of 1915 because of alterations to the transporting of troops from France. There were to be no more early arrivals as the men would arrive at Victoria between 4:00 and 5:00 p.m. The opportunity for entertaining them was thus reduced to a few hours but, noted the magazine, "the opportunity of speeding our countrymen on their way remains." The hospitality offered by members in their own homes was no longer possible with the personal touch which had impressed so many of the visiting soldiers. Instead the church members, consistently referred to as the "ladies," had to prepare an early dinner in the hall. When fed, the soldiers would troop up from the hall, meeting the congregation coming down from the evening service who would give them a cheer as they departed for stations. Once, when the boat trains were cancelled, the troops were offered accommodation in the hall: "St Columba's Hall has seen many interesting sights, but seldom anything more interesting than the happy warriors "tucked in" on what they thought were the most comfortable spots." One slept under the grand piano.

With the work at St Columba's so well-known among Scottish battalions it was not surprising that the *Edinburgh Evening News* picked up on the story. The newspaper ran a piece entitled "Scottish Soldiers in London, A Congregation's Kindness." A correspondent who was a serving officer said approvingly that no pressure was put on the guests to join the evening services and there was nothing of the "Holy Willie" about the work. "Some men refuse to join the party from the station in the morning," continued the correspondent, "fearing apparently that the hospitality offered is but evangelising disguised, but the bulk of the men have greater discrimination and greater faith in the downright goodwill of their would-be hosts." (*Edinburgh Evening News,* 13 November 1915, p.4)

It is worth reflecting on the fact that the work at St Columba's would have been a totally new, unexpected and sometimes challenging experience for those involved. A rigid social class structure in 1914 was profoundly shaken by the onset of war. A predominantly middle-class congregation with an aristocratic element was rolling up its sleeves and ministering to soldiers from all sections of society, many from much humbler backgrounds than the regulars at Pont Street. They were arriving from the Front muddy, tired and no doubt troubled by their experiences in the trenches. Most would never have visited the capital before, let alone spoken to smart Londoners. Now they were being invited by hostesses to dinner in their affluent Belgravia homes.

Having catered for around 200 men on some days in late 1915, *Soldiers on Furlough* had grown to a scale which required the direction of a committee nominated by the Kirk Session. The assistant minister Rev. Douglas Robertson was the secretary and Mary Blackwood was the treasurer. The work depended on hard graft by many church volunteers but also continuing generous financial contributions. There was to be no break on Christmas Day:

> Could we bear the thought that the men from Scotland had on that day only the sombre refuge of a railway station or the doubtful hospitality of a public house? There must be someone to welcome them and cheer them on their way. And who could do so more fittingly that the representatives of the Church of Scotland?

A New Year message in 1916 by Dr Fleming reflects on social changes brought about by the war:

> The great masses of the people, high and low have steadily … moved towards the higher choice of self-repression and zeal for the common good. Most of all in the trenches have the highest and humblest, the rich and the poor, learned the lesson of brotherhood, wholehearted and unreserved.

He called on his church flock to face the coming year "bravely and hopefully" with the possibility it would be "the year of the Great Peace."

Instead, it was the year of the Somme, Verdun and new horrors in a continued stalemate on the Western Front.

January 1916 saw no ebbing in the flow of soldiers through St Columba's. It was noted that on one occasion "our accommodation was severely taxed for a few hours." The February magazine has a lengthy description of the work on one of those days which conveys the hustle and bustle of activity and conversation:

> Down one side of the hall there were two long rows of tables where 60 or 70 men were having a substantial meal. On the other side some were writing; telegrams were being sent off to every part of Scotland; in every corner gossiping groups were telling their stories; one was examining some souvenir of the battlefield; one was listening to some other tale of the trenches. Here a Scot from the far north was being advised about his trains; there another had found a friend from his own town. And still they were coming in; fur-coated, mud-stained, sturdy figures hung round with innumerable instruments of war, they seemed to have walked straight from the trenches into the bright light of St Columba's Hall ... Our object and desire is not merely to give them food; nor is it merely to save them from the dangers of the streets; there are some who would fall if there were no open door, but, after all, the majority need no such adventitious aids to virtue. Rather we seek to meet them with that open friendship which is the expression of the respect in which the community holds these men who have made such great sacrifices in the common cause.

Official recognition for the work came in April 1916 when Major General Sir Francis Lloyd, General Officer Commanding the London District, visited the hall and made presentations of the London District Badge. Typical for the times the badges were given to the men who went to the stations to meet the soldiers rather than the women involved in providing the hospitality. It is at least noted that "although many of the men are now the proud wearers of the badge, they fully realise that it is among the ranks of the ladies that the workers are to be found who are 'starred' as indispensable." By June the church had looked after a total of 5,000 men since the scheme started just under a year earlier.

Two years of war had not dampened enthusiasm for leisure activities on the Home Front. The magazine records that the church cricket team had played 10 matches by midsummer of which eight had been won. The most recent game had seen the very rare feat of a hat trick with the first three balls of the match by McPherson and four wickets by Murdoch. It is not clear whether the players were church members too old to be called up or too young. The tennis club, meanwhile, was pressing ahead with the Ladies' Championship for the Gerard Cup and an appeal for more new players. Three soldier members had visited the club's courts at Wormholt Farm "all looking bronzed and fit and it was particularly pleasant" to see them playing.

Detailed records of Scottish troops who had passed through St Columba's were kept. These enabled the organisers to look out for news of their former charges. Casualty lists in newspapers were scanned and notes of sympathy were written to the families of guests. Wounded men in hospital in London were visited and many

St Columba's volunteers help a soldier with his pay book. (St Columba's Church of Scotland)

were said to be glad to see familiar faces from St Columba's. A mother answering a letter enquiring about her wounded son wrote back: "Boys like mine brought up in a country place have very little idea of London, and I am sure it must be a relief to many a mother besides myself to know that there are kindly folks to look after their boys."

The enthusiasm and determination of St Columba's members, mainly women, was impressive even by the high standards of commitment to voluntary work on the Home Front during the war. An urgent appeal from the pulpit was made for a large number of woollen hose tops for the London Scottish Regiment. Willing knitters came forward at once according to the magazine. Mrs Fleming and her daughter Christian were among those thanked. Stocks of woollen hose tops and socks were held at the church and parcels containing sometimes 500 or 600 pairs were dispatched to any Scottish battalion at the Front who requested them. Each week nearly £25, funded by an appeal, was spent sending parcels to Scottish prisoners of war in Germany and appeals for further donations to continue the work were made.

It was as well they were energetic and unflagging in their willingness to serve. On the last weekend of November "our accommodation was taxed to the utmost." The Moderator of the General Assembly of the Church of Scotland was in attendance for the annual St Andrew's Festival Service and addressed what was said to be a large body of men who were "deeply stirred by his eloquent and encouraging words." A letter from a colonel commanding a battalion of the Seaforth Highlanders said the work done by St Columba's for soldiers proceeding on leave was much appreciated.

By the end of 1916, the roll of honour published in the monthly magazine extended to 241 names of those who were serving and those who had lost their lives. Twenty-six had been killed. Brief notes were written on some of those who had fallen including Corporal Ian MacLaren, described as "one of the fine band of men who left our Cricket Club in the early days of the war … he lost his life while gallantly leading the men of his platoon."

January 1917 was the busiest month to date for *Soldiers on Furlough* with 1,000 men entertained. St Columba's was by now known to every Scottish battalion serving in France. A lengthy letter from a mother thanking for the welcome at the station and hospitality to her son paints a colourful picture of the church's work:

> They were driven off to find a sumptuous repast waiting for them and (not at all a minor delight) the opportunity of making themselves clean and tidy for the home folks. An entertainment of song and music followed, then a drive back to the station in time for the train. It was all like a fairy tale. God bless your efforts on behalf of these brave boys.

Church members took satisfaction when there were chance meetings amongst the soldiers. Three times in the space of a few weeks brothers met unexpectedly in the hall. On one occasion brother spotted brother at the church door – one was coming back from saying goodbye to his dying mother, the other was heading home to do the same.

Soldiers having dinner at St Columba's, looked after by the hospitality team. (St Columba's Church of Scotland)

A sermon by Dr Fleming reveals his view of the spiritual nature of the work with the troops:

> We do not preach to them at the railway stations. We do not content ourselves with saying – Thou shalt not do this or that. We say – Here is shelter, here is light, here is food, company, entertainment, the warm spirit of Scottish welcome. We crowd out the evil influences with good; and when the devils tap on the door, the good spirits that are in possession simply reply – 'House Full' – 'No room'

The soldiers seemed to respond positively to the Christian message when it was promoted to them. A visiting Canadian chaplain, arriving in the church hall, confirmed that in a letter to a Canadian newspaper: "My eyes beheld a sight they shall not soon forget. There were seated in the most reverend manner some 150 young Scotsmen just out of the trenches with the mud of the Somme scarcely dry on their clothes. They were singing from the psalms so dear to their native land."

Tributes in the magazine to those of the St Columba's flock who had fallen in action were always moving, but one especially so as the soldier in question was just 21 and had helped with the *Soldiers on Furlough* work. Private William Macgregor Moffat, the only son of the postmaster of Troon in Ayrshire, had come to London originally to work in the Civil Service. He was described as a "true son of the Church" who had come forward for preparation for First Communion in 1915. Before enlisting he had been among the groups who met soldiers arriving on leave trains at Victoria. An old friend writing to the church said; "the memory of his cheerful disposition and undoubted abilities, of his clear outlook on life and of his readiness to answer the call of duty remains treasured in the hearts of those who, knowing him best, loved him most."

Rev. Robertson, like many at the church, felt the loss of Private Moffat deeply:

> He had become a very faithful member of St Columba's. He came to us with a keener interest in his Church than most of our young fellows have when they reach London, and he would have made one of the best of churchmen. He played regularly in the cricket team, and I used to think of him as one of those who could be trusted to set a good example by regular attendance at Church and Bible Class.

Rev. Robertson was by the middle of 1917 serving in France. He had played a central role in the launch of *Soldiers on Furlough* and the magazine reported that he was greatly missed and that he had "a peculiarly happy way of addressing words of welcome to our guests, and of entertaining them." By June that year, St Columba's was welcoming its 9,000th guest. At the end of July, the 10,000th soldier was recorded, almost exactly two years since the first tentative visit to Victoria Station.

A sizeable proportion of the 10,000, it seems, were on their second or even third visit to St Columba's. A member of the Black Watch, who 17 years before had attended the church Sunday school, was pleased to meet his former teacher at the front door on welcoming duty. Another soldier, enquiring at the station about St Columba's, was asked how he knew about the church's offer of hospitality. He replied: "It is known about, up and down the line out there." Heather sent from Scotland to the church was gratefully received by the men for "a piece in the bonnet."

"No wonder we don't want to come back to the Front when we get such hospitality shown to us," was the sentiment expressed in one especially moving letter from a grateful Glaswegian soldier. His leave had been traumatic as he had got back home to find his only child, a two-year-old daughter, very ill. A few days later she died. Back in France he wrote fondly to his hosts at St Columba's:

> I hope this finds all the ladies that gave us a good time all well, especially the violinist – my word she was great. Give her my respect and best wishes, and I don't forget her Lullaby she played. I can fancy I hear her yet, as I sit in my little wooden shanty here, amongst the thundering of our big guns.

Tragedy was to strike another musician involved in the church entertainment. In recording the death of wounds of church member Lieutenant H.S. Graves, the magazine notes that sympathy will be with his sister Phyllis "whose beautiful singing is such a delight to our Scottish *Soldiers on Furlough*" and who had almost at the same time lost her fiancé in France.

Harry Graves was "a keen golfer ... of the kind who never hesitated when the call came to the sterner contests of battle." His father Frank Graves was the organist at Kinnoull parish church in Perth. Typical of many of his generation, Harry had moved from his home in Scotland to London to take up a job in banking and became an active peacetime member of the London Scottish Regiment. He headed out to the Front with the London Scottish in the early weeks of the war and was wounded in the famous action at Messines. Commissioned into the Black Watch, he died of wounds in November 1917 during the Battle of Cambrai.

A Gordon Highlander, who had lived abroad before the war, told the church volunteers that with no friends or relations to go to he had not hitherto asked for leave. But, he added, "all the Scotsmen at the Front talk so much about St Columba's, that I made up my mind to come and see the place for myself."

A tragic death a long way from the Front was also reported. A company sergeant major who had proposed the vote of thanks in the hall at the end of the evening's entertainment was on his train home later that night. He was killed when the carriage door opened unexpectedly. The church organisers had his home address and were able to write to his widow vouching for his presence in the hall and promising to help secure her pension.

The rising volume of soldiers catered for every weekend was beginning to cause problems at the local Knightsbridge underground station. Already crowded trains were unable to take on board all the St Columba's visitors. A plan was made with the local railway operator to send an empty train as soon as the men arrived "having been marched there to the skirl of the pipes and often to songs of their own."

A page from *The Graphic* depicts a New Year celebration for Scottish soldiers at St Columba's. (Reproduced by permission of the National Library of Scotland)

Mothers and wives were sometimes entertained on the way from Scotland to visit wounded relatives in London or France. Arrangements were made for them to be met at stations if word came through from Scotland that a visitor might be left stranded. Church members would also stand by to provide meals on weekdays, often at short notice, to soldiers who had missed leave trains and turned up unexpectedly at the hall.

The scale of the work, far greater than could possibly have been imagined in the early weeks back in 1915, was only possible with sufficient financial donations. Yet St Columba's was never struggling thanks to the continuing generosity of friends and admirers near and far. From a "lone shieling on a misty island" (Stornoway) came £2, from another donor a cheque "in loving memory of my only brother." From the widow of a soldier entertained at the church a few weeks before his death, came a letter explaining that her "wee son" had emptied out his money-box and asked for the pennies to be sent "to the lady for a poor soldier-man." A Scottish bank in London conducted a whip round among staff and sent in a cheque.

A single church collection one Sunday raised £160. A general appeal was made in a letter, signed by Dr Fleming and some of the aristocratic members of the Kirk Session, and sent to the Scottish press; "we feel that the work we are doing is for

Scotland as a whole, and for the Dominions, many of whose soldiers of Scottish origin come to us." This brought in another £760 which was said to be a "large sum."

The 20,000th Guest

The March 1918 edition of the magazine contains a well-deserved tribute to the work of Mary Blackwood, the driving force and leader of so much of the wartime work at St Columba's. At an event to mark the 20,000th guest of *Soldiers on Furlough,* a presentation was made "as a token of high esteem and in appreciation of her devoted labours." A flower basket adorned with ribbons of tartan of Highland regiments was given to Miss Blackwood who "maintained that the success of the work was due to the loyal co-operation of all."

The 20,000th guest, as it turned out, was a Private John Lee of the Highland Light Infantry. After being greatly fussed over during his meal he was presented by Miss Blackwood with "a handsome trench knife (suitably inscribed)," presumably not intended for offensive purposes. Private Lee and other men in the hall were given a souvenir card prepared for the occasion.

Mary Blackwood was also president of the scout troop at the Caledonian Church, Holloway. Scouts were rewarded with badges for wartime voluntary work which included helping with *Soldiers on Furlough.* This involved joining the church members welcoming incoming troops at stations, guiding them towards Pont Street and helping in the hall. Cameron describes the role of the scouts bidding farewell to the guests: "with a piper, (they) guided the Jocks from Pont Street to Knightsbridge tube station, where more than once the company would break into sets of the eightsome reel to the piper's music while waiting on the platform."

The church's work with soldiers on leave was graced with a royal visit. Princess Louise came on two consecutive weekends to see how hospitality was offered. As well as addressing the soldiers, she "also spent several hours going about among them man by man, in her own perfectly charming way, and talking to them about their welfare and the Scotland which Her Royal Highness and they love so well."

A member of the St Columba's congregation who achieved subsequent fame for her war work close to the battlefields was Dr Elsie Inglis. She was the founder of the Scottish Women's Hospitals, run by female doctors but working with the French and Serbian authorities because they were rejected by the British Army. A regular collection for the group was undertaken at the church for the sponsorship of beds in the hospitals. The death of Dr Inglis in 1917 was followed by an extensive tribute in the magazine:

> one of our most treasured memories will be of that keen, clever face of hers in St Columba's of a Sunday – with that far, wistful melancholy in it, added to its firm determination, which we knew … our Scottish Florence Nightingale, of whom we shall be for ever proud.

On their arrival from the front line, Scottish soldiers were brought to St Columba's from various railway stations around London. (St Columba's Church of Scotland)

The major German offensive on the British lines in March 1918 led to a cancellation of all leave and the flow of visitors to St Columba's dried up for a time. There was to be no rest period for the church volunteers, however, as they organised tea and concerts for Scottish wounded recovering in London. Eighty-five were picked up from hospitals in motor buses and brought to the church to be entertained by pipers, dancers and singers "to try to make the men forget for a time the horrors they had been through on the battlefield." The enterprise was to continue even after leave for front-line troops resumed.

The ingenuity of the St Columba's congregation in the war years was evident in unexpected ways. A church member Lady Marjorie Dalrymple was involved in introducing a Danish-designed lightweight artificial leg to the UK. This served the purpose of helping amputees with a temporary solution before a permanent artificial leg was fitted. This hollow cylinder-shaped device, with a wooden peg at the bottom, was said to be easy and painlessly possible to wear. Lady Dalrymple asked through the magazine for volunteers to come forward to help assemble these artificial legs, such was the demand from hospitals.

The July 1918 edition recorded that the total number of *Soldiers on Furlough* guests had hit 23,000. Numbers of men had, apparently, commented that, apart from nurses in hospitals, the workers in the church hall had been the first British women they had spoken to for three years. One guest had remarked; "thank you for all your kindness to us and your friendship." More than 700 wounded had been entertained in eight weeks. James K. Munro received a special mention for his work collecting soldiers from hospitals. Some were paralysed from the waist down so could not get to the top deck of the buses to enjoy the fresh air. Mr Munro had carried them up and down on his back. Many of the wounded guests had recently arrived back from prisoner of war camps in Germany.

A Scottish Sergeant wrote to Dr Fleming after his visit:

> I had not been home for a period of three and a half years, and I do not think anyone can realise what a kind reception means until one has had a similar experience. I know I cannot find words to express my feelings on the matter … the kindness shown, and above all the absence of that awful thing 'charity' touched me very much.

The presence of a piper to play them to the station accompanied by a boy scout was always popular. One evening the piper had continued to play on the platform of the tube station and "suddenly men stepped forward and on went the dance. Would that the scene could have been portrayed on canvas." Sprigs of heather sent by well-wishers in Scotland were snapped up by the departing soldiers and placed in their bonnets for the march to the station.

Peacetime, but the Work Continues

The Armistice was signed on Monday, 11 November 1918 and the following Sunday there was a service of thanksgiving at St Columba's. Dr Fleming's sermon, reprinted in the magazine, was a towering piece of oratory even by the standards of his usual powerful rhetoric:

> With reverent homage we lay our tribute of gratitude on the graves of the men and women who have died. Highland glen and lowland strath will hear their tread no more. And round the re-built family altars of the homes from which they set out so proudly they will be missed when the roll-call comes. Here, where so many of them sang the songs of Zion, their voices will never again resound. They are dead. But they are immortal. And because they paid their lives for our liberties and bought our safety with their blood, we shall hold them in an everlasting remembrance.

Lady Haig was a guest that day. Three hundred men from different Scottish regiments greeted her with "rounds of cheers." Expressing her delight at meeting them and her pride in their achievements she continued; "though hostilities were over, much depended upon the Scottish soldier in times of peace, and she trusted they would continue to set that wonderful example to the country they had displayed on the battlefield."

The hall, meanwhile, was "decorated with flags of Great Britain, Scotland, the Navy and Mercantile Service, and all the Allies, tartan sashes were draped round the pictures, and a fine portrait of HM the King was lent to us." The mood amongst the men was said to be "very joyous" and some guests who had travelled for seven weeks from Mesopotamia only heard news of peace when they arrived at Waterloo station. "The voices of the men singing the 'Old Hundredth' carried, we were told, right up the street; and it brought a lump to one's throat to watch those strong, keen, grand fellows singing those words which are one of the great heritages of every Scottish man and woman."

Peace may have broken out, but the work of *Soldiers on Furlough* continued with troops returning for demobilisation or on leave from the Army of Occupation in Germany. December was a record month with over 3,000 men entertained. Christmas Day saw 400 arrive but when they had settled down for the concert a further 100 with three officers appeared without notice at the door. All alternative accommodation was full so they had been guided to St Columba's. True to tradition the church volunteers did not turn them away: "Every room, passage and stair was packed with kits, and at 6.30, 500 happy men marched off with our guides to the skirl of the pipes on their way to the trains for the north."

Brother continued to meet brother unexpectedly in these gatherings in the hall. The magazine described one such encounter: "On a recent Saturday, while one of our guests was on the hall platform singing, another emerged from the box where he was shaving, and standing at the door remarked "I thought I knew that voice; that is my brother; we have not met for four years."

Official recognition for Mary Blackwood came at last from the War Office. She was mentioned in the official *Gazette* for her "magnificent work" in managing and inspiring the hospitality at St Columba's. A social evening in May 1919 celebrated the work of all the volunteers involved in *Soldiers on Furlough*. There was praise again for Miss Blackwood who was presented with a thistle brooch and other gifts. A basket of flowers was handed to her by Anne Stewart "one of the tiny band of workers who started the work in July 1915." Speeches were made and letters from absentees read out. It was noted that female volunteers would often walk long distances to get to the church for the 6:00 a.m. breakfasts because Sunday buses had not started running.

In later years Mary Blackwood would be remembered by one who knew her as "someone with a strong personality and the valuable ability to recruit and motivate helpers for good causes – it was largely due to her initiative and work that St Columba's was able to provide the outstanding hospitality and support which is on record." She continued to be an important figure in church life after the war including holding the post of Secretary of the Amateur Dramatic Society.

Another prominent figure in the wartime work was Mrs MacLeod, organiser of the concerts for the guests. The magazine recorded the "very deep debt of gratitude" for her work and reported that a guest had remarked "she is like a mother to us." Another, "one of our most devoted workers," was Miss McLennan. After train timetables changed, leaving little time to get across London for services to Scotland, she would take sandwiches and scones from the hall over to Victoria Station. Her commitment and zeal for the work was summed up thus: "few realise how many Scottish soldiers, who have been enticed away to the public houses, have to thank Miss McLennan for regaining their trains, and saving them from falling into the hands of the Military Police."

By this stage the number of soldiers accommodated since the start of the hospitality work had reached 43,000 with a steady stream of troops continuing to return from the former battle zones. By the time it was wound up more than 48,000 had passed through the doors. Cards recording every visitor had been meticulously kept up to date and filed. The final church Roll of Honour was published with the 64 who had lost their lives among the 352 names of those who had served King and Country. Among those listed was John Buchan for his work as Director of Information. So too Lieutenant James Steele who had been wounded in 1916 and returned to service. He was to play a pivotal role in the rebuilding of the church after the original building was severely damaged by enemy action in the Second World War. His son Stuart is a church elder to this day.

Stuart Steele's mother Peggy Leonard was one of the church volunteers. She had joined St Columba's in 1913 after moving south from Glasgow to join the civil service. She appears in some of the photos of the wartime hospitality teams along with two friends Nettie Kennedy and Miss A.R. MacAuslane. Stuart remembers them as close family friends in subsequent years. His mother recalled how they wrote letters for some of the soldiers to their families and girlfriends.

One soldier to enjoy the hospitality at St Columba's on three occasions was Robin F.V. Scott, later to return as minister at the church in 1938. George Cameron says in his short history *St Columba's (Church of Scotland), Pont Street*: "a certain Miss Phyllis Graves had more than once as a singer entertained the troops in the hall where now she sat beside him as Mrs Scott at the Welcome Meeting." This was the same Miss Graves referred to earlier whose brother Lieutenant Harry Graves had died at the Front. It was none other than Mary Blackwood who at that social occasion had produced the three cards with Rev. Scott's presence recorded.

A volunteer at St Columba's, John Golder, in a piece for a Kilmarnock newspaper, praised those who "had given time and money and loving thought to help thousands of men whom they never knew." His conclusion on the significance of the work and the achievement of the church members is as good as any:

> The men who consecrated their lives towards the security of the lives and liber-
> ties of the dear ones at home have not been slow in expressing their gratitude for
> the kindly service rendered by their compatriots in the great city of London, and
> shall hold it in lasting remembrance.

Appreciation of the work was not restricted to the Scottish press. In a feature entitled "The Scot on Leave in London" for *The Graphic*, a nationally renowned illustrated news publication, the author A. Mackintosh talks of a "little Scots oasis in London," which he describes as an inspiring spectacle:

> It is delightful to watch these Scots when, with kit on back and ready for the
> journey, for which they have been prepared by a parting cup of soup, they range
> themselves with St Columba's helpers round the hall and sing Auld Lang Syne.

How warmly they clasp hands these men of a race supposed to be cold, how cordially they "tak' a cup o' kindness yet," and how vigorously they acclaim "a richt guid willie-waught Better lo'ed ye canna be," they sometimes sing as they tramp out into the street on the way to the tube for Euston, St. Pancras, or King's Cross, the London railway stations dearest to the heart of Scots, and better loved could no soldiers be than those are by their compatriots.

The Graphic, 29 December 1917, p. 852

The next day, one of those soldiers, Private Hugh M. Bennie, left behind a note of his own gratitude, which the *Magazine* duly published:

A TOMMY'S THANKS

When I cam' oot the station,
In great big London toon;
A fine, big man cam' up tae me'
Before I could luik roon.

Says he, "If ye're frae Scotlan',
I'll tak ye tae a place,
Whaur ye can get some grub tae eat,
An' wash ye're hauns an' face."

Sune on a bus we loupit,
Some ither chaps an' me,
Awa' tae St. Columba's Kirk
We rattled on wi' glee.

We got a wash – we needed it –
An' then took by the haun
An' set doon at a table,
The sicht, man, it wis graun.'

Wi' parritch, pies ·an' tea an' bread
We filled oorsels fu' up;
Wi' a' the bonnie lassies
Sayin', "Hae anither cup."

God bless the dear, kind ladies,
The gentlemen an' a',
We never wull forget ye,
When we are faur awa'.

Not only wull we think on ye,
We'll dae a guid lot mair;
For often on oor bended knees
We'll breathe an earnest prayer.

St. Columba's Hall, London,
30th Dec., 1917

Mary Blackwood, seen in centre with white medal, who led the hospitality effort at St Columba's. (Courtesy of St Columba's)

2

The Men in Hodden Grey: The London Scottish Regiment

Andrew D Parsons

The date was 30 October 1914. A fleet of the instantly recognisable open-topped London buses pulled up in front of the medieval Cloth Hall in the Belgian city of Ypres. Hundreds of the buses had been requisitioned by the War Office and sent to the Western Front as improvised troop transport. The soldiers boarding the buses were also instantly recognisable as Scottish, unmistakable in their kilts and glengarries.

These were not Regular soldiers from one of the famous Highland Regiments. They were Territorials from London. They were part-time volunteers who did military training on evenings and weekends. Only twelve weeks before these Londoners had been boarding these same buses at home and heading off for work and not to war. These men were no ordinary Londoners, they were part of a selective club drawn from Scotsmen resident in London. They were particularly distinguished by their uniforms. They wore Hodden Grey kilts and glengarries, they were the citizen soldiers of the London Scottish Regiment.

This is one telling of the story of the London Scottish Regiment in the Great War. It is the story of the Regiment in the context of the Scottish community in London from which the members came. It is the story of some of the individuals who served, their connections within this community and their experience of war. It looks at some of the institutions of the Caledonian community in London and their support for soldiers serving in the

A war-time silk cigarette card showing the badge of the London Scottish Regiment. (Trustees of the London Scottish Regiment)

London Scottish Regiment. This is the Scots in Great War London in uniform. The London Scots (14th County of London Regiment) were boarding buses to move up to the front line to the Ypres Salient near the Flanders village of Messines. On 31 October the London Scottish became the first territorial battalion to engage with the enemy in the First World War.

One of those on the bus was Douglas ("Duggie") Lyall Grant who came from an established London Scottish family, worked in banking, lived in Wimbledon and followed his father into the Regiment. He was an avid sportsman and enjoyed cricket and shooting but his passion was rugby football. Although not in the 1st XV he was pre-war member of London Scottish FC (LSFC). He would become one of the great personalities from the Regiment and LSFC. Although he was a Lieutenant in 1914, he had enlisted as a private soldier in 1909 and went straight into the Pipes and Drums, having learned to play bagpipes at school at Glenalmond in Perthshire. He would have much in common with 17-year-old Piper Archibald Angus, who had only just left Edinburgh Academy and had been the boy Pipe Major in the school band. Lieutenant Lyall Grant survived the baptism of fire on Hallowe'en at Messines. Piper Angus did not.

Lyall Grant went on to be awarded the Military Cross for gallantry in 1915. He was then taken prisoner in 1916 and remained a POW until 1918. Light-hearted accounts of his time at the Front and in captivity were published anonymously in the *London Scottish Regimental Gazette*. Of these, more later. Repatriated after the war, he carried on with the Territorial Army and commanded his Regiment from 1926–1930. More significantly he was one of the prime movers in restarting LSFC, serving as honorary secretary 1913–39 and then president 1939–63.

Lyall Grant would also have known Private James Ross outside of the Regiment, as they were teammates at London Scottish FC. Ross was a former Scottish rugby inter-national and club captain. Ross was killed at Messines. Another member of the rugby club was 21-year-old Private Robert Bruce Kyle from Station Road in Barnes. He too, was killed at Messines. Kyle was a member of the congregation at St Columba's and was one of 10 from the regiment on the church's memorial. Sergeant Norman Mcleod Brown survived Messines but was killed on Christmas Eve. He also worshipped at St Columba's. Brown also appears on the London *Camanachd* (Shinty) Club Memorial along with one other London Scot, Private William Cowie who worshipped at Crown Court Church of Scotland.

As if the irony of going to battle on the same omnibus that used to take them to the office wasn't enough, the London Scottish were heading for their baptism of fire on the very night they should have been celebrating. Hallowe'en was always the annual all-ranks dinner at Headquarters on Buckingham Gate in Westminster. Prizes were given, speeches were made and doubtlessly there would have been singing and reeling and general merriment. The regimental comforts committee, led by Mrs Constance Malcolm, wife of the Colonel Commanding the Regiment in France, sent haggis to the troops in crates labelled "Boots." Too few of the London Scots who boarded the buses in Ypres got to enjoy the haggis when it finally caught up with them several days later. Almost half of the 800 men who went into battle on Hallowe'en 1914 were either killed, missing or wounded. So, while the London Scottish were being fêted for being the first Territorials into battle, in hundreds of homes across London, Scots families were grieving.

Background

The Regiment was very much a product of Victorian London's Scottish community. The London Scottish Rifle Volunteers was founded in 1859 by Lord Elcho, later the Earl of Wemyss and March. Support for the creation of the Regiment, both moral and material, came from the Caledonian Society of London, the Highland Society of London and the Royal Scottish Corporation. It was to be a Highland Volunteer Regiment in everything but geography. The recruits who were to fill the ranks would be found exclusively from London's Scottish community. The uniform was consciously modelled upon that of the romantic ideal of the famous Highland Regiments. Lord Elcho chose the Hodden Grey, a plain, grey, homespun cloth for his new Regiment's uniform because it was a form of camouflage and it avoided arguments about whose clan tartan to wear. The Hodden Grey then became a unifying feature and its distinctiveness was a point of pride for those who wore it. They were London's kilted soldiers.

In 1886 the Regiment moved into a purpose-built drill hall at 59 Buckingham Gate. It was at this headquarters in Westminster that the territorials trained in peace time and young men volunteered in wartime. During the Second Boer War 1899–1902, some 200 London Scots volunteered for, and served in South Africa, many with the Gordon Highlanders. In 1914 it was here that recruits were examined and attested. Soldiers would pass through on their way back home from leave, courses or hospitalisation. Reunions were held at "59" after the war and the names of those who fell, 1,542 of them, are carved, in relief, on a large wooden memorial that still dominates the Regiment's home.

In the years immediately before the First World War the *London Scottish Regimental Gazette* published a full-page directory of Scottish societies in London. There was definitely an awareness of being part of the larger Scottish community in London and many members of the Regiment belonged to more than one organisation. Such was its position among these Scottish societies in London, that while the Regiment faced up to war on the front line, the rest of London's Scottish community supported it by finding new recruits, providing comforts in wartime and continuing to succour veterans and dependants after the armistice.

The Regiment has been called the "standing evidence of the patriotism of London Scots." It was of course not the only patriotic Scottish club in London, but it was the only voluntary Scottish organisation in London whose main purpose was to bear arms in defence of the realm. (By contrast the Scots Guards, were professional Scottish soldiers located in London.) In this regard, the London Scottish Regiment holds a unique place amongst the exiled Caledonian community in London in their experience of the First World War. Members took great pains to describe it as a Scottish regiment and identified themselves as Scottish soldiers in dress, music and tradition. It was a huge head-turner on the streets of London to see a column of kilted soldiers marching past Buckingham Palace to the music of the Pipes and Drums. The Regimental History (*The London Scottish in the Great War*) boasted that the "Battalion … represented before London, in visible form, the Scottish people."

Birth or Parentage

It has to be said that the London Scottish Regiment in 1914 was not representative of the Scots living in the city, let alone of the general population of London. What was then still a single battalion was a very narrowly self-selecting organisation. The recruits had to be Scots of either "birth or parentage" and there was a joining fee. The rank and file were mostly educated at public schools or universities and were very much white-collar workers. The majority listed their occupation as "clerk." In *Tommy: The British Soldier on the Western Front 1914–18* Richard Holmes quoted one Londoner who wrote that:

> amongst foremost London Clubs before the War could be numbered the head-quarters of half a dozen of the leading Territorial Battalions. Such regiments as the Artists Rifles, the Civil Service Rifles, the Honourable Artillery Company, the London Rifle Brigade, the London Scottish and the Kensingtons … In those days the offices in the City worked longer hours than they do now; and Saturday mornings off were by no means so prevalent. At the same time the amusements offered were less and sport was not so well organised … Accordingly the young men in the banks, insurance offices, the Civil Service and the City generally joined the Territorial Battalions as much for their social activities and their facilities for exercise and sport provided as much as for any other reason. Friends would join the same battalion almost on leaving school … and certainly the last thing on their minds was that they would shortly be fighting for their country in a great European war.
>
> Edward Bryan Latham: *A Territorial Soldier's War*, 1967, p. 1

For the London Scottish, there was the small matter of the joining fee or member-ship subscription. This was a hangover from the days of the Rifle Volunteers when the battalion seemed to be a rather heavily armed social club but continued up until conscription was enacted in 1916 and such levies were prohibited. The solicitor A. Stuart Dolden recalled paying one pound as a joining fee upon enlisting in 1914 at a time when a private soldier's pay was a shilling a day. No.1607 Private D.A. Stewart enlisted in 1912. He was educated at the Whitgift School in Croydon and declined a place at Cambridge University in favour of articling to a firm of accountants. Thus, Stewart must have been one of the very few chartered accountants to have earned the

Distinguished Conduct Medal when he served as a Lance Corporal at Givenchy in January of 1915.

Professional Men

On the eve of war, the London Scottish was composed of well-educated, largely professional men of Scottish birth or parentage who could afford the membership fee. Other socially exclusive battalions of the London Regiment, such as the Artists' Rifles and the Inns of Court ceased to be active service units at the Front because they could not provide a regular supply of recruits. Both ended the war as officer training units. Even within London, it is not hard to imagine that the stream of similar recruits would run dry before too long. But the London Scottish were further hamstrung by their insistence (their cadre of actors notwithstanding) on ethnic exclusivity.

It took in excess of 6,000 soldiers to populate the single battalion establishment of 1,000 men over the duration of the war and into 1919, by then, the London Scottish had two battalions at the Front and a third (reserve) battalion as a depot at home. At a conservative estimate, 15,000 men passed through the ranks of the London Scottish over four years of war and in three theatres of operation. There was no way then, that the available pool of pre-war young Scottish articling clerks and university leavers could fill the vacancies in the Regiment as they were needed. The definition of "London Scot" needed to be refined.

Recruits of the London Scottish Regiment and its pipers march through London in the early years of the war. (Trustees of the London Scottish Regiment)

The pre-war social composition of the Regiment was part of the problem. It may now sound amusing that No.1791 Private Marryat Ross Dobie, an Oxford graduate in classics who was later to be Head Librarian at the National Library of Scotland, wrote in his diary in 1914: "On arriving in the trench I threw away *Claude d'Antioch* and *Récits des Temps Mérovingiens* and a tin of bully beef." Not surprisingly, Dobie was commissioned to the Intelligence Corps in 1915. He was not an isolated case. In fact, throughout the course of the war, the London Scottish lost more men to the commissioning process than to the enemy. 1,542 all ranks are listed on the war memorial and more than 2,750 men were commissioned from the ranks, some to the London Scottish, some to the Infantry but many to the rest of the army and others to the Royal Flying Corps and the Royal Navy. These were hugely capable individuals who, with even a minimum of military training and experience, were better placed to lead in a time of mass mobilization. The Gunn brothers, (No.2240) Kenneth and (No.2139) Marcus, both members of the Twickenham Rowing Club, were commissioned to separate battalions of the Black Watch and both were killed in 1916. Another pre-war volunteer and Messines veteran was solicitor No.2267. Private Thomas MacDonald Eggar. He was commissioned into the London Scottish and then seconded to the Air Ministry. Eggar drafted the Act of Parliament which created the Royal Air Force (RAF) on 1 April 1918, by merging the Army's Royal Flying Corps (RFC) with the Royal Naval Air Service; from five RFC squadrons at the outbreak of war, the RAF by early 1919 had 114,000 airmen, 4,000 combat aircraft and 150 squadrons. Interestingly, when Stuart Dolden was offered a commission he decided that he couldn't leave his comrades in the trenches and refused. The Old Whitgiftian accountant who won the Distinguished Conduct Medal, Douglas Stewart, was commissioned to the Cheshire Regiment in 1915 and killed in 1916. After the announcement of his DCM the Regiment's War Diary, now in the National Archives, recorded on 11 June 1915: "during the last three weeks the very large number of applications for commissions from the ranks have been forwarded by the Commanding Officer resulting in the loss to the Battalion of a large number of its best men."

Alexander Fleming, the discoverer of penicillin, was a pre-war London Scot who earned the Territorial Long Service Medal as a private. He resigned in April 1914 to concentrate on his career and was disappointed when war was declared not to be allowed to rejoin his old Regiment having been directed to the Royal Army Medical Corps (RAMC) instead. Fleming's Territorial Force Efficiency Medal is displayed at the National Museum of Scotland next to his Nobel Prize. When Dr Angus MacNab, the Medical Officer, was killed at Messines in 1914, three medically qualified privates allegedly tossed a coin to decide who would lay down his rifle and take over treating troops. Private Eric Wright won (or lost …) the toss. Wright was a Cambridge educated medical officer of health from Romford. He later died in 1915 while serving as a medical officer in a hospital in Egypt.

Other men would have to be found. The first draft of reinforcements from outwith the Regiment came from 200 men from the 2nd/9th Battalion Highland Light Infantry (The Glasgow Highlanders). They were posted to the London Scottish in

While its 1st Battalion were fighting in France, the London Scottish Regiment's 2nd Battalion halts at the windmill on Wimbledon Common during a route march, 24 October 1914. (Trustees of the London Scottish Regiment)

early September 1916, after the carnage of the first day of the Battle of the Somme in July but before the significant actions around Combles in late September. The London Scottish were fortunate in that the Glasgow Highlanders had a similarly long history as a volunteer regiment and recruited from the better educated sons of Glasgow's middle class.

A longstanding relationship with the Gordon Highlanders was formalised in 1916. Adjutants and instructing staff had been sourced from the Gordons since Victorian times and many London Scots who served in South Africa served as Gordon Highlanders. Drafts went both ways and from 1917 London Scots could also find themselves posted to battalions of the Gordon Highlanders. On balance, however, more Gordon Highlanders filled vacancies in the London Scottish than the other way around. In truth, the regiment could not afford to be too fussy as trained soldiers were needed at the Front regardless of birthplace, accent or cap badge. Notably, the 2nd Battalion was heavily reinforced by Gordons when they returned, depleted, from Palestine in 1918. The drafts of Gordons ensured that the 2nd Battalion was able to fight through the last 100 days.

Hollywood's Finest (In Due Course)

The London Scottish had some reputation prior to the war which made it attractive for young men in the capital to join. Four actors destined to be true film stars before and after the Second World War all served in the ranks of the Regiment.

Claude Rains (1889–1967) would later star in the film *The Invisible Man* (1933), but is most often recognised playing the French Captain Renault alongside Humphrey Bogart and Ingrid Bergman in *Casablanca* (1942). But his name belied the fact he was a London boy, born in Camberwell in 1889, brought up in Fulham. By 1911 his father Frederick had morphed from organ builder to a career in the brand new moving picture industry, and Claude himself was assistant manager at the Haymarket Theatre. He joined the 3rd Battalion of the London Scottish in 1916, and later that year was gassed near Ypres, and lost most of the sight in his right eye.

Herbert Marshall (1890–1966) was born in London but travelled as a child with both parents being actors in repertory theatre. He also joined the 3/14th London Scottish in 1916, was severely wounded at the Second Battle of Arras on 9 April 1917, was stood down a year later with the Silver War Badge for those honourably discharged due to wounds or sickness, and eventually lost his leg. With a prosthesis he walked with a slight limp that didn't prevent him starring as a romantic lead alongside Garbo, Dietrich, Crawford and the rest of Hollywood's finest.

Ronald Coleman (1891–1958) first joined the London Scottish in 1909. Badly injured at Messines, but lucky to survive when a shell exploded nearby and sent him flying, he too was discharged with a Silver War Badge and went on to star in Hollywood and win an Oscar in 1948.

Still instantly recognisable, Basil Rathbone MC (1892–1967) was born in South Africa to British parents who moved back to Hampstead in 1895. He enlisted in the 2nd Battalion in 1915, giving his profession as actor. A year later as so many of the London Scottish did, he moved on, in his case for a commission as an intelligence officer with the Liverpool Regiment. Perhaps that was the career move that fitted him for his most famous role as the first major screen Sherlock Holmes.

The Regiment's four famous actors – subjects of the National Archives blog entitled "The Hollywood Battalion," give the regiment a retrospective sheen of glamour; but the odd thing as that none of the four appear to have had much if any Scots blood.

Likewise, Sir Cedric Hardwicke (1893–1964), leading Shakespearean actor and doyen of the British film industry, who also served in with the London Scottish from 1915–1921. So what was the attraction? Was it a simply that the regiment's Victoria headquarters were convenient for London's theatreland?

Sports

One example of the interconnectedness of the exile community is that of the London *Camanachd* (Shinty) Club. Like the London Scottish Football Club and many other organisations, we know the names of those who fell because they were memorialised. Less is known about those who served and survived. Two of the 11 names on the London *Camanachd* Club war memorial, housed in Crown Court Church, were also members of the Regiment. Both men also are commemorated on the Rolls of Honour in their respective churches. No.1057 Sergeant Norman Mcleod Brown was a pre-war

Territorial from Kirkcaldy, played shinty and worshipped at St Columba's. He was killed on Christmas Eve 1914 having survived Messines. No.2783 Private Cowie, from Brechin, died of wounds on 28 September at the Battle of Loos. There must have been a few of their fellow club members in the Regiment. In 1920 the *London Scottish Regimental Gazette* announced that "It is proposed to continue the Shinty Match on Wimbledon Common on Boxing Day. This year a team of all-comers in tartan kilts will compete against a team wearing Hodden Grey."

Another nexus of the Scottish community in London was the London Scottish Football Club, although by no means all soldiers in the club served in the London Scottish Regiment: of the 103 names on the LSFC memorial, only 10 or a dozen had served at one time with the Regiment. Similarly, not all rugby players serving in the Regiment played for LSFC. For example, Captain T.D.O. MacLagan MC and Bar, a Glaswegian and a member of the Regiment since 1902, was captain of the Civil Service RFC. He was killed in Palestine serving with the 2nd Battalion in 1918.

Many more rugby players such as Lyall Grant served with the Regiment and survived. No.1058. Private Ernest Alexander Kinross turned out for the LSFC 1st XV in 1914. At the Front, on New Year's Eve of that year, he recalled that an inter-company rugby match was interrupted by an order to move immediately and they departed, still in their kit, covered in mud.

Much later, when in reserve billets at Le Transloy in September 1917, the *Regimental History* recorded: "Several games of Rugby were played and it was soon discovered that the Battalion still possessed a great amount of talent for this fine game."

Recruiting and Willie Martin

One of the unsung heroes of the Scottish war effort in London was Willie Martin, a Gaelic speaker from Stornoway. Martin came to London in the 1880s and worked in the shipping industry. He joined the London Scottish Rifle Volunteers in 1887 and resigned from the Corps in 1912 with rank of Colour Sergeant. On the outbreak of war and at the age of 49 he re-enlisted, was commissioned and made quartermaster of the reserve Battalion. He did not serve overseas and as a lieutenant, he did not achieve high rank. Willie Martin's real contribution, however, was in his role as recruiting officer.

It could be argued that few others embodied the inter-connectedness of the Scottish community in London more than Willie Martin. From his arrival in London he took an active part in Scottish social life and was a member the Sutherland Association, Ross and Cromarty Association, *Camanachd* (Shinty) Club, Hon. Secretary of the Gaelic Society 1900–07 and he served for almost 30 years in the London Scottish Regiment. During the Boer War he organised parcels for soldiers at the Front and was the recruiting sergeant for the London Scottish for the decade before he retired. A tribute published in the *London Scottish Regimental Gazette* on his second retirement in 1917 boasted: "The history of Scottish Recruiting, especially the raising of two battalions and the London Recruiting of the Highland Brigade at Bedford, centres round our late Quartermaster. [He is credited with] the negotiations which cumulated in the meeting of London Scots in the Royal Corporation Hall."

It is claimed that it was Martin who began lobbying for permission to recruit a second battalion in late August 1914. He was the interlocutor between the Regimental hierarchy and local London Scottish worthies such as Willie Grant of the Highland Society of London and Thomas Moncrieff, Secretary of the Royal Scottish Corporation. A second battalion was fully recruited by 2 September and it was suggested then that efforts should be directed towards recruiting for the Highland Brigade at Bedford. Few people dreamed that the war would last past Christmas and future recruitment was not a priority.

Once the second battalion was established, the *Gazette* published statistics about the recruits. Occupationally, the men who rushed to the colours in the first weeks of the war were very similar to the pre-war volunteers. There were 420 clerks; 226 commercial men; 264 professionals; 101 undergraduates; 10 engineering apprentices and 1 member of parliament. Forty percent were Scottish born and 60 percent claimed Scottish parentage. Sixty individuals were Gaelic speakers.

A year later the *Gazette* reported that on 4 November 1915 "There was a meeting with the object of stimulating recruiting for Ours under the auspices of the Federated Council of Scottish Associations in London in the Royal Scottish Corporation Hall." No less than the Secretary of State for Scotland, Rt. Hon. T. MacKinnon Wood MP, said "We have got to fill up the ranks of that Regiment sadly depleted in the fields of Flanders and of France. We have got to make up for the thousand officers that this regiment has sent to the army." Previously the Council had focussed its attentions on marshalling the resources of the community in London to provide comforts for not only soldiers of the London Scottish Regiment, but for Scottish servicemen across the Army and Royal Navy. The Scottish community continued to support the Regiment and made this concerted effort to keep it supplied with recruits. Willie Martin's active participation in the community was a critical, if unheralded, player in this recruiting effort.

Matters of Faith

The Presbyterian faith was one of the defining features of the Regiment's self-identity. As much as the kilt, glengarry and bagpipes were unmistakable outward symbols of "Caledonia" so was the Church of Scotland. Membership in the Church of Scotland was certainly not a prerequisite for membership in the Regiment. The records of both St Columba's and Crown Court Church show that of the members of those congregations who served, only about 10 percent served in the London Scottish Regiment.

There was an institutional relationship. The Regimental chapel was, and is, St Columba's, the Regimental chaplain was the incumbent at St Columba's and there was an annual battalion church parade at Pont Street every April. After the war this church parade was moved to Remembrance Sunday and has remained a tradition to this day. In 1914, the Regimental Chaplain was the Rev. Archibald Fleming appointed in 1903 and was previously acting chaplain to the volunteer battalion of the Royal Scots in Edinburgh from 1898–1902. For reasons of age (he was 50), possibly health and most probably having the responsibility of his own large congregation, Padre Fleming did not travel overseas in the First World War. He remained a Chaplain to the Forces and ministered, amongst many others, to members of the Regiment at home.

The Rev. John MacWilliam Vallance was born in Greenock, and educated at Oban High and St Andrews University. He was ordained in 1911 and received the call to Caledonian Church, Holloway. Rev. Vallance ministered to the volunteers of the 1st Battalion, he travelled to France with the Regiment in September 1914 and he was present at Messines. The only problem was that Vallance was still a civilian and not officially an Army chaplain. This is a marvellous example of the extemporised nature of the first months of the war and the fact that officialdom really didn't know what to do with a territorial battalion on the Western Front. Vallance was recognised as a temporary Chaplain to the Forces and received the 1914 Star, War and Victory medals. Vallance was relieved in March of 1915. It is doubtful that a Regular army regiment would have been able to "smuggle" a civilian clergyman to the Front, in time of war.

Rev. J.S. Stewart ministered to the 1st Battalion from March 1915 through Loos and the Somme until August 1916 when he was relieved by the United Free Minister, Rev. David Colville Lusk. Rev. Lusk was from Edinburgh and before the war he had ministered to the Presbyterian students at Oxford University. He served with the 1st Battalion from mid-1916 to 1919, through Arras, 3rd Ypres, Cambrai, the Ludendorff Offensive in 1918 and the last 100 days. He was awarded the Military Cross and bar for gallantry as well as being Mentioned in Dispatches. Rev. Lusk continued as Regimental Padre after the war and resigned only in 1936.

The 2nd Battalion began with the appointment of the minister of Brondesbury Presbyterian Church, the Rev. E.B.H. MacPherson. In 1920 a memorial window was dedicated to the memory of 34 parishioners of that church who fell in the war including Captain James C. Miller, who fell at Cambrai in November 1917 and No.3184. Sergeant Alick F. Patterson who was posted to the 2nd Battalion and fell in August 1918 in Belgium. All three were neighbours in Cricklewood. Rev. John Edward Reilly MC was the one Methodist minister attached to the Regiment and was with the 2nd Battalion in the UK prior to deployment in June 1916. Another Presbyterian, the Rev. James Mitchell, whose peace-time church was St Andrew's in Reading, accompanied the 2nd Battalion through most of the war from 1916–18. He was especially remembered as the padre who was with the battalion throughout the campaign in the Holy Land. The Rev. G. Lindsay Leslie notably delivered the Immortal Memory at the battalion's Burns Supper in Jerusalem in January 1918, "within the hearing of the guns of the enemy"

On 2 November 1919 a service in memory of the fallen of the London Scottish Regiment at St Columba's was conducted by the Revs. Fleming, Lusk, and

MacPherson. The lesson was read by the newly-ennobled Earl Haig, newly-appointed as the Regiment's Honorary Colonel, and later to become an elder of the church. The London Scottish honoured their own, in their spiritual home at Pont Street, and in their own indomitable style. Pipes would be played, kilts would be worn and the worship would be that of the Church of Scotland.

Pipes and Drums

It is a testament to the *esprit de corps* of the London Scottish that while the personnel of a battalion changed over the course of four years of active service, the spirit of the organisation remained. The Regimental history suggested that "it was as if the mere donning of the kilt made at once a London Scot, imbued by the instinct of the old traditions." Of course, there was more to it than just the kilt. Soldiers who served in the earlier campaigns later held significant roles as officers and senior NCOs and maintained standards and acted as guardians of traditions. That is one of the great strengths of the British regimental system. The soldier is defined by his regiment and not the other way around.

To see how this happened, we can look at one small sub-unit, the Pipes and Drums, and draw corollaries for the manning of the Regiment as a whole. On the outbreak of war, 14 of about 20 pipers and drummers volunteered for overseas service. Pipe Major Robert Robertson (No.120) was one who remained behind and organised the band of the reserve battalion. Robertson, already in his late 40s, was an architect and a member of the Caledonian Club. Many other pre-war Territorials assumed positions in the reserve battalion to build that battalion up with the surge of recruits in August of 1914 and perpetuate the regimental ethos.

The pipers and drummers of 1914 were used as front-line soldiers. Four were killed at Messines: No.3085 Piper Archibald Angus, a native of Chile and at age 17, the youngest to be killed that day; No.142. Corporal J. Carey, from Dundee; No.1008 Lance Corporal Eric Glenn Chapman, who also played rugby at London Scottish FC, and No.1341. Piper Douglas Parkyn. No.1870. Piper J.F. Bennie and No.139. Lance Corporal Harry G. Latham would be killed in the weeks that followed. The remainder were either wounded or invalided before the new year and by Easter 1915 there were only two pipers in the battalion. While regular drafts from the 2nd Battalion kept the 1st Battalion up to strength, pipers were harder to come by.

It is a proud boast that through the course of the war in excess of 2,750 other ranks were commissioned to be officers in the Army, the Royal Navy and in the Royal Flying Corps (and eventually into the new RAF). For example, No.1331. Private James W. McHattie survived Messines and was commissioned into the 5th Battalion York and Lancs Regiment in December 1915. He was killed while attached to the RAF in April 1918. McHattie is commemorated on the Crown Court Church war memorial. In this regard, having the reputation of being a "white collar corps" was a curse as the typical pre-war London Scottish soldier was what the War Office considered to be ideal officer material.

In contrast, some remained in the ranks and returned to the Front. No.1477 Piper Charles Oram was a clerk at the stock exchange in civilian life. He was invalided home after Messines in 1914 and was posted to the Reserve Battalion for convalescence. Oram then joined a draft for the 2nd Battalion and travelled to Salonika in 1917. Oram was one of the pipers to play into the liberated city of Jerusalem and later became Pipe Major of the 2nd Battalion. Pipe Major Oram was a member of St Columba's Church.

The problem with recruiting and retaining pipers continued. By the Battle of Loos on 25 September 1915, only two pipers remained and they were both employed as runners. No.1938. Piper Alexander Joss was a product of the Royal Caledonian Schools which was a fertile source of recruits. Joss was wounded at Loos and then commissioned to the Army Ordnance Corps. The other piper was a war time volunteer, No.4167. Piper Donald Pinnington. He was also wounded at Loos and then commissioned into the Royal Navy. Even by September of 1915, the flow of recruits who had rushed to the colours in the first months of the war were beginning to dry up.

By 1916 and the Battle of the Somme, the 1st Battalion still had plenty of familiar old faces but many of the pre-war territorials, the ones with the connections in London's Caledonian community and memberships in other Scottish organisations, were disappearing from the Regiment having been killed, wounded, or commissioned. The vacancies were being filled by recruits who were perhaps more representative of the general population. The pipers and drummers were employed as stretcher bearers which was not always safer than serving in an infantry platoon. On 13 May 1917, at Arras, the Regimental Aid Post received a direct hit and two piper / stretcher bearers were killed. No.3329. Piper Andrew Paton was 26 and from Glasgow and No.7765 Piper Simon Campbell was 19 and from North Lochboisdale, South Uist. On his enlistment papers his occupation was listed as a footman in Chelsea. The social profile of recruits was shifting but they were still Scots and unified by the Hodden Grey, a unique cap badge and the perpetuation of tradition and hard won regimental prestige. The individuals may have changed but the London Scottish Regiment as an institution persisted.

The Battle Honours

The soldiers of the London Scottish wore a brass badge on their shoulders bearing the number 14 over a semi-circle with "County of London." The London Regiment was a massive 28-Battalion Regiment encompassing all of London's Territorial Infantry Battalions, most with their own unique cap badges, uniforms and traditions. For example, the 15th London Regiment was the Civil Service Rifles, the 16th, the Queen's Westminsters and the 18th, the London Irish Rifles. The official designation of the London Scottish was 14th County of London (The London Scottish) Regiment. Often this was shortened to 1st/14th Londons and when a second and third battalion were recruited they were known as 2nd/14th Londons and 3rd/14th Londons.

The 1st Battalion London Scottish, relieved of front-line duties, march back for a rest, Arras, 1 April 1918. (Trustees of the London Scottish Regiment)

The 1st Battalion served on the Western Front from September 1914 until the armistice, after which they formed part of the Army of Occupation until May 1919. The 2nd Battalion provided drafts to the first until June of 1916 when they too were sent to France. In December 1916 they were moved to Salonika and then to Egypt where they fought through the Palestine campaign under General Allenby in 1917–18. The Victoria Cross was awarded to two men of this battalion during the Palestine Campaign. The 2nds returned to the Western Front in July of 1918 and finished the war in Belgium. A 3rd battalion served at home as a training and administrative depot but did not serve overseas.

The London Scottish proceeded from Southampton to Havre on the SS *Winnifredian* on 15 September 1914 and were the first territorial regiment to arrive in France. Initially, they were given mundane jobs such as unloading trains and guarding prisoners until push came to shove and a crisis on the Ypres Salient near the village of Messines gave them their opportunity. On 31 October the London Scottish held their section of line against repeated enemy attacks and gained fame as the first Territorial infantry regiment to engage with the enemy in the war.

Almost half became casualties that night, either killed missing or wounded. The Medical Officer, Captain Angus MacNab was reportedly bayonetted while tending to the wounded. MacNab was a New Zealander and a celebrated eye specialist at Moorfields Hospital. He was a member of St Columba's. Another member of the congregation was No.2144. Private A.G.R. MacKenzie who lost his right leg that night. He was 35 and an architect. No.1823. Private Andrew Smith was 20 and from Ballater. He also worshipped at St Columba's. He was posted as "missing" and for a while, it was thought he was safe as a prisoner of war. His remains were never found and his name is commemorated on the Menin Gate Memorial to the Missing in Ypres along with 100 of his comrades from 1914. He may be the same A. Smith who appears on the LSFC memorial.

Lieutenant Duggie Lyall Grant began keeping diaries in the early days of the war, and the *Regimental Gazette* in December 1914 published, anonymously, his carefully redacted account of the Regiment's "baptism" at Messines, without of course mentioning the location by name.

> October 30th [1914] – We're off! Suddenly yesterday over the border and now away six miles to the trenches. No more because we are falling in ... I scrawled a line this morning which was all I had time for, now in the afternoon we are sitting by the roadside, with guns popping all around, and not knowing what we are going to do. ... The guns are incessant, and the whistle of the shell is really rather entertaining – up to now! There is at the moment very heavy infantry fire. I have got a rifle and bayonet, which is a good job – it gives you something to hang on to. The fellows are very cheery, and I cannot see the slightest sign of funk, though there is bound to be when we get actually shelled. ... The din is getting worse every minute. Will continue this later as at the moment my hands are frozen. Later – just off to the match – will get this through by someone.

He goes on to describe the action in detail in the entry for 2 November entitled indeed "The Match." and his description brilliantly details how the soldier in the field knows only what he can actually see or hear around him and has no idea about the grand scheme of things. Afterwards:

> I then met the Adjutant and heard for the first time what we had done. He said ... the General ... told him that the 'Scottish' the day before, in getting to their position, had done what two out of three Regular Battalions would have failed to do, and with a steadiness such as he had never seen surpassed, and that by keeping the Germans at bay all night, although finally being driven back through being outnumbered, we had saved the guns.

No mention of course of the hundreds killed or wounded or missing in action.

Over the coming months Lyall Grant would be a regular contributor to the *Gazette*, his positive reports from the Front no doubt doing much to keep up spirits at home, and to aid the constant challenges of recruiting men to fill the gaps left by the fallen.

The 1st Battalion was an enigma in that initially it didn't belong to any higher formation and it was circumstance, heavy casualties, that found the Territorials from London serving with the regular battalions. They considered it a great honour to be serving with the 1st Coldstream Guards, 1st Scots Guards, 1st Black Watch and 1st Cameron Highlanders in the 1st Guards Brigade of the 1st Division. Supported by regular drafts from home, the 1st Battalion carried on in the front line through the Battles of Givenchy and Festubert in the winter of 1915. It was with the 1st Division that the London Scottish fought at Loos in September 1915.

Already by the Battle of Loos, London Scots had been commissioned elsewhere and returned to the Front. Lieutenant James Kennedy was a 35-year-old originally from Inverness-shire. He enlisted in the London Scottish when war was declared and was sent to the Western Front in March 1915. He was commissioned to the Cameron Highlanders in August and died of wounds on 26 September 1915. Kennedy's name is on the same memorial in Crown Court Church as the Shinty-playing Private Cowie. The rugby-playing medical officer to the London Scottish, Captain George Grant, RAMC, member of the London Scottish Football Club, also fell at Loos.

In January of 1916, the London Scottish were moved to the 56th (1st London Territorial) Division which was composed of other battalions of the London Regiment. It was with the 56th Division that the London Scots were launched into the Battle of the Somme, at the northern extreme, in a feint attack at Gommecourt. That first day was a disaster for the British Army and casualties in the Scottish totalled 590 killed, missing and wounded. Other battalions fared even worse in the carnage, but that would be no consolation to the families of the dead. No.2310. Corporal Alexander MacDonald was 29 and from Aberfeldy. He is commemorated on the Thiepval Memorial to the Missing. No.5804. Private William Young was 32, a native of Banffshire, he lived on Battersea Church Road. He is buried in Gommecourt British Cemetery. Both worshipped at Crown Court.

The Battle of the Somme lasted until November when the 51st Highland Division finally took the ground at Beaumont Hamel. The London Scottish were engaged significantly between 9 and 27 September in the area of Ginchy, Leuze Wood and Bouleux Wood, ultimately taking the town of Combles. In the fighting from July to when they were finally relieved on 8 October, the Battalion had lost as many casualties as on the first day of the Somme. No.1581. Sergeant Major R.M.L. Walkinshaw was a pre-war territorial from Leith who worked in London as a civil servant. For his gallantry and leadership in these latter battles he was awarded the Military Medal and appointed Regimental Sergeant Major. He was also a member of Crown Court.

The Canadians assaulted Vimy Ridge on 9 April 1917 but that was one small part of the larger Battle of Arras. The Scottish fought from 9 April to 11 May in the area of Neuville Vitasse. Second Lieutenant W.S. Crawford was killed, and the adjutant, Captain W.A. Young was wounded. No.6776. Private William H Leibow, a dental mechanical technician from Perth, who lived in Kingston upon Thames, was wounded in the head at Arras but survived and was commissioned into an English regiment. All three men were members of St Columba's.

The Third Battle of Ypres, popularly known as Passchendaele, was fought between 31 July and 10 November 1917. The London Scottish were, for a short period fighting in the area of Langemarck before moving back to the Arras Sector. No.2045. Private James Mitchell, from Dumfriesshire, was one of those London Scots who was posted to an English regiment upon arriving on the Western Front in 1917. He was sent as one of a draft to reinforce 26th Battalion (City of London) Royal Fusiliers in July 1917 and was killed with them on 21 September 1917 at Passchendaele. A member of St Columba's, he was an only son and left a widowed mother.

The 1st Battalion's commander, Colonel E.D. Jackson DSO, considered the Battle of Cambrai to be his "Hallowe'en" moment, or most significant action. The battle was fought in the week leading up to St Andrew's Day. Despite suffering significant casualties over the week, a depleted London Scottish Regiment withstood a determined enemy counterattack on 30 November 1917. Padre Lusk and RSM Walkinshaw were awarded the Military Cross in that action.

In 1918 the 1st Battalion experienced the lows of the Ludendorff Offensive which was the Germans' last-gasp effort to breach allied lines and force an armistice. The Scottish saw very heavy fighting defending the line at St Eloi near Vimy Ridge in March. No.515717. Private James Stewart Gordon, 32 years old and originally from Fochabers, was killed there on 29 March and No.510449 Private J.J. Watson was wounded in the same battle. They worshipped at Crown Court.

The battalion saw significant actions at Boiry-Becquerelle in August, Bullecourt in September and were back near Cambrai in October where they ended their war. The 1st Battalion was sent to the town of Hilden outside Cologne as part of the Army of Occupation and finally arrived back in London in July 1919.

The 2nd Battalion had a very different yet no less storied war. It was populated by the same demographic as the 1st Battalion, pre-war territorials and Scotsmen resident in London and it was not unusual for soldiers to have served in both battalions. The 2nd Battalion arrived on the Western Front in June 1916 as part of the 60th (London Territorial) Division. They were used for holding and defending trenches but did not have an attacking role during the Battle of the Somme.

In December 1916 the 60th Division was moved to Salonika to face the Bulgarian Army in the mountains around Lake Dorian. In June 1917 the 2nd London Scottish was transferred to the Egyptian Expeditionary Force under the command of General Allenby and prepared for the Palestine Campaign.

The 2nd Battalion next saw action on Hallowe'en, on the third anniversary of the Battle of Messines. Nineteen men who fought at Beersheba were survivors of Messines. By early December the British were on the outskirts of Jerusalem and that city was taken on 9 December 1917. In the fighting for the approaches to Jerusalem No.510051. Corporal Charles W. Train, another Messines veteran, single-handedly neutralised two Turkish machine guns and was awarded the Victoria Cross.

The battalion marched eastward. After Jericho had fallen on 24 February, they pushed across the River Jordan on 23 March and on 26 March took the town of Es Salt. On the night of 30 April, the London Scots attacked the heavily defended hilltop position of El Haud. No.511828. Private R.E. Cruickshank saw that his platoon was pinned down and volunteered to get help. He was hit by enemy sniper fire four different

The 2nd Battalion London Scottish temporarily occupy Es Salt on their way to Amman in Transjordan, before being driven back by Turkish forces on 24/25 March 1918.
(Trustees of the London Scottish Regiment)

times while attempting this rescue and was awarded the Regiment's second Victoria Cross. No.511895. Private William Beveridge, a member of the Crown Court congregation, was killed in this action.

The London Scottish were finished with the Palestine Campaign but not finished fighting. In June 1918 the battalion sailed for Europe and the Western Front, were posted to the 30th Division and were back in action at Dranoutre in Flanders on 21 August. The 2nds continued through Belgium and on to the River Lys and ended the war near Avelghem, crossing much of the same territory that the 1st Battalion had fought over in 1914.

Benevolence

The troops at the Front were well supported by the wider community at home.

They received reading material and knitted goods from St Columba's and later from the Federated Council. The Regiment's own welfare fund, *Mrs Malcolm's Fund*, (Constance Malcolm's own husband had left his solicitors' practise in Wimbledon and went to the Front with the Regiment in 1914) was launched with a letter to the *London Scottish Regimental Gazette* in September 1914 headed: "Comforts for our Boys at the Front"

Dear Sir, May I appeal through your columns to the friends of the London Scottish to help me to keep them supplied with comforts while on active service. The London Scottish Old Comrades Association, who are helping me with the clerical work will be glad to afford all information to friends interested.

The congregation of St Columba's was generous right from the start. The October 1914 *St Columba's Church Magazine* records that even before the 1st Battalion left for France: "a request for (socks) for the London Scottish on the eve of their departure for France … was attended to and eighty pairs and three dozen good shirts were sent by return." In the same issue there was an appeal for newspapers: "Will members of the congregation undertake to post, in each case on the evening of the day of issue, to the Front, for the use of the London Scottish."

It wasn't only the troops at the Front whose welfare was being catered for by the congregation. In September 1914 a collection was taken for the purchase of an other-ranks' recreation tent for the home camp of the Reserve Battalion. Subsequent issues of the magazine gave regular updates on the "St Columba's Tent" and recorded donations of writing paper, books and magazines provided for the soldiers.

The first list of subscribers to Mrs Malcolm's Fund had 49 names and raised £320/13/0d by 25 September. The Fund sent haggis for the first Hallowe'en in France. In the first 12 months of operation it raised £2,765/8/1d and was regularly supplying oatmeal, compressed soup, chocolate etc. Knitted goods were always required and a special appeal in September 1916 was particularly poignant: "Hosetops are still much needed, the barbed wire on 1 July played havoc with them," a soldier wrote describing the 1916 Hallowe'en Dinner at the Front provided by the fund. The menu included: "Malcolm soup, roast beef and veg, haggis and currant pudding sweets and cigarettes." The "Malcolm" in the soup most definitely referred to their benefactress and not to their now former Colonel. In addition to socks, hose tops and blue touries for the bonnets, cigarettes and tobacco were supplied in vast quantities as well as soap, razors, stationery and sporting equipment. In 1919 Mrs Malcolm again used the pages of the *Gazette* to offer thanks: "The success of this fund has been due, not only to the generosity of the subscribers and workers but also to the untiring energy and devotion of Major Lyall Grant [Father of Duggie] who has … superintended the buying and forwarding of various comforts to the two battalions at the Front."

It was appreciated. Mrs Malcolm wrote to the *Magazine* in 1914: " … will you convey to the members of your congregation who have very kindly contributed to the comforts sent both before the battalion left for France and again now, my most sincere thanks for all the beautiful things sent." The troops called her "our fairy godmother"

The Federated Council had been established in 1914 to organise and marshal the charitable efforts of the Scottish community in London and to act as a single distributor of donations. At the end of its first year of work it was reported in *St Columba's Church Magazine* in December 1915 that amongst other things, they had distributed "10,314 pairs of socks down to 6 copies of Burns poems and 1 concertina." The London Scottish, amongst many others, benefited from the Federated Council's largesse.

After the war the Scottish community continued to support the dependants of soldiers killed or disabled by war service and those veterans in need of assistance. When it was wound up in 1919, Mrs Malcolm's Fund had raised £5,196/14/11d. The unspent balance was transferred to the War Memorial Fund.

Those Scots at home in London still played an enormous role in the war effort, as can be seen in the example of providing for the welfare of the soldiers of the London Scottish Regiment.

POWs

The sheer numbers of First World War POWs were a logistical challenge to captors. Altogether, as Michael Moynihan points out in his collection of diary extracts *Black Bread and Barbed Wire*, over 170,000 British soldiers spent time in captivity, including 6,842 officers. (The Second World War total was over 190,000.) POWs appreciated food parcels and anything else sent from home.

A separate Regimental fund was created in late 1915 "to see to the needs of the 17 of our men known to be interned in Germany. … to show them that they have not been forgotten." The Prisoner of War Fund, run by the Regiment's Old Comrades Association, set up a separate subscription and sent tobacco, cigarettes, parcels of cocoa, cheese, condensed milk etc. and a parcel of warm clothing was sent to each prisoner via Mrs Malcolm's Fund. This number grew as the conflict continued. One hopes that No.3742. Sergeant J. Beattie, a member of Crown Court Church, received a package. Beattie was taken prisoner in August 1916 on the Somme and was interned at Ohrdruf. Captain Duggie Lyall Grant was interned at four camps including Holtzminden. In 1918 the organisers were able to report that "Haggis has been sent to all prisoners for Hallowe'en and Christmas parcels containing plum pudding, turkey, roast beef, etc. are being arranged for." The fund was wound up in 1919 having raised £3,397/19/6d with the balance of £508/14/6d transferred to the War Memorial Fund.

Lyall Grant spent almost two years in camps. His capture in June 1916 seems almost banal, as he describes it: stationed away from the Front as an embarkation officer at Boulogne, he had been home briefly on leave in Wimbledon, and set out after breakfast to return by aeroplane from Farnborough. His pilot, on his first trip to France, got lost, inadvertently crossed over into German-occupied territory and they were duly shot at. Believing they were on course for St Omer, and this must have been "friendly fire" from their own side, they decided the safest thing was to land in the nearest field. "Little did I think," wrote Lyall Grant ruefully, in a diary from which the *Regimental Gazette* published extracts in the 1920s, "on leaving home yesterday morning that by seven I should be in German hands."

The illicit diary – an extraordinary 50,000 words was eventually sewn into his kit waistband and inside his bagpipes so he could smuggle it out when he was freed in April 1918 – reveals much of the daily life of the officer as POW.

While other ranks were forced mostly into labour camps, officers were generally reasonably well accommodated but as Moynihan points out, being left idle "was itself a test of character and mental stamina for this privileged class." With extraordinary verve and a determination ("The only thing is to make the best of a bad job and when down in the mouth think of Jonah – he came up all right"), Lyall Grant passed his captivity doing all he could to be spared not only boredom but "another day of much internal fighting against the depression that must not be allowed to get the upper hand." Boarding school being a fresh memory for many, time was passed playing games – versions of everything from tennis to rugby and fives to hockey being established with teams and leagues and prizes and rules adapted to the playing conditions. Thus, Lyall Grant's entry for 6 September 1917:

> Quite an event today was the start of RUGGER. The ground can hardly be called suitable being only 50 yards long by 25 wide, while a pump and an electric light pole are obstacles to be avoided however we had a good enough game with eleven a side and got hot, dirty and scraped.

Six weeks earlier: "Played my monthly Medal round on our new golf course." In between all the sport were regular light entertainments: "24 November [1917] the concert passed off well and the sketch [entitled *The Artist's Model*] was quite a good show. I fancy I must have looked rather sweet as the "Model" in a small ballet frock and tights, with a wreath on my head."

POWs would also draw on others' skills, several times Lyall Grant took up Spanish lessons and for a time even had lessons in shorthand.

Boarding school also accounts for endless puerile japes to keep spirits up. We can imagine other prisoners sniggering as he persuaded one Commandant that his goose-stepping on parade was indeed not meant as an insult to the German hierarchy but caused by physical disability.

Moynihan is sure that much would have been left out for fear of reprisals if his scribblings were discovered, so the diary is largely silent on topics such as escape committees, or ill-treatment which undoubtedly did occur, in favour of complaints that the wine on sale in the POW mess was expensive and execrable and that camp commandants were profiteering. But the diary did its job in sustaining the determination to be positive.

Mealtimes mattered and even parties were hosted and attended.

> 2 August [1916]. In the morning our mess had two Russians for breakfast. The meal provided by the Germans consisted of one thin slice of black bread and some washy coffee. Our menu for our guests was Fruit and Cream, Porridge, Fish, Sausages, Bacon, Tomatoes, Various Potted Meats and Game, Toast, Butter, Jam and Marmalade – all from parcels of course.

And not only were the Scots and other British POWs better provided for from home than their fellow inmates from other countries; they were better looked after than the local populace. Beyond the wire, food shortages and rationing were rife, and at one camp the guard was doubled, not to prevent escapes but in fear that locals might try to break in to steal food!

The *Regimental Gazette* will have appreciated the diary, as he had been such a regular contributor in the years before capture.

Moynihan, writing ten years after Lyall Grant's death in 1968 at the age of 80, concludes his extracts thus:

> his first wife died in 1920, his dearly beloved eldest son was killed in the Second World War. He worked all his life for a living, in turn as a Merchant Banker, a paint salesman and a whisky salesman. During the Second World War he saw plenty of action as Officer-in-Command of a troopship at the Sicily landings and elsewhere … but to his friends he was always … living exuberantly in the present …
>
> Lyall Grant joined the London Scottish as a humble piper and finished up as Commanding Officer. And apart from the London Scottish Rugby Football Club … it was in the Regimental Headquarters … . that he was most in his element. There the memory of him lives on. Memories of sporting prowess, of his after-dinner speeches that set the table aroar, of the bagpipe parades and horseplay as the drink flowed. It seems no great remove from [the camps at] Gütersloh and Crefeld.

In his history of London Scottish FC, *The First 100,* Frank Morris, who knew him in his later years, wrote of the man who served as secretary and then president for 50 years broken only by those 22 months as POW, that "he was always as interested in the doings and welfare of the lowest recruit as of the most famous internationalist, and when he said as he often did that every member of the club was important he spoke with the utmost conviction and sincerity."

War Memorial Fund

In October 1918 an appeal was made for a London Scottish War Memorial fund. As the war ended it was obvious that there would be a great number of individuals in great need. It was not only the families of those who had fallen but the soldiers who returned wounded, disabled or otherwise and their dependants who would suffer distress, permanent and poignant.

A committee was formed of members and ex-members of the regiment, representatives of the Royal Scottish Corporation, the Caledonian Society and other Scottish societies. Louise, Duchess of Argyll was patron and Arthur Balfour (former Prime Minister and war-time foreign minister) agreed to be the honorary president. Lord

Balfour of Burleigh was honorary treasurer. Colonel Bernard C. Green CMG was appointed president and Rev. Fleming was chairman. The Royal Scottish Corporation, represented by Thomas Moncrieff and James Paton, assumed the role of almoner and looked after the funds raised.

The object of this fund was unambiguously to help the living, to assist those lives left in the wake of war in a time before a social welfare safety net existed. It was considered that the relief of suffering and destitution took precedence over any monument, however important a permanent tribute to the fallen may be. The objects of the fund were:

1. Assistance for the widows of the fallen.
2. Sending their children to schools and colleges befitting the position of their parents and helping them to start in their careers
3. Making life easier for the invalid and the old
4. Re-starting returned soldiers in civil employment
5. Assistance for the many thousands of wounded who found themselves thereby handicapped, to get a footing with some sort of remunerative employment.

In the 1918 *Gazette*, Lady Frances Balfour, wife of former Commanding Officer Colonel Eustace Balfour (brother of the former prime minister), wrote an appeal for the war memorial and referred to it as a "sacred obligation" and that it should have an aim of raising £50 000, which would be worth slightly more than £2m 100 years later.

Although a Scot herself, Lady Frances cautioned; "We must always remember that the London Scottish contain many Anglicised Scots both in church and in local upbringing and it would be a very serious mistake to remember the deeds and claims of this great Regiment only from a Scottish perspective"

By the end of 1920, and on the 18th list of subscribers, the fund had risen to over £36,000. Amongst other donors were the poet John Oxenham, private soldiers, senior officers, bereaved parents, Scottish companies and a separate list from the Highland Society of London. Caledonian societies in Shanghai, Bangkok and New Zealand sent contributions. Colonel R.J. Ogilby DSO, late commanding officer of the 2nd Battalion, gave his army pay for the previous two years. The London Robert Burns Club donated the profits from their 1919 Hallowe'en concert at Central Hall, Westminster.

The War Memorial Fund continued distributing grants to deserving cases long after the war. In fact, it still exists to this day in the form of the London Scottish Benevolent Fund. A poignant reminder of the how the fund did exactly what it was created to do is documented as recently as the 2017 *London Scottish Regimental Gazette*. In December 2016 the executrix of the estate of a Mrs Madge Trusler wrote to say: "My Mother died in August this year and left a small bequest to your charity in her will. I enclose a cheque in accordance with her wishes." The origin of this bequest can be found 99 years earlier when Mrs Trusler's father was serving in the 1st Battalion.

He was No.515220 Private John David Johnston, a printer from Battersea who volunteered on 10 December 1915 aged 21. He was mobilised in March 1917 and joined the 1st Battalion in France on 19 June 1917. He was wounded in part of the 3rd Battle of Ypres (Passchendaele) on 17 August in the trenches at Half Way House near Hooge. According to the Regimental History: "A carrying party was badly caught in this bombardment; received a direct hit and lost an Officer seriously wounded; eleven other ranks killed and ten wounded." Madge's father received shrapnel wounds to the right thigh which later resulted in an amputation of that leg. He was discharged from the Army with a war pension in April 1918 and died of tuberculosis in 1934, according to the family, "having never fully recovered from his war injury."

The covering letter explained that as Madge was awarded a scholarship to the Grey Coat Hospital School in Westminster which covered fees but not associated expenses such as books uniforms and sports equipment. Her widowed mother applied to the War Memorial Fund and was given a grant to cover these expenses for every year while her daughter remained in secondary education. In gratitude for the practical benevolence of the Regiment's War Memorial Fund 80 years before, Madge Trusler left a bequest in her will.

Physical War Memorials

The laudable aim of the War Memorial Fund was to finance people and not objects. However, there was still a desire to have a permanent physical memorial to fallen comrades. A completely separate fund was started in 1920 for the physical war memorials but prioritising the living may explain the relatively modest memorials this Regiment has to their fallen in the First World War.

The Home and Overseas Memorial Fund commissioned three memorials and contributed towards a fourth. The single memorial on the Western Front is located at Messines, on the site of the Regiment's baptism of fire on 31 October 1914. It is a simple Celtic cross made of grey Aberdeenshire granite with the cap badge and all the battle honours from both battalions inscribed on the front. It was unveiled by the King of the Belgians on 5 May 1925.

Secondly, a bronze plaque was unveiled by Earl Haig in St Columba's Church in 1922 but was destroyed when the building was bombed in the Second World War. The current church has the London Scottish Memorial Chapel in which can be found memorial rolls bearing the names of all fallen London Scots.

Thirdly, there is the splendid memorial at the Regimental Headquarters. This wooden monument dominates one wall of the current Drill Hall and on it is carved the Battle Honours and, in alphabetical order, the name and rank of each of the 1,542 officers and men who fell in the Great War. Earl Haig, as Honorary Colonel, unveiled this memorial on 21 January 1923. It was designed by Captain Archibald Chisholm and the work superintended by Major Robert Jardine, both members of the Regiment. To this day, every London Scottish soldier and ex-member will come to attention before this memorial upon entering the building and upon exiting. Eventually, in 1934, a brass memorial plaque was dedicated at St Columba's Church commemorating the men of the 2nd Battalion who fell in the Palestine Campaign 1917–18. Colonel Ogilby then took it to Jerusalem and unveiled the plaque at St Andrew's Scots' Memorial Church where it can be seen today.

Conclusion

The London Scottish Regiment was uniquely of the Scottish community in London. The pre-war territorials of the Regiment were middle class and educated. It was a white-collar club. The volunteers had to be Scottish by birth or parentage. They were all London residents. Many belonged also to other Scottish organisations in London such as the churches, sports clubs or county associations.

As the war progressed, the original members were either killed, wounded or commissioned outwith the Regiment. Those who filled the ranks as reinforcements joined a regiment with prestige, tradition and unusually high *esprit de corps*. The personnel changed but the London Scottish Regiment remained as an institution. The wider Scottish community in London contributed to the maintenance of this *esprit de corps* and unique identity by their contribution of troop comforts and general benevolence. The Scottish community continued to support the regimental family in peacetime with financial and other help for the families of the fallen and veterans in need of assistance. The Regiment was very much of the Scottish community in London.

The London Scottish Regiment marks Hallowe'en every year with a dinner at its headquarters in Westminster. Pipes are played, kilts are worn and haggis is eaten. On one wall there is a large oil painting by Richard Caton-Woodville depicting the action of 31 October 1914. Young London Scots are shown on the battlefield with bayonets fixed and wearing their glengarries and kilts of Hodden Grey. Close by is a painting of that ubiquitous London bus loading London Scottish soldiers outside the Cloth Hall in Ypres, by George Duncan Macdougald 1880–1945. Macdougald enlisted in the London Scottish Regiment in November 1914. This canvas was painted in 1936 from an original photo, commissioned and presented to the Regiment by Lieutenant Colonel James Patterson MC. On another wall, on the memorial, are the names of all those who fell in the Great War, looking down on the current generation. These Great War London Scots are not forgotten.

3

Great War Generosity: The Royal Scottish Corporation

Justine Taylor

The Way It Was

"The Scot has a tendency to migrate southwards," the moderator of the General Assembly of the Church of Scotland told his audience in November 1916 at the annual fundraising dinner of the Royal Scottish Corporation, one of London's oldest charities. To laughter, he said, "That is for the good of the south," adding that this was "in many ways for his own advantage." But, he reminded his fellow guests, there were also less fortunate Scots who made their way down to London and who were then "made to feel the pinch of adversity." It was these Scots in need whom, during the Great War and many years before and since, the Corporation has stepped in to help.

This charitable institution, operating publicly under the name of ScotsCare since 2005, was established by royal charter in 1665 and has origins dating back to the union of the crowns in 1603. The Scots who had arrived in London with James I would not have been entitled to the parish relief introduced at the end of Elizabeth I's reign. This restricted aid to those born in a local parish and the initial subscription charity, known as the "Scots Box" by 1611, helped to fill this welfare gap. The charity's formal title is the rather wordy "The Scottish Hospital of the Foundation of King Charles II" and it opened a hospital or workhouse in Blackfriars for poor Scots artisans in 1673. A general charity was established after the closure of the hospital in 1700 and the Corporation's new "Hall" was eventually purchased at Crane Court, off Fleet Street, in 1782. The charity further evolved by following social issues and trends, to complement, but not subsidise, public welfare services available for poor immigrant Scots. Four royal charters, a number of significant leaders and other benefactors throughout its history, as well as some sound property dealing and equity investing since the late-1700s, have sustained the Corporation through four centuries.

Home Front Help

The charity's first report of the war, in November 1914, gratefully thanked generous donors but noted that "Distressing appeals arising directly or indirectly from the war will inevitably come before the Management in the ensuing months, and these must be provided for in addition to the ordinary work of the Charity." This ordinary work reflected what had been the case for many years, namely the distribution of pensions to elderly Scots, allowances to widows with young children and comforting handouts of various forms to the generally needy or homeless Scot. And during 1914–19 there was still a Scottish immigrant population in London worthy of this charitable attention. Reflecting a move to the suburbs, the 1911 census gives a total of around 90,000 Scots living in London and the surrounding counties of Middlesex, Surrey, Kent and Essex. These numbers were at a similar level in 1914 and throughout the Great War.

The Corporation's indigent pensioners (there were 365 in April 1916) generally "embraced all classes," according to the charity's active secretary Thomas Moncrieff, although in 1912 some were described as being selected from "a class of persons who have occupied a respectable social position," with many women having been domestic servants who had outlived their original employers. The pensioners also had to have a certain level of income and had to have lived for 20 years within 12 miles of the Hall. They were usually aged 65 or over, but "in cases of complete physical or mental disability," those aged 55 and over might also be accepted.

Family poverty in London's East End – Raymond Street, Wapping, 1918; the Corporation had long supported similarly poor widows, increasing its aid during the war to enable their children to fight life's "battles." (London Metropolitan Archives, City of London)

In the years leading up to 1914, financial juggling was required to alter the Corporation's income eligibility criteria as the government's social welfare reform expanded in two ways. Firstly, the Old-Age Pensions Act was passed in 1908, giving pensions of 5s. a week (7s.6d. for married couples) to men and women from the age of 70, who had been resident in the UK for at least 20 years and who had an annual income of less than £31/10s. Recipients also had to be of good character. Any person on poor relief, or known to be an habitual drunkard, or an inmate of a mental asylum or who had been out of prison for less than 10 years was ineligible. The Corporation's allowances had to be removed or reduced and its annual reports from 1911 and throughout the Great War all carry similar wording, repeating the refrain that the management had given "the Governors the fullest assurance that neither now nor hereafter will any overlapping take place and help will not be continued unless called for by the circumstances."

Secondly, in 1911 another government social welfare reform was introduced in the form of the National Insurance Act. This brought working people medical and unemployment benefits for the first time in return for an individual payment of 4d. a day, plus an employer's contribution. The Corporation reported that "the same scrupulous care will be applied" in this case but expected that it would affect the charity to a lesser extent; "owing to the age and physical state of the persons who form the bulk of the Corporation's recipients," it did "not anticipate any appreciable relief from this act for many years to come."

As the war progressed, and in 1916, following an increase in the government pension amount, Thomas Moncrieff made calculations for turning the pensioners' monthly payments into weekly amounts, hoping to find a margin that could somewhat improve the allowances of the "minorities under seventy." He had long thought that "the years in the sixties when earning powers diminish until seventy when national benefit becomes applicable are now the most serious time of all for the Corporation's beneficiaries and demand of us vigilant care that unnecessary hardship does not fall on the individual." In January 1917 it was agreed that the £13 pensioners under 70 should receive 6s. a week and the £18 pensioners 8s., with both returning to the usual 5s.6d. when they reached 70 in order not to disqualify the pensioners from the government scheme. From April 1918, when the government raised the maximum allowable annual income, the Corporation's pensions for those over 70 could also be returned to their original weekly 7s.6d.

This war-time spending on pensions was occasionally brought down by pensioners themselves asking to return their allowances. Deaths of pensioners also reduced the relief expenditure. At the beginning of 1917, the harshest winter on record for 22 years caused the elderly pensioners' death rate to rise exceptionally and the Corporation recorded that 49 individuals of an average age of 74¾ had died. By the end of 1918 the death rate had returned to "normal" with a recorded 29 deaths. This was despite the deadly influenza pandemic then raging around the world, but which seemed to affect the young more than the old.

The elderly London Scots, however, – "their well being is our constant care, their well being our pride" – appear to have been hardy souls and were often recorded as living into their 80s, 90s and beyond. Moncrieff remembered in December 1923 "at least four centenarians" in his time as secretary and a near fifth that year. This lady was the liveliest of the lot having years before helped her father carry the mails on foot in any sort of weather from Braemar to Ballater. He recalled her climbing the Monument in the City of London to celebrate her 96th birthday around 1919, accompanied by her 73-year-old daughter, whom, he said, "lagged far behind." One centenarian of 1915, William Haining, had arrived in London at the age of 14. He had been known as the "Waterloo bairn" in his Scottish village and in all the surrounding countryside when he was born on the day "Napoleon's portentous career was dashed into irretrievable ruin." Another claimed the chieftainship of Clan Macnab and looked the part sufficiently to become an artist's model for Lord Leighton and other painters at the Royal Academy. Many pensioners, remembered Moncrieff, were also failed inventors. One elderly man thought he had found a new way for aircraft to fly to New York in around 90 minutes. Described as charmingly sweet and placid, during the Great War he had "directed his efforts to death-dealing explosives and propounded such schemes as would have annihilated the enemy at one fell swoop;" he was surely a man ahead of his time.

Children and their mothers had long been a key focus for the Corporation, with education one of its early priorities. A good education, and the Scottish experience of it, perhaps enforced by church attendance, was thought important in providing an understanding of how to make London work to one's advantage, monetary or otherwise. Having trained orphans and the able-bodied Scots poor in its original hospital, the Corporation had established a "school fund" in 1812, using donations from Scots in India and East India Company directors in the City of London to pay children's school fees. In 1891, when schooling became state funded, these educational grants were added to the fund for widows of deceased Scotsmen with young children. When the Great War began, these widows' grants were working well and ready to support needy, fatherless families on the Home Front.

Employment prospects greatly improved but food prices rose as the war went on. In early 1916, governor Robert Henderson recommended that allowances for children should be increased, with the maximum age of receipt raised. He knew that the charity's governors had long thought the current amount insufficient to cover the high cost of food, sometimes requiring a mother to go short so that her children should have enough to eat. And money, he thought, could be found to fund the payment improvements. Demand had decreased so that the 174 widows helped in 1898 for an amount of £618 had gone down in 1915 to 76 for £303. Henderson considered that the decrease in numbers was probably because of "the abandonment of the London area by large public works, such as shipbuilding and heavy engineering, in which there were employed a high proportion of younger Scotsmen." He also thought that the recent acts for national insurance and workers' compensation, the fact that more children were being accepted into the Caledonian Asylum and that there were "more numerous and better opportunities open to women workers" had also been "a favourable influence in keeping down the numbers" of grant applications. The changes were agreed in

April and the widows' payments, now to be weekly instead of monthly, became 3s. for one child, 4s.6d. for two children and 6s. for three children or more, plus an additional 1s.6d. for each child after the first three.

The ages of the children were also extended from 12 until 14, since attendance at school was now compulsory up to this age, making it an "irresistible case for continuing the help." In raising the maximum age, the Corporation also ensured that "provision was made to cover the early years of training in recognised trades." It also encouraged the widows to help their children: "The future benefit to their children, as well as to the state, in being enabled to enter the ranks of skilled rather than casual workers, will be steadily kept before the mothers." At its November 1916 festival dinner, Lord Balfour of Burleigh, the charity's treasurer, enlightened the Corporation's guests on the public advantages of the changes to the widows' grant scheme, especially "that the children should have a longer time to prepare for the battle of life so that they would not be tempted to drift into what are called blind alley occupations."

Indeed, the Corporation had for many years also helped those who had found themselves up these "blind alleys", having been in the capital for only a few days or even hours. In 1911 the charity had given out lodging and food tickets to 2,000 casual callers, but when war began many of these homeless and workless men found employment and the workhouses also soon emptied. However, much-needed help was again required as the war ended and its after effects were keenly felt. The secretary Moncrieff reported that he had himself witnessed homes at the end of the war "in bitter winter weather" which had "no food or firing or bedclothes, and with practically no stick of furniture left to pawn." He had met yet another desperate young mother, "with the barest remnants of clothing for herself", who had pawned the shawl in which her baby had been wrapped to buy bread for her other crying children.

In the immediate post war years, the new cases showed fewer widows, but many more unemployed men. These years saw even more "acute distress" as the price of "bare necessities" and housing problems during an acute shortage of accommodation in London also "pressed heavily on the deserving Scottish poor." The Corporation also saw homeless men arriving in rags and provided them with suits of clothes from donated second-hand items. In 1923 especially, much larger numbers of poor Scots than expected had clamoured for the Corporation's relief because of post-war unemployment, causing "a heavy and serious drain" on the charity's resources. This year alone, some 7,000 applicants for temporary relief had come to the attention of the Corporation, many of them homeless, unemployed men. Moncrieff noted that not one was turned away without something, although money was rarely given. A number of these men were former soldiers applying to the charity looking for work. One successful case of November 1926 was described as an "Ex-Scots Guardsman in need of work. Bank Messenger or such like."

Careful vetting of these applications had always been a tradition of the charity's administration; it would never help just any Scot. "Sturdy beggars" and vagrants were expressly forbidden aid as early as the Corporation's 1665 charter and those helped by the charity, according to its earliest tenets, had to be "sober and industrious"

The Corporation's new building facing Fetter Lane by the late 1920s; this had been rebuilt in a Scottish baronial style during 1878–80, after a devastating fire in 1877. (Royal Scottish Corporation)

rather than "'idle and extravagant." In the early 1900s and 1910s, whilst dealing with additional numbers of cases as a result of the war in South Africa, governors of the Corporation had occasionally been victims of unscrupulous begging letters and scrutineers were appointed to investigate new cases and pension applications to weed out these "impostors." The appeals for help during the Great War were still carefully double-checked to uncover such "scroungers" as the charity continued to see a number of bogus applications. At the Corporation's 1916 St Andrew's Day dinner, the Duke of Argyll, chairman of the feast, reiterated this fact in his speech, saying that amongst those who came to make a living in London "there must be a certain Scottish jetsam thrown upon the shore of London life." But, he added, not all of "that jetsam perhaps is very wholesome and that is why it is necessary to look into special cases and scrutinise them and see that no bad applications of our funds are made." Indeed, the committee of management was pleased to report at its meeting on 10 January 1917 that "the notorious begging letter writer, W.A. Sinclair, who has been very active in recent months, has been again prosecuted;" he was sentenced to a year in prison.

The long-serving beadle, George P. Smith, a former sergeant in the Seaforth Highlanders, was responsible for discovering a rather ingenious impostor during the war. This 20-year-old man who gave his name as Malcolm Douglas MacDonald, claimed he had been born in Aberdeen and that he had served with the band of the Argyll and Sutherland Highlanders. He appeared to have lost both feet and was also supposed to have a bayonet wound in his stomach. Financially supported by a

Red Cross worker and other "ladies", he had been sent to convalesce on the south coast. The Corporation was asked if it would step in and continue the help for this badly wounded man. Enquiries at London hospitals could find no trace of him and the charity ordered the soldier to be brought to its Hall for examination. The former regimental musician then "stumbled up the stairs at Crane Court, aided by a pair of beautifully constructed crutches", whereupon the beadle questioned "MacDonald" about his marching tune. When his whistle did not fit, his feet were found and the police were called to pick him up for fraud.

Courts and Committees

The Corporation's third charter of 1775 had acted as a re-incorporation of the charity after a period of decay and instituted a presidential system and a greater number of governors. The Scottish nobility had also become a presidential fixture in the late-18th century and from the mid-19th century certain active members of the Caledonian Society of London took administrative control. This state of affairs continued during the Great War, with key governors' and administrative meetings at this period comprising annual general and general quarterly courts plus the monthly finance committee and committee of management meetings, the last numbering 24 members; honorary physicians, surgeons and chaplains were also in attendance.

The first meeting of the committee of management after the declaration of war had taken place on 13 August 1914. At this meeting, the secretary "was empowered to take all necessary steps to ensure, as far as possible, that distress caused by the war among Scottish people in London is brought to the notice of the Corporation." The committee met monthly to consider the appeals (usually between 20 and 40), the finance report and pensioners' deaths. Allowances were paid monthly after a thanksgiving service, when the pensioners also received soup and tea. From July 1915 a number of gifts of heather were also periodically distributed to the elderly men and women, often donated by Lady Helen Murray. The war did not impinge too much on the operational aspect of the charity's meetings until October 1917 when the hours of court and other meetings were changed to earlier in the afternoon, "In view of the darkness of the streets and the difficulties in travelling."

On 14 July 1915 the committee approved the insuring of the Hall "against enemy aircraft" for £10,000 or more "as required." In the desire to save as much money as possible for a new building, little or no money was being spent on the cramped old offices at the Hall and in January 1916 work on wiring the Hall and installing "electroliers" was deferred until after the war, although the secretary was asked to "extend the improvement obtained for the existing gas fittings." Nevertheless, the staff, who were hampered in their work with "bad lighting, bad heating and other inconveniences," never apparently grumbled to the governors. Another expense, however, came in May 1916 when, after many years, the Highland Society of London asked for the return of its safe and Moncrieff was tasked with finding a replacement.

A War Bonds poster of 1918 fixed to the National Gallery in Trafalgar Square; the Corporation took care of its investments throughout the war. (London Metropolitan Archives, City of London)

At the outbreak of the war the charity's investment account had stood at £105,000, with £97,000 in its main investment account and £8,000 invested in a building fund. After August 1915 the Corporation's investments were moved out of consolidated stock and into new government war loans. By the end of 1916 the books showed a reduced total of around £92,000 and in March 1917 the charity was urged by its stockbrokers, Hedderwick and Storey, to take money out of the war loans and re-invest it in the 2½ percent Consols, Mr Hedderwick noting that "in the case of a Body such as the Royal Scottish Corporation which is practically to continue for ever, it stands to reason that their investments should be as permanent as possible." By 1920–21 the charity's accounts did indeed show a good return, with a total investment of £207,000 (not including the building fund). Legacies had been received and annual subscriptions and other donations had also held up well throughout the war, despite the fact that the Corporation lacked the usual offerings from the Royal Caledonian Ball, which was not held during these years of conflict.

The President and Treasurer

The president and treasurer who headed the charity and its finances during the Great War were former prime minister the Earl of Rosebery and his fellow statesman Lord Balfour of Burleigh. The fifth earl of Rosebery, born Archibald Philip Primrose in London in 1847, was a Liberal prime minister for 15 months from 1894 until 1895. He had been a Corporation governor since 1868 and was elected treasurer from 1885 until 1903, becoming the charity's president from 1903 until his death in 1929. Educated at Eton and Christ Church College, Oxford, he had been sent down from university in 1869 for owning a race horse. Sport was his passion – besides a lifelong involvement in horse-racing, he was for 10 years president of London Scottish FC rugby club, then president of the Scottish Football Association and honorary president of Heart of Midlothian FC. He became the fifth earl in 1868 on the death of his grandfather and sat amongst the Liberal peers when elevated to the House of Lords, gaining a "reputation as Scottish Liberalism's leading crowd-puller." Rosebery covered Scottish interests as an Under-Secretary at the Home Office for 1881–83, served as foreign secretary in 1886 and accepted the challenging post of chairman of the newly created London County Council (LCC) in 1889.

In 1892 Rosebery again served as Foreign Secretary and, when Gladstone retired in March 1894, he took on what he saw as the "inherited" role of prime minister, as well as a budget he could not change. Whilst prime minister he came close to a nervous breakdown brought on by long months of constant insomnia in March 1895. This insomnia and his melancholic disposition had not been helped by the deaths of his father when he was three, his younger brother in the Sudan in 1885 and his beloved wife, Hannah de Rothschild, in 1890. Although his early political career had promised much, and he had a charismatic and magnetic personality, Rosebery found no great success and made his last appearance in the House of Lords in 1911. He publicly supported the war effort from 1914, but he no longer wished to serve in government; he had really performed at his best in the LCC chairmanship, away from the strains of national politics.

Rosebery's two sons were also politicians. The eldest, Harry Mayer Archibald Primrose, as the sixth earl would eventually follow in his father's footsteps as president of the Corporation in 1947. He had been commissioned into the Grenadier Guards when a young man, had been elected MP for Midlothian and had then sat in the House of Lords as the earl of Midlothian. He re-joined the Grenadiers on the outbreak of the Great War and was appointed aide-de-camp to General Allenby, accompanying him to Palestine in June 1917. Wounded and decorated, he was awarded both the Military Cross and the Distinguished Service Order. His younger brother, Neil James Archibald Primrose, was elected MP for Wisbech in 1910. He was appointed Under-Secretary of State for Foreign Affairs in 1915 and served as Joint Parliamentary Secretary to the Treasury in 1916–17 and was made a privy councillor. Primrose became a captain in the Buckinghamshire Yeomanry and was awarded the Military Cross in June 1916. He died of wounds received at Gezer in Palestine on 15

November 1917, when leading his unit against the Turkish army during the successful third Battle of Gaza. This shock did not help his father's health and Rosebery suffered a stroke in November 1918 that severely debilitated him and left him almost blind. His death in 1929 hit the Corporation hard; it would miss in its long-serving president "a wise counsellor, an honoured friend and colleague."

As the Corporation's treasurer, Lord Balfour of Burleigh maintained an active interest in its financial dealings during the Great War. He had taken on the role in 1903 when Rosebery had become president. Alexander Hugh Bruce was the sixth Lord Balfour of Burleigh and had been a Corporation governor since 1877. Born in Alloa in 1849, Balfour of Burleigh had been educated in Musselburgh, at Eton and at Oriel College, Oxford. He began his public career soon after leaving university and represented Scotland in the House of Lords from 1876. He is described in his entry in the *Oxford Dictionary of National Biography Online* (*ODNB*) as "an able Conservative," seemingly an unusual trait amongst his fellow Scottish peers at this time.

Balfour of Burleigh was an establishmentarian and showed "shrewdness, business ability, and sound knowledge of local government." He was good at cutting through detail and much of his work consisted of participating in or chairing royal and other commissions that produced authoritative and influential reports. He had performed well as Secretary of State for Scotland from 1895 until 1903, but was generally a non-political operator. Notably for the period covered by this chapter, he was a member of

Liberal politician and prime minister in 1894–95, Archibald Philip Primrose, 5th Earl of Rosebery and 1st Earl of Midlothian KG KT PC, was the Corporation's president from 1903 until his death in 1929. (Royal Scottish Corporation)

the government's committee on post-war commercial and industrial policy for 1916 and 1917. A trusted leader of the Church of Scotland for 50 years when he died in 1921, the Corporation had also benefited greatly from his "influence, sagacity and wise counsel." It remembered that, despite other important calls on his time, Balfour of Burleigh had presided "constantly'" over the monthly management meetings and had provided "a vision of an intensely patriotic and kindly nature" and this would continue "as an example and impulse" to his fellow governors.

Two other high-profile Corporation officers, elected one of the six vice-presidents of the Corporation in November 1914, were another former prime minister Arthur James Balfour, who was still a busy politician, and Arthur, 11th Lord Kinnaird, another London-born Scot; most renowned as a footballer who played once for Scotland and in nine FA Cup finals, he was doubtless much more valuable to the Corporation as a banker and philanthropist.

Perhaps more so than the president, the treasurer and the vice-presidents, the lynchpin around which everything revolved at the charity's headquarters in Crane Court was its secretary Thomas Moncrieff. Born in Arbroath, he had arrived in London in 1885 to work for the Home Office and then the Prison Commission. Having been in post at the Corporation since 1898, Moncrieff had developed a "wide experience of the conditions in which the poor live and their battle in life." He also found time to be a great supporter of other London-Scottish charitable causes during the war and afterwards led the move to rebuild and reorganise the Corporation's premises. His fellow Scots in the Caledonian Society appraised his presidency in 1919–20, noting "his strong character, his unfailing urbanity, his paternal and loving care of the pensioners, his sound judgement in difficult cases."

Working closely under Moncrieff was Alexander Macnaughtan, the "visitor and collector" who visited the elderly pensioners and also gathered donations. A long-term and continuing illness since around 1915 meant that Macnaughtan was forced to retire in May 1917. Miss E.C. Kerr had been appointed the Corporation's first female visitor in 1915 to help Macnaughtan. She guided the Corporation through the administratively gruelling days of the first old-age pensions and also appears to have instituted a programme of volunteers to help her in the important visiting task during the Great War. The six honorary physicians, four honorary surgeons and the nine honorary chaplains by the end of 1914 could all be called on to volunteer for these duties. One of the nine chaplains was the Rev. Alexander Macrae, chaplain to the 2nd Battalion Scots Guards and a former minister of Crown Court Church. He had been the senior chaplain to the Corporation for over 35 years when he resigned in 1933, during which time he had "served the aged recipients with the utmost devotion."

Other Benevolent Scots

Many generous patrons and patronesses had followed in the footsteps of the charity's 17th-century benefactors who had frequented the taverns of Covent Garden, and the

Corporation's subsequent history reflects the story of Scots and their social and business networks in London. When the Scots Hall in Crane Court was destroyed by fire in November 1877, it was soon rebuilt, and from 1880 the Hall became home to a number of other Scottish organisations and a rallying point for Scottish generosity which continued during the Great War and beyond.

The most important and long-lasting social event, maintained despite wartime conditions, was the Corporation's annual festival dinner in celebration of St Andrew's Day, held in the King's Hall at the Holborn Restaurant. Notes of the proceedings and speeches of the 252nd dinner on 30 November 1916 give a flavour of this glittering occasion, which raised £4,228 for the charity. The Duke of Argyll presided, and the principal guests on the top table included the High Commissioner for Australia and his agents-general for South Australia, Western Australia and Victoria; the High Commissioner for South Africa; the Deputy Minister for Canadian Overseas Forces and the Deputy Director of Canadian Supply and Transport; the Consul General of Montenegro and the Minister for Panama. Closer to home, three other principal guests were the Lord Advocate, the Moderator of the General Assembly of the Church of Scotland the Right Rev. John Brown, and Brigadier General J.D. McLachlan DSO (who would become the first British military attaché in Washington DC in 1917, once the Americans entered the war in April that year). The pipers of the Royal Caledonian Asylum provided the music at the dinner, whilst two of the Corporation's honorary chaplains said grace and offered thanks.

The Australian High Commissioner toasted the imperial troops and praised his "brither" Scots in these forces. "Though they be hard as steel in their affection and love of their own country, they know a world situation when they see it ..." MacLachlan in turn toasted Britain's Navy and Army, as well as the new technology available for fighting a now global war. "Of course at the beginning of the War", he said, "one did not realise exactly the way things were going to turn out. People of this country did not realise before the war broke out that manufactured machines had to a very great extent replaced manpower." The general public had previously considered itself quite apart from the military sphere, he commented, but "now the Army and the nation are one and the same." Scots were also renewing acquaintances all over the world on this wartime St Andrew's Day, the Duke of Argyll next reminded the dinner guests, even in Paris: Field Marshal Sir Douglas Haig had been invited to the celebration being held in the French capital; "I think it was a very enthusiastic person who thought that Sir Douglas Haig could go on an occasion of that kind. But, gentlemen, he went one better, because I understand he said that, 'While I regret very much I cannot be there myself, I am sending three Scottish officers and three pipers.'"

Besides this annual dinner and (usually) ball in London, a further means of raising money was via another long-standing Scottish networking body in the capital, the Caledonian Society of London. Many of the society's senior figures during the Great War were also extremely active in relieving distress through the Corporation, including, amongst others, secretary Thomas Moncrieff. A friend of Moncrieff, George William Paton (Sir George from 1930) was president of the society from

1913 until 1919. He had also been a life-managing governor of the Corporation and a member of its committee of management since November 1914, later becoming one of the vice-presidents. Also a director of the Caledonian Asylum, he would be appointed an elder of St Columba's with Earl Haig in 1921. Originally from Greenock, Paton had worked in shipbuilding before moving to the Diamond Match Company in Liverpool. This firm later merged with Bryant & May, of which he eventually became chairman. Paton, like Rosebery, amongst other charity colleagues, lost a son in the First World War, one of a number of the younger generation of Corporation governors killed in this conflict who would be sorely missed from the ranks of long-term benefactors and future capable officials.

Fallen Young Governors

Captain George Henry Tatham Paton was Paton's only son and one of the very youngest governors. Serving in the 4th Battalion Grenadier Guards he was killed in action on 1 December 1917 during the Battle of Cambrai in the attempt to retake the village of Gonnelieu. The news had been received at the charity's meeting of 12 December. The older governors remembered that even in his boyhood, Paton junior had shown "the warmest interest" in the Corporation's work and his death "had deprived the committee of one who showed promise of becoming a valued and devoted colleague." His father, wishing to remember his son's "all too short life and the splendid end granted to him," gave two new £18 pensions in his name. News of his award of a Military Cross had previously been received on 12 September, whilst the award of his posthumous Victoria Cross was brought to the notice of the Corporation's committee of management on 13 February 1918.

At the same 12 December 1917 meeting the committee was also informed of the death of another young governor, the Honourable Arthur Middleton Kinnaird MC, killed in action on 27 November. Kinnaird had been a lieutenant in the 1st Battalion Scots Guards and was the fifth son of vice-president Lord Kinnaird, appointed in November 1914; Lord Kinnaird's heir, the Honourable Douglas Arthur Kinnaird, also serving in the 1st Battalion Scots Guards, had been killed on 24 October 1914. As we have seen above, the death of Neil Primrose, son of the Corporation's president, the Earl of Rosebery, on 15 November 1917 proved a severe blow to his father's health.

Several other young friends of the charity who died had also been remembered at Corporation meetings earlier in 1916 and 1917. On 12 July 1916 the governors had learned of the death of the son of Surgeon-General William Gerard Don, one of the charity's honorary surgeons. David Fairweather Don, aged nearly 23, was a second lieutenant in the 14th Battalion Sherwood Foresters and had been attached to the 2nd Battalion South Wales Borderers when he was killed in action on 1 July whilst leading his men towards enemy trenches. This particular action took place near the village of Beaumont Hamel at Y Ravine, one of the strongest German positions along the Somme Front. David Don's body was never found but he is remembered on the

Thiepval Memorial. The Surgeon-General had served in both the Navy and the Army and it had taken some time before his son could obtain permission to leave employment and follow in his father's footsteps. In fact, as the news cutting pasted into the charity's minutes records,

> During these days he was absolutely miserable. He was simply eating his heart out, and it was just as though a burden were rolled from his shoulders and a weight lifted from his spirit, when the last obstacle was removed and he became a Soldier of the King. When the summons came for him to leave our shores he was like a schoolboy in his eagerness to go and to play his part well in the great struggle of the nations.

Aged 33, the Rev. Robert Alexander Cameron MacMillan was yet another young governor who was killed. A native of Ullapool, MacMillan had received a DPhil from Glasgow University and was the minister of St John's Presbyterian Church in Kensington from 1913 until 1917. As chaplain to the 2nd Battalion Cameron Highlanders during 1915 and 1916, he had served in Salonika and France before being commissioned as a second lieutenant in the 2nd Battalion Seaforth Highlanders, embarking for France in early 1917. "I cannot see much use in preaching at present," he had previously written from London. "I have nothing to say. How can I stand up and preach courage to young men when I haven't myself done what they are willing to do? So you must not be surprised if you hear that I have joined." He was killed in action at Fampoux, near Arras, on 11 April 1917; initially reported missing, his body was found five weeks later. The writer John Buchan paid tribute "to one of the greatest and most heroic spirits" he had known. "But I never knew one half of his greatness till the outbreak of War."

> He was one of those who, when they give, must give everything, … How are we to speak adequately of those who have made the great sacrifice. He has given his life for his country. Do you realise the tremendous meaning of that phrase? Most of us do not give our lives; they are taken from us slowly, bitterly and unwillingly. But he, and others like him, gave their lives cheerfully and freely …
>
> Mrs Fraser of Leckelm, *Records of the Men of Loch Broom*
> *Who Fell in the European War 1914–1918, Profile 49*

Help for Scottish Soldiers & Sailors

John Douglas was another active Corporation governor and Caledonian Society member whose son, Lieutenant William Loudon Douglas MC of the Royal Flying Corps, was another young governor serving in the war; he survived. By August 1914, his father had become well known as the central point of contact for Scottish societies around the world. He was a Corporation vice-president and had been a member of its committee of management for over 30 years. "A most sincere man", he had, it was said, a great love of his country, of justice and fair play and of his fellow human beings, and "if he could not suffer unworthy Scotsmen gladly, he was always ready to gently scan his brother man, and look for the best rather than the worst in humanity."

John Douglas and his fellow Caledonian Society member and Corporation official, Thomas Moncrieff, took on additional work early in the war when they involved themselves in a new project. Continuing what had been started "in a small way" at the Corporation, the Federated Council of Scottish Associations in London was officially formed in October 1914 to care for serving Scottish soldiers and prisoners of war. Douglas became its chairman whilst Moncrieff was honorary treasurer. The council was especially keen to stop unwanted charity, particularly since early in the war smaller regiments had received too much and the larger regiments no parcels at all. Douglas's report to the Council's fifth annual meeting in 1920 summarises its wartime and early post-war activities, and a slightly abridged version of this fascinating account is reproduced in the Appendix:

> It was the aim of the organization to regulate indiscriminate and local distribution of comforts by associations and individuals. The system was successful in checking overlapping and preventing a large amount of waste, and the whole-hearted co-operation of all associations was asked so that no Scottish soldier would have to complain that, while others received many articles and threw some of them away, he had no friends and had to go without.

By March 1915 Douglas could report that the council had taken on the direct distribution of socks, other woollen garments and "comforts" to the soldiers of 38 battalions "at the different fronts." Donations and contributions of these items, many handmade by wives and friends of members, came from Scots in London, Scotland, England and Wales and also from a number of Scots abroad, including 2,000 pairs of socks and money from the St Andrew's Society of the River Plate in Buenos Aires. By the end of the war, Douglas calculated that the final number of articles totalled over 75,000, including 37,619 pairs of socks. Other distributed articles included "shirts, mufflers, mittens, gloves, hose tops, helmets, coats, towels, bandages, medical comforts, soup squares, pipes, tobacco, cigarettes, soap, games, sets of bagpipes, and other musical instruments," and books. Some more specialised articles like "football accessories" were procured by the association and paid for by the officers and soldiers themselves. The remaining 137 pairs of socks were finally distributed to the Corporation's "deserving" poor in 1919.

In December 1915 the Federated Council had also started to send food parcels to Scottish prisoners of war in German camps and to "friendless Scottish soldiers in Turkey, Bulgaria and elsewhere." The associations within the council were also each encouraged to adopt a number of prisoners of war. The efficiency of the operation was such that the 48th Highlanders of Canada (the Toronto Highlanders) also asked the organisation to deliver supplies for their 221 prisoners. Additionally, bread was distributed through the

Wounded soldiers being entertained in a London hospital garden by Scots Guards pipers in 1917; as many Corporation Scots did, the Belgian parents of the dancing girl, Raymonde Oury, helped the war effort by visiting wounded soldiers in London hospitals. (Private Collection)

Bureau de Secours in Berne, Switzerland, and the prisoners thereafter received "the best bread in a fresh condition." The council was also able to trace men when relatives had had little luck – one mother in Scotland had tried for six months to find her son; the council found him in a German hospital in a matter of weeks.

Working from the Corporation's Hall, Moncrieff also arranged council outings for badly wounded soldiers in London hospitals, giving a little pleasure to a total of over 13,000 men. These soldiers were taken by bus and car to the grounds of the Caledonian Asylum and other private gardens and places of interest in and around London. Visits to wounded Scottish soldiers in London hospitals also began, aided by the English County Folk Visitation Society, which sent cards daily telling the council of new arrivals. From 1914–18, over 6,000 men in 100 hospitals in London, Middlesex, Surrey, Kent and Essex were visited by around a hundred volunteer visitors, who also prompted many soldiers' reunions with their wives and mothers. Over 47,600 men had benefited from the council's aid by 1919 and the total cost of all activities during the war had been just over £4,700, well covered by donations of £5,000. Goods received and sent abroad were estimated to have cost around £10,000.

Despite the Armistice of 11 November 1918, the war did not end for serving soldiers until 1919, during which year they were finally demobilised and gradually sent home and their units disbanded. The Corporation continued to help such veteran, discharged and serving Scottish soldiers in need, using its own funds if the recipients were based within the prescribed 12 miles of the charity's Hall or by means of two administered trusts if the men lived or were serving else-where, namely the Kinloch Bequest and the St Andrew's Scottish Soldiers' Fund.

The latter military charity was origi-nally established in 1915 to help Scottish soldiers of the Aldershot Garrison. Dated 20 August 1915 and signed by Lord Kitchener, as the Secretary of State for War, the first 99-year lease concerns a portion of land at Stanhope Lines, at a rent of £18 a year, on which site would be built "the Presbyterian Soldiers' Home" at a cost of "at least" £6,000. Balfour of Burleigh was one of the original trustees and more names were added in 1917 for what was now being called the "St Andrew's Soldiers' Home." These included Corporation governors mentioned elsewhere in this chapter, espe-cially John Douglas, Thomas Moncrieff (as chairman) and George Paton.

Making use of another older fund administered in London for two hundred years, the Corporation has been able to

Lord Balfour of Burleigh had been Secretary of State for Scotland 1895–1903 and was an active treasurer of the Royal Scottish Corporation from 1903 until his death in 1921. (Royal Scottish Corporation)

help poor and disabled Scottish soldiers and sailors far from the capital by distributing allowances from the Kinloch Bequest. During the period of the Great War, its benefi-ciaries were often veteran servicemen of previous wars of empire and those of the 1914–18 war were helped long after this war's end. Like the school fund, the bequest forms another of the charity's connections with British India. William Kinloch, a native of Arbuthnott in Kincardineshire, and a wealthy Calcutta merchant, died on board ship in July 1812 during a voyage home after 16 years in India. He left the residue of his estate, amounting to nearly £77,000 (equivalent today to just over £6 million), to the Corporation which it received in 1818. A Corporation committee was established to manage Kinloch's fund and distribute the interest as well as the stipu-lated capital percentage as pensions; the bequest was to be wound down and finally distributed once the capital had reduced to £2,000.

A few years before the outbreak of the Great War the fund's administrators were keen to amend the scheme of the bequest in line with recent developments in govern-ment welfare and the falling numbers of potential beneficiaries. In 1902, after the South African War, the government began the provision of permanent pensions to servicemen who had lost legs, arms or their eyesight to a level that took their individual incomes over the £20 limit of the bequest. Further service pension improvements in 1904 led to more Kinloch beneficiaries being removed. The old-age pensions of 1909 meant that those aged 70 and over, who received an Army or Navy pension, also had to leave the Kinloch list. As a result, fewer applicants had easily been provided for since 1904 from the interest of the fund alone, leaving its capital untouched. A sub-committee reported in June 1911 that the bequest could "no longer be fully distributed"; its capital now amounted to £36,200, yielding an income of £905 from annual interest, with its pension pay outs having fallen to around £495 a year – not to mention "the gradual extinction of the class of applicant eligible under the Scheme." But, the sub-committee noted, there had arisen a "most deserving class of disabled soldier or sailor," notably those under the short-service system, especially in the Army, who received no pensions or only short temporary pensions after their discharge, "and who are unable to earn a livelihood from no fault of their own." These "deserving men in distress" could much better be reached if the Kinloch scheme could be amended.

A new scheme was applied for and granted in June 1913. The new conditions allowed the Corporation to appoint a local support agency, such as the British Legion, to help find and manage beneficiaries. It was confirmed that, as previously, appeal candidates had to be Scotsmen who had served in the Navy or Army, who had become disabled through no fault of their own and who were in need and deserving. They could still not be inmates of Greenwich or Chelsea Hospitals, nor could they be in possession of, or entitled to, an income from other sources amounting to or exceeding £31/10s. per annum; nor could they have during the previous six calendar months received poor-law relief other than medical relief. Additionally, they could not be a patient of a mental hospital, nor be in receipt of medical help as an inmate of a poor relief institution (but men could become eligible if they recovered from their mental and physical disabilities). Preference would be given to those who had been maimed or wounded in the service of their country. Men could be removed if their qualifications on further investigation did not fit the bequest's requirements and also if, "in the opinion of the Committee", they were "guilty of insobriety, breach of regulations, or immoral or improper conduct." Candidates were to write formally to the secretary with their personal details and dates of service, providing supporting evidence. The maximum annual income and weekly shilling amounts of the allowances were periodically raised during the war and £5 could also be paid towards medical and other comforting costs during a final illness and a funeral.

As the outbreak of hostilities brought job opportunities, those pensioners still capable of work had their pensions stopped or reduced. Fourteen applications were considered on 21 October 1914, the first meeting after the declaration of war. These included that of James Cott, aged 45, who had no Army pension but was receiving 3s.1d. from Kinloch. Recently called up to guard bridges, he was now receiving 30s. a week and it was decided to suspend his Kinloch pension during this employment. A widower named Paul MacPherson, aged 64, had been accepted for recruiting duty in Aberdeen at 17s.6d. a week. Having to pay board and lodging for himself, he also paid to "keep home on a small croft where his sister lives"; his Kinloch pension was continued, but would be reviewed.

Rather than employment, though, it was unacceptable behaviour that removed some men from the pensions list or prevented others from being granted help as new applicants. Kinloch pensions for the old soldiers in Glasgow during the 1900s had sometimes been paid through the city's police force, usually as a result of the "intemperance" of the pensioner. One old soldier's pension had also been paid in this way, not because he was a drunkard himself but because he was "aged" and it was his much younger wife who was regarded by the Kinloch committee as "very unsteady." On 29 March 1916 a pensioner had his allowance reduced because he had been "'constantly in and out of the Poorhouse" for the past year. Another, who had been given money for a room, would receive no further grant because he "had refused to leave a common lodging house."

The minutes of 3 October 1917 mention the case of John McFarlane, aged 64, who had been in the Black Watch for nine years and (like many other cases) had served in Afghanistan. His two sons serving at the Front sent back large allowances, but their financial support was being reduced "by regular parcels to France"; the bequest awarded him 5s. a week. Some of the appeals for help are more heart-breaking. The meeting of 2 October 1918 considered the application of one of the youngest men to apply. John MacKay, aged 37, was described as having served for 15 years in the Seaforth Highlanders. Discharged as medically unfit in 1914, he was now suffering from tuberculosis in the Seaforth Sanatorium. He received 5s. a week as National Insurance and had an Army pension of a shilling a day which constituted his entire income to keep a wife and three children. Given a weekly Kinloch allowance, back-dated to January, he was expected to remain in the sanatorium's care for at least another six months. MacKay's death was instead reported on 26 March 1919 when a £5 grant was given for his funeral. The same amount was similarly granted for that of James Walkinshaw who had died "quite friendless."

The case of William Hutchison, married, aged 67 and a native of Kilncadzow, South Lanarkshire, was reported on 18 January 1935 and he was granted a weekly Kinloch allowance. He had enlisted in the Highland Light Infantry in 1896 and had served with this unit for some months before transferring to the Scots Guards. He then spent over seven years with this regiment, re-enlisting in 1914 and being discharged in 1916 after service in France. Described as "steady and reliable," he received no Army Pension and was suffering from chronic rheumatism. He had been separated from his wife for 11 years and had lost two of his sons in the Great War; another two sons and one daughter "'are married and unable to assist." A similarly poignant story that won over the governors on 9 February 1938 was that of John Tate of Edinburgh, who was unmarried and aged 73. He served in the Labour Corps since June 1915 until discharged as unfit in June 1918. He had a gun-shot wound in his left leg and was described as "Honest, sober and trustworthy." His war pension was 8s. a week and he received an old-age pension. From these sources, Tate paid "7/- per week for a cubicle in a lodging-house" and was "in need of boots and clothing."

Even long after the end of the Second World War, cases in Scotland of suffering old soldiers from the first war were still coming to the attention of the Kinloch trustees in the Corporation's London office. An application of early 1959 came from Robert Pagan, a veteran of the Argyll and Sutherland Highlanders. He was then suffering from "heart trouble" and had received a bullet wound in his leg and had shrapnel in his back as a result of service at Ypres in October 1917. His referee stated that Pagan had "suffered dreadfully for many years with a patience and fortitude which I personally witnessed and wondered at"; he was awarded a pension from the Kinloch Bequest in April.

Unusually, a record of Pagan's Great War service has survived and is preserved amongst the so-called "burnt documents" at the National Archives. These papers reveal that Pagan had been a gamekeeper from Thornhill in Dumfries when he enlisted aged 17 at Dunoon on 31 August 1914. As a private in the 2/8th Argyll and Sutherland Highlanders he arrived in France in August 1915 and his game-keeping skills were finally noticed in July 1917 when he transferred to the Lovat Scouts as a sniper. In 1916 Lord Lovat had formed what he called the "Lovat Scouts (Sharpshooters)" specifically with sniper skills. In addition to the 10th (Lovat Scouts) Battalion of the Cameron Highlanders, these sharpshooters comprised initially nine (and later 14) detachments of 21 men, which operated across the Western Front, attached at divisional level and occasionally to corps. Very little information on the snipers' exploits has survived and it is therefore largely unknown how these bands operated. Robert Pagan's Kinloch case thus provides us with the rare story of a member of one of these small sharpshooter groups. From 4 September 1917 he appears to have been attached to the 22nd Wing of the Royal Flying Corps (RFC) and was wounded on 31 October towards the end of the long third Battle of Ypres (or Passchendaele). He was hospitalised on 2 November with "bomb wounds" to his left knee and left thigh. Invalided to England on 4 November on board the hospital ship *Newhaven*, Pagan arrived at the 4th Scottish General Hospital at Stobhill, Glasgow, on 16 November. He recovered well enough to serve again in France from June 1918 until February 1919, being demobilised at Perth a month later. Pagan appears to have quickly obtained a suitable position on a Scottish estate, sending a change of address to the Army authorities on 19 March as "Kennels, Ardkinglas, Cairndew, By Inverary, Argyllshire," 40 years before his appeal to London for help.

Today

It might be estimated that the Corporation, more recently known as ScotsCare, has helped well over a million Scots and their families from its earliest times until today, when around 340,000 Scots can be counted as living in and around London. Since 1974 the revised charter limitation has meant that help can now be given to first- or second-generation Scots living within 35 miles of Charing Cross. As children of second-generation Scots, the third generation are now also helped up to the age of 18. In 2017, the charity spent over £2.4 million providing stability and support to those most in need. It owned 84 sheltered and other flats in three areas of London and distributed grants to around 1,000 London Scots, especially for children's clothing and household items. ScotsCare also continues to administer the two military funds for the benefit of Scotsmen and Scotswomen of all three services, wherever they may be serving or wherever they may now be living as veterans.

The Corporation was once rather picturesquely described "as a small seed planted in an alien soil." The resulting plant has grown steadily over the years, proving the point that rich and poor Scots have never been far apart. Nevertheless, attracting generous supporters and creating and filling the niche where the charity can flourish will be crucial to ScotsCare's future survival. Above all, we must remember in this centenary year that the passing of time since the Great War has brought no lessening of the "pinch of adversity" for London's vulnerable Scottish community and its young children.

4

The Flower of Youth: London Scottish FC

Paul McFarland

London Scottish Football Club's Great War experience was pitched into the wider folklore of Scotland when renowned critic and poet Mick Imlah published his short poem on the subject in *The Lost Leader* – his last collection rushed out before motor neurone disease claimed him at 52 in 2008.

> *London Scottish* (1914)
>
> April, the last full fixture of the spring:
> "Feet, Scottish, Feet" – they rucked the fear of God
> Into Blackheath. Their club was everything:
> And from the four sides raised that afternoon,
> The stars, but also those on the back pitches,
> All sixty volunteered for the touring squad
> And swapped their Richmond turf for Belgian ditches.
> October: mad for a fight, they broke too soon
> On the Ypres Salient, rushing the ridge between
> "Witshit" and Messines. Three-quarters died.
>
> Of that ill-balanced and fatigued fifteen
> The ass selectors favoured to survive,
> Just one, Brodie the prop, resumed his post.
> The others sometimes drank to "The Forty-Five":
> Neither a humorous nor an idle toast.

Of course, poetry is not gospel. Permissible poetic licence and no access to Club records meant much was conjecture. We have not identified Brodie the prop. He doesn't feature in the 1913–14 team photograph, but then nor do some other regulars. No matter: John King, a pre-war member of both London Scottish Football Club and

Regiment, wrote to the *London Scottish Regimental Gazette* in June 1919 that of the 60 players in the four teams (no substitutes then, a team was 15 only), over the whole duration of the war, 46 had been killed.

This essay is therefore not about London Scottish FC during the Great War. In reality, the Club was put on hold. Within days of the declaration of war most of the players had gone – swapping their Richmond turf not just for Belgian ditches but French ones too, or for the heights of Gallipoli, or for the dunes of Palestine, or for the new world above, flying flimsy-framed two-seaters over enemy lines, or patrolling the chilly North Sea in anticipation of that one great battle. No rugby to play, no players to play it.

We do not know how many London Scots served, but the Club's history, captured in Frank Morris's 1978 book for the Club's centenary, gives us a flavour from the first meeting convened after the war. This was not held until 30 July 1919, a full five years after the previous one. Club secretary Duggie Lyall Grant, himself back from four years on both sides of the Western Front, as piper and soldier in the London Scottish Regiment, and for almost two years as prisoner of war, "gave some illuminating statistics, admittedly incomplete, of members' activities during the War."

> Of the 451 members in 1914 [which may or may not include those who had not paid their subs and were being threatened with sanction at the 1914 AGM ...], only 271 had ultimately replied to his questionnaire ... Of these 271, 53 had been too old for service, and one too young, five had been medically unfit and four had been retained for duties of national importance, leaving 208, of whom 205 had served in the forces. Of these 69 had died.

And they are among the 103 names on the Club's war memorial (later research suggests there should be at least 104 ...). The roll-call continued:

> 52 had been wounded (37 of them once, 11 twice and four three times) and between them they had gained most of the honours that were going including one CB, two CMG, six DSO (one with bar, 26 MCs (four with bar)

and so on, and not forgetting two Croix de Guerre and one Serbian White Eagle!

Only 29 playing members had responded, and Lyall Grant ventured that the Club would struggle to get more than two teams out, but in the end three took the field from the autumn of 1919.

Prior to this general meeting of members, the committee had decided to form some sort of memorial, and work had begun collecting names. Some of these we now know nothing about. They may not have featured in the first team, and so are not to be found in the pre-war team photographs or in the occasional match reports in the *Richmond and Twickenham Times*, but the lives of others were illuminated by their deeds.

What we do know however is that while other gatherings of Scots in London focused efforts on the Home Front and on providing comfort, support, succour ... for the Club, well, there really wasn't a club for five years. Frank Morris's history silently acknowledges this: the 1913–14 season closes in the chapter *The End of an Era*, and 1919–20 opens the next chapter *Between the Wars*. The five empty seasons between are captured in a page turn.

For rugby's London Scots didn't stay at home, they went to war, and this is their story, the stories of some who died and of some of their pals, who survived and achieved.

In the Beginning

It is often assumed that the rugby club was formed out of the regiment. The London Scottish Regiment pre-dates the rugby club by 19 years, but the rugby club was in fact the love-child of the St Andrews Rovers. On 10 April 1878, a handful of Scots who played football for them met at the long-ago demolished Mackay's Tavern, in Water Lane, near Ludgate Hill and, seemingly upset at the Rovers' policy of admitting non-Scots, decided to break away and form a new club called for the avoidance of any doubt, London Scottish Football Club. Strictly, any rugby club founded after the formation of the Football Association in 1863 has to be designated RFC, a rugby football club. But the London Scottish FC founders, while adopting at that first meeting the plan to play according to the rugby football code, kept open the option of fielding teams for the round ball game too. The option remains to be exercised.

Not only that, but the avowed desire for a club solely comprising Scotsmen was dispensed with long before such insistence on racial purity had become illegal. The Club was officially made "open" well before the end of the 20th century; but even at its start, we find non-Scots including Canadians, South Africans and even Englishmen pulling on the sacred blue jersey. That the Club now also fields three teams of girls would then, of course, have been unthinkable, heretical …

However, to the Club's immense benefit, the Scottish Rugby Union had decided quite early on that a Scotsman living in London – which of course included an awful lot of professional and volunteer soldiers – wishing to be considered for selection for the national team would have to, as a pre-requisite, join the London Scottish club. Scotland Rugby's reliance on London Scottish players continued right up to the advent of professional rugby 20-odd years ago. The first international match, Scotland v England, took place in 1871 and London Scottish was founded seven seasons later. Almost a quarter of the nearly 1,100 Scotland players have also played for the Club.

Moreover, the ties before the Great War were stronger and tighter than ever before or since. In the first decade of the century, Scotland teams regularly fielded up to 10 men from the Club. Ten of the 12 men to captain Scotland between 1905 and the outbreak of war also turned out for London Scottish, as did three of the four Scotland captains to be killed. There are two Scotland captains in our 1913–14 team photograph: David McLaren Bain, captain in 1914, and Charlie Usher in 1920.

Yet, while the Regiment cannot be said to have spawned the Club, there was and remains what today we would think of as much shared DNA. One of the three founders of London Scottish Football Club, Neil MacGlashan, was in the Regiment, and a second, George Grant, joined in 1879. Four more of the initial members were also members of the Regiment, and this pattern would continue right through to 1914 when war was declared. We know of at least eight members of both Club and Regiment who were at Messines on 31 October / 1 November 1914, one of the regiment's battle honours.

London in 1914

London Scottish FC's members were not typical of London's burgeoning populace. London a century ago dominated Britain if anything even more than it does now. With a population of over seven million, more people lived there than in all the great cities of the rest of Britain combined.

Recruiting poster for Rugby Union footballers, published in December 1914. (© IWM, Art. IWM PST 7806)

The 90,000 or so Scots living in London in 1914 were part of an established immigrant tradition: London was home to tens of thousands of French, Italians, Germans; while Jews from Russia and Eastern Europe had for decades been escaping persecution and coming to work in the rag trade. It was a cosmopolitan city much as it is now, reliant on immigrants from north of the border and anywhere else to oil the wheels of commerce and to work in the significant industry the capital had in those days, as well as in the professions; but it was also a deeply divided city, the poor vastly outnumbering the wealthy. It was a city not expecting war, preoccupied by worker unrest leading to strikes and by suffragette demonstrations.

But when war came, gentlemanly pursuits such as playing rugger and cricket ceased immediately, and in the months to come there would be no Derby, no Goodwood, no Ascot. Only professional football, still the working man's game, persisted, not as if there were no war, but in the belief that the working man needed his Saturday afternoon relief. The 1914–15 league season was played out in full, as was the FA Cup, in the belief that morale would be boosted and even that recruitment would thus be encouraged. Leagues and cups were then postponed till 1919 but football clubs were encouraged to keep playing friendlies and for example to put out teams that included workers in munitions factories, setting a precedent for football in the Second World War when wartime cups as well as friendlies attracted huge crowds desperate for light entertainment and relief from austerity, the blitz and fear. We forget that for periods in both wars, eventual defeat looked the more likely outcome.

Meanwhile, rugby by contrast was held up as an example of men doing their duty: one recruitment poster claimed that 90 percent of rugby players had joined up and aimed to shame other "British athletes" to follow suit.

1913–1914 Team Photograph

The Club has a team photograph for each of the pre-war seasons. They are not a roll call of all the players in all four teams, but a snapshot of the 1st XV who happened to be playing on the day the camera came. Of the XV in the 1913–14 team photograph, taken prior to a match versus United Services, most were already in the army and only two of the XV were not commissioned either at the start or once war was under way. Officers of course took the brunt of the war: the historian Dan Snow, in an essay for the BBC online magazine debunking WW1 myths, has shown that 12 percent of casualties were from the ranks but 17 percent of officers were killed (including 200 generals), and that probably explains why a rugby club such as London Scottish seems to have suffered disproportionately. Five of that XV were killed and all but one of the rest seems to have been wounded.

Yet this was neither particularly disproportionate nor unfortunate. The calculations of Ewan Cameron, Professor of History at Edinburgh University, are generally accepted. Cameron believes 690,000 Scots served during the First World War, and 65 percent of those Scots volunteered between 1914 and 1916, compared with 52 percent

London Scottish 1913–14: the Club 1st XV assembled before the match against the United Services. (*Left to right, back row*): Private J. Ross London Scottish Regiment, Killed 1/11/1914, Messines, Scotland 5 caps; Captain A.B.S. Legate, Cameron Highlanders, Believed Wounded; Brigadier R.M. Scobie KBE CB MC, Royal Engineers, Wounded, PoW, 3 caps; Captain I.M. Moffatt-Pender, Seaforth Highlanders, RAF, Wounded, 1 cap; Major A.M. Jackson MC, Royal Engineers, Killed 27/4/1917, Béthune; Brigadier C.R.M. Hutcheson DSO & Bar MC & Bar, Royal Field Artillery, Wounded 1914–18, Killed 29/4/43, North Africa; Lieutenant J.L. Huggan, Royal Army Medical Corps, Killed 16/09/1914, Chemin des Dames, 1 cap. (*Front row*) Brigadier G.C. Gowlland, Royal Engineers, Wounded, 7 caps; Captain E.A. Kinross, London Scottish Regiment and York & Lancaster Regiment, Survived; Lieutenant General C.M. Usher DSO OBE Légion d'Honneur, Croix de Guerre, Gordon Highlanders, Wounded, PoW, 16 caps and Scotland Captain; Captain L. Robertson, Cameron Highlanders, Killed 03/11/1914, Ypres, 9 caps; Major R.D. Robertson, Gordon Highlanders, Wounded, PoW, 1 cap; Lieutenant W.A. Stewart, Royal Army Medical Corps, Wounded, 4 caps. (*Seated*) Squadron Leader A.W. Symington MC, Kings Royal Rifle Corps and RAF, Wounded, 2 caps; Captain D.M. Bain, Gordon Highlanders, Killed 3/6/15, Festubert, 11 caps and Scotland Captain. (*Ranks, awards and honours shown cover those also earned after 1919*). (London Scottish Football Club)

in the rest of the UK. Scotland's higher proportion of volunteers led to proportionately more Scottish deaths per head of population than among the English, or for that matter the Welsh or Irish.

The pattern continues into rugby – 31 Scotland international players were to die compared to 28 who had played for England. Eleven who had contested the last pre-war Calcutta Cup match on 21 March 1914 at Inverleith in Edinburgh (England won 16–15) would be killed: six Scottish and five English, including both team captains. That Scotland team also featured 10 current or past London Scottish players.

In the 1913–14 Club photograph we find 11 of the XV were current or past Scotland internationalists. Thirteen served as officers; of Scotland's 31 killed in action, 26 were officers. In the years before the Great War, the men who played for Scotland tended to be educated at private schools, were university educated and/or in the professions or the army. The London Scottish player profile was identical. Twenty of that 31 had played for London Scottish, as had 20 of the 55 Oxbridge Blues who were killed. On the Venn diagram of war dead, at the intersection of Scotland, London Scottish and Oxbridge Blue are the names of 12 men.

The First to Fall

If you stand at the graveside of Lieutenant R.F. "Ronnie" Simson, at Moulins, near the Chemin de Dames, and gaze northwards, out beyond the little churchyard where 10 of those beautiful Commonwealth War Graves Commission stones have been planted among the family monuments of French villagers, out towards the rolling landscape once pounded by German guns, you can't help but feel the presence of those men, the men who "fought and died, for their wee bit hill and glen."

For this isn't the flat plains of Flanders, with landscape remarkable for its lack of remarkable feature (only those who have cycled there believe Flanders has hills). Beyond this little valley, beyond the trees on the skyline, is the Chemin Des Dames, the ridge where once, Caesar defeated Gaul; it's also the ridge where Napoleon won a key Battle at Craonne exactly 100 years before, the ridge where in September 1914 the Germans pulled back from the Battle of the Marne to the Aisne River and everyone dug in, the French shelling the German line so thoroughly that they destroyed the statue erected to Napoleon only months before. It was the ridge where trench warfare began, the ridge where the first British soldiers who had played rugby for their country, then died for their country, including the first of the 1913–14 London Scottish team to be killed.

Ronnie Simson, though, wasn't in the XV the day they took that year's team photograph. Born in Edinburgh on 6 September 1890, he must have loved his rugby, turning out for Blackheath, London Scottish, the Army (he had entered the Royal Military Academy (RMA) at Woolwich at 19), and in 1911 for Scotland. EHB Sewell described him as: "a fine, tall centre with excellent hands and a long, raking stride, and a very keen nose for a chance of a try. He had the flair for doing something with the ball, making an opening before parting with it to his wing." The shell that exploded under his horse, as they reconnoitred a new position for his Royal Artillery battery on 14 September 1914, accounted for them both.

Lieutenant Ronnie Simson does feature in the three previous seasons' team photographs, alongside the next London Scot to be killed. For just two days later and a few kilometres away, Dr James Laidlaw Huggan of the Royal Army Medical Corps (RAMC) was hit by a shell after he had escorted 60 badly wounded German POWs to safety after their shelter had been incinerated by German artillery fire. The Victoria Cross recommendation was declined: he had been saving German lives not British or French ones. Lieutenant Huggan is commemorated in a nearby memorial; the shell had left nothing recognisable to bury.

Like so many of his team-mates as well as comrades, James Huggan was a middle class Scottish boy, learning his rugby at Jedforest, his father being a local engineer. A stellar sporting career at Edinburgh University, where he won an athletics Blue and played the round ball as well as oval ball games, didn't hinder a first-class honours in surgery. He joined the RAMC in 1912 and, while in London and playing now for London Scottish, got his solitary

Scotland's Lieutenant Ronnie Simson, Royal Artillery, was the first international rugby player from the British Isles to be killed when he died on 14 September 1914; in total 87 were lost, of whom 31 were Scotland caps and 20 had played for London Scottish FC. (Image supplied by World Rugby Museum, Twickenham)

call-up for what no one knew would be the last international for nearly six years. Reports at the time thought a berth on the wing would be his for years to come, after he had scored one of Scotland's three tries in that agonisingly close defeat to England.

Scotland must have been playing expansive rugby: their other two tries came from the other wing. John George Will, brought up in London, was playing his seventh match for his country, and as he too would be killed, also his last. Will had turned out for Cambridge in the Varsity matches of 1911, 1912 and 1913 and was earmarked as skipper for the soon-to-be-cancelled 1914 clash. We don't know when he played for the Club, but most likely he combined Varsity and Club each season. The rule that

Scotsmen living in London and ambitious to play for their country play for London Scottish was not a bad recruitment tool for the Club!

His father's address was given as Bethnal House Asylum, Cambridge Road in London. Dr Will was the medical superintendent, not a resident ... young John meanwhile went from Cambridge to the Western Front with the Honourable Artillery Company (HAC). Popular like the London Scottish Regiment among middle class young men, the HAC combined part-time military service with a social life. When John Will joined in August 1914, however, military service was no longer a pastime. He was in France within a month. He at least survived the early hostilities and, like many who had started in the volunteer regiments, earned himself a commission into the regulars in 1915; he then joined the increasing number of commissioned officers drawn to the excitements offered by the new Royal Flying Corps.

Nigel McCrery, who brought together international rugby's war dead in his book *Into Touch,* believes he has cracked the mystery of John Will's death. Back at the Front as a fighter pilot, after a spell in England as an instructor, he appears on 25 March 1917 to have been in a group of two planes attacked by the Baron von Richthofen's so-called *Flying Circus,* and while the Red Baron claimed his companion, his brother Lothar shot down Will. This was never confirmed at the time, as the crash location could not be located. Huntley Gordon, quoted in *The Unreturning Army* had the rest of the story:

> In December, a newly-advanced artillery battery came upon a cross made from a propeller with "2nd Lt JG Will RFC" painted round the hub; Second Lieutenant Gordon added "He was the wing three-quarter known before the war as *the Flying Scot* ... the grave must have been made by Boche airmen, a curiously chivalrous act, for they can hardly have thought we would advance far enough to see it." His obituary recorded that "The cheery alertness which was so characteristic of him in the football field was part of his very nature ... So much alive was he that it is difficult for us to believe he is now for ever still and silent."
>
> *The London Hospital Gazette*, October 1917

The story leaves one wondering if Second Lieutenant Will knew his young fellow London Scot Donald (D.A.D.I.) MacGregor. Only 18 at the outbreak of war, he had perhaps only a season in the junior sides before joining up. Also a flyer, he survived till 30 November 1917 when he fell victim to the Red Baron himself. John Will certainly knew another flying Scot – Lieutenant William Middleton Wallace had earned four caps, and played alongside Will in all three of Scotland's 1914 matches. An observer and photographer rather than pilot, he was shot down over Sainghin, France on 22 August 1915.

One of those three tries that day at Inverleith was converted by Frederick Harding Turner, a former London Scottish skipper who had subsequently returned to his native Liverpool. One of several forwards of that era who were also goal-kickers, he had captained his country during the 1912–13 season, but for the 1913–14 opener at

Cardiff Arms Park, his fellow London Scot and fellow front row forward David Bain, took charge.

Freddie "Tanky" Turner was another Blue. Educated at that perennially fine rugby school Sedbergh, for three seasons he combined rugby at Oxford University and London Scottish, gaining his Blue in 1908, 1909 and 1910 as captain before embarking on a 15-cap Scotland career. Having returned home to work in the family printing business, he joined the Liverpool Scottish and headed to France in November 1914. Ten weeks later a sniper shot Lieutenant Turner near Kemmel in western Flanders. Stephen Cooper in his World Rugby Museum blog *Rugby from the Front, 1914–1918 (July 1915)* recorded that "Turner's body, buried with care by fellow rugby man and double Victoria Cross winner Noel Chavasse, was lost as fighting continued to rage around the churchyard burial ground."

That Wales match (Scotland lost 24–5) proved to be Bain's 11th and last cap. He would miss the Calcutta Cup in 1914 but go on to be a captain in the Gordon Highlanders. He may have played rugby for the Gordons too – Ruth Duncan, the Gordons' museum curator, credits Bain's club team mate Lieutenant Colonel Dudley Ralph Turnbull DSO with introducing the game to the regiment. Captain Bain perished in northern France on 3 June 1915, Turnbull from a sniper's bullet at Passchendaele on 1 October 1917. The Gordons was a popular choice among clubmen. At least nine of the 104 served with them.

John Will, David Bain and Tanky Turner were among the many who combined playing for the Club with rugby at and for Oxford or Cambridge University.

These men were indeed a class apart: Scots who grew up in and around London, or who descended on the south-east of England, studied at the premier universities, played rugby for university and at London Scottish and as often as not for country too. Their pals were another distinct group, Scots like Ronnie Simson and James Huggan, who had already joined the military and likewise split their rugby fun between regiment – or the combined United Services or Army teams – and their beloved Club.

David Bain brings us back to that 1913–14 team photograph. Four others in it also appeared in that 1914 England match, but survived the war. Charlie Usher, who lost his brother John Milne Usher, would resume his playing career too, back in the Club side to play Blackheath in October 1919, and captained his country throughout the 1920 Five Nations tournament.

As the entire XV in the photograph were either already in the Army or joined up at the outbreak of war, most were in the initial British Expeditionary Force that went straight to France. Five would perish. Five more would not only survive but continue their military careers through to the Second World War. Apart from General Charlie Usher, three more rose to brigadier.

The young Captain Colin Ross Marshall Hutchison survived more than four years on the Western Front in the Royal Field Artillery. In 1943, now aged 50, Brigadier Hutchison (DSO, MC and bar) would be killed in the desert war in North Africa. Hutchison had also turned out again for the 1st XV after the resumption of play in 1919. Like Charlie Usher he had a younger brother Donald Herbert Hutchison, also at the Club, who would not have that opportunity: Donald Hutchison only made it to August 1915 when he was killed at Ypres.

Messines

The same weekend in September 1914 that Simson and Huggan were to be the first London Scots and the first Scotland players to be killed, the Volunteers of the London Scottish Regiment set off for France. Six weeks later, the Regiment "won" the first of its battle honours, sent out on Hallowe'en to attack the German position at Messines during the First Battle of Ypres. They were the first territorials to go into battle. Of the 800 to leave the trenches, 300 failed to return in one piece, being killed, wounded or recorded as missing.

Four of those to die were from the Club. Lieutenant John Charles Lancelot Farquharson was another of the Club's many Oxford men, an old Alleynian from Dulwich College awarded his Blue while at University College in 1903. Though his parents lived in Woking, he resided in London's Vincent Square, and was a manager for Thos Bolton & Sons, Copper Refiners. He had enlisted in 1907 as a private but had risen to Lieutenant by January 1914.

A few years below him at Dulwich had been Albert Luvian Wade. Bertie Wade played at the Club for at least four seasons but was also a talented painter and frequented the artists' quarter in Paris. In a letter to a friend he described his last leave in Paris: "they all remembered me and all seemed pleased to see me again, that it fairly brought tears to my eyes, but then I always was a sentimental ass." Lieutenant Wade was killed near Arras in April 1917.

Likewise, 20-year-old Private Robert Bruce Kyle. One of many born abroad (in Colombo, Ceylon, where his father was an engineer) he was sent home to Kelvinside Academy, Glasgow and Royal High School, Edinburgh. He then joined his now widowed mother Agnes in Barnes and worked on the Foreign Desk of the Hong Kong and Shanghai Bank. He enlisted in the Regiment in January 1913, volunteered for duty at the outbreak of war, left for France on 15 September 1914 and was reported missing on 1 November after the Regiment's charge at Messines. He was finally reported killed in action in February 1915.

Lance Corporal Eric Glenn Chapman, aged 22, was the son of James and Margaret H. Chapman, of Whetstone, London, and lived in Crouch End. A clerk at Parr's Bank in London, he had enlisted in the London Scottish Regiment in 1909 and was also a piper. He was buried at Wytschaete Military Cemetery a kilometre or two from the Messines memorial.

Two days later the same Ypres Front claimed another of our men from that 1913–14 photograph. Captain Lewis Robertson was the 31-year-old son of an Edinburgh wine merchant, but as a professional soldier had graduated from the Royal Military College Sandhurst back in 1903. He was commissioned into the Queen's Own Cameron Highlanders, and living in London, was a 1st XV stalwart for 10 seasons; he also turned out regularly for the army, and was capped nine times between 1908 and 1913. He had already survived the Battle of the Aisne in September 1914.

Meanwhile his namesake and team-mate (and former club secretary) Robert Dalrymple Robertson survived. He missed Messines, having been wounded and taken prisoner at Mons on 28th August 1914, but cleverly aggravated his wounds to persuade the Germans he was unfit for further combat and to release him early in 1915. He swiftly recovered and was at Gallipoli later in 1915. Captain Robertson had been born in Woolwich, and was also a professional soldier when war broke out, having graduated from Sandhurst and been commissioned into the Gordon Highlanders in 1911. He won his one cap against France in 1912. He stayed in the army after the war, retiring initially in 1935, and then signing on again for the Royal Naval Volunteer Reserve during the Second World War. He died at Battle in Sussex in 1971 aged 80.

Three more London Scots, F.P. Robertson, A.B. Jebb and A.W. Mather survived the carnage of Messines, but were killed later, creating a pattern of their own: club rugby players who were also pre-war territorials, who went to war initially with the London Scottish Regiment, then transferred to the regular army.

Lieutenant Arthur Beresford Jebb lived in Putney, though we know him to have been a native of Glasgow. He enlisted in the Regiment in 1913 and was badly wounded at Messines. He recovered to be back in France the next year, now commissioned into the Royal Field Artillery, and was killed on 18 June 1916. He is buried near his old team mate George Grant at Mazingarbe, in northern France.

Likewise, having joined up in his teens in 1909, Lieutenant Frederick Percival Robertson, son of a Hendon doctor, was still a private with the London Scottish at Messines. Unscathed there, he was subsequently wounded in early 1915, then got his commission into the Lancashire Fusiliers and was killed on 3 March 1916. He was buried in northern France.

Captain George Leonard Grant, BA, MRCS, LRCS, was another to transfer. A private in the London Scottish and travelling to France with the regiment on 15th September 1914, he was transferred to hospital work and commissioned into the RAMC. He too survived Messines, but he would die of wounds in France in October 1915.

Grant was one of a number of the men to do the London Scottish "double" of regiment and rugby club who had joined the regiment in the ranks rather than as officers. That they were officer material was in most cases evidenced by the fact that most were commissioned within months of the war commencing. If they survived long enough.

The wonderfully named William Gladstone Burn was a surveyor born in Edinburgh in 1890 or 1891. Having moved to London and living in Tufnell Park, he joined the weekend soldiers as far back as 1908, but in 1913 switched from the London Scottish to the Kensingtons (i.e. from the London Regiment 14th Battalion to the 13th) as Second Lieutenant. Thus, he missed Messines, but went to France in November, took on a role in signals, was promoted to Lieutenant and was killed in action in Flanders in May 1915.

Private Jimmy Ross was surely officer material. After all he had won a Blue for Oxford in 1897, captained the university in the 1898 Varsity match, captained the Club in 1901–02 and again in 1904–05 and been capped five times at forward for Scotland. He was on the bus to Wytschaete that Hallowe'en. His body was never found. He is listed among the 54,391 names on the Menin Gate, as is another Ross, known to us now only as R. Ross, who played for the Club and died with the regiment at Ypres in May 1915.

A few weeks later the continuing conflict around Ypres would claim yet another international. Second Lieutenant Patrick Charles Bentley Blair was the son of a minister in Dumfriesshire who had fetched up at Cambridge via Fettes College. He was capped five times but also secured a first-class degree and thus a position in the Egyptian Civil Service. He gave that up though for a commission in the Rifle Brigade at the outbreak of war. He was scaling a German parapet at the head of his men, when a shell ended his chances of a glittering career. One of his predecessors as a Scotland prop was Captain Rowland Fraser. They teamed up in the Cambridge front row against Oxford in 1910 – Fraser's third Blue (and he was captain too), Blair's first of four. Fraser also joined the Rifle Brigade. He would be one of the 60,000 to die in the first hours of the Battle of the Somme.

Somewhere nearby are the never-found remains of Private Bernard Tod, another teenage volunteer with the regiment in around March 1913. From school he joined the staff of Steel Bros. & Co., Ltd. East India Merchants, of 6, Fenchurch Avenue, E.C, but went straight to France in September 1914. He was another to survive Messines, but not for long. He was killed at Givenchy two days before Christmas. He was 18.

The last to be killed after surviving Messines was Lieutenant Alan William Mather from Putney. He had enlisted in the Regiment in 1912 aged 18, and the *Regimental Gazette* for 1913 lists him as a bugler. After Messines he rose to the rank of Sergeant, before in June 1916 being commissioned into the Black Watch. He survived not only Messines but Loos – which was the Club's blackest day, seven team-mates all being killed – and the Somme, only to die in a freak flying accident over Lincolnshire, less than two weeks before the Armistice. He is one of many who must have turned out for the rugby club at some point but perhaps not for the 1st XV.

That so many London Scottish rugby players – survivors as well as at least 11 of those killed – joined the London Scottish Regiment was hardly a surprise given their common roots and a generation of parallel history. That many enlisted as privates looks strange when their team-mates mostly were commissioned; in fact, as we have seen, if they survived long enough, they often transferred to commissions in the regular army.

However pre-war, when these men were just training on a midweek night and with the odd weekend away, it seems that life in the ranks was more attractive, carrying less responsibility than a commission; we can only guess, but did the weekday comradeship of the ranks better replicate the Saturday comradeship they enjoyed at the rugby club?

And the Army

Though the players were mostly in uniform within weeks of war being declared, they didn't all join up together like one of the so-called "Pals' Battalions" such as Heart of Midlothian Football Club. In the words of Robbie Burns many had long before decided to "go and be a sodger."

Indeed, beyond the London Scottish Regiment, the rugby/army connection could not have been stronger. Of the 14 men on the British Army's international roll of honour who were capped for Scotland between 1896 and 1914, only one did not also turn out for London Scottish. This wasn't just a Great War connection either: in the century from 1896, 34 of the 42 soldiers capped by Scotland were also London Scots, the last of them Rob Wainwright in 1992, who also captained Scotland and was, like three of his pre-Great War predecessors at the Club H.G. Monteith, J.T. Simson and J.L. Huggan, a medic in the RAMC.

It wasn't just the top-level players: by August 1914 many of the men turning out for London Scottish, and not only for the 1st XV, were already serving soldiers or reservists. The 104 who died belonged to more than 40 different units, including seven different ships of the Royal Navy, and at least five finished up in the Royal Flying Corps or its successor the RAF.

Born Abroad …

Indeed, such was the preponderance of soldiers in the Club's teams that some may not even have been paid-up members and regular players. One such may have been Major Alexander McLean Jackson of the Royal Engineers, who was killed at Béthune in northern France in April 1917. Maclean was a Canadian or more precisely a Newfoundlander (this weather-blown British dominion not joining with Canada till 1949) who came to London to St Paul's School in 1910 and by 1912 was at the RMA in Woolwich.

Jackson appears in that 1913–14 London Scottish team photograph alongside other graduates from the RMA: Ronald Scobie, and Colin Hutchison. These two and Ronald Elphinstone Gordon all played alongside Jackson for the RMA against the Royal Military College at Sandhurst in 1912 and in several other matches for the RMA. These army pals were all first or

Major Alexander MacLean Jackson MC, killed 20 April 1917, aged 24; Jackson was a Newfoundlander of Scottish descent, schooled in London, who served with the Royal Engineers and played for London Scottish FC. (Private Collection)

second-generation Scots, and even Jackson had a Scottish granny, Christina St Clair MacLean, born in Edinburgh in 1831, but while others in the photograph crop up regularly in team sheets for other matches we have been able to check, Jackson does not. So perhaps he just got roped in to that game against United Services, and posed in a borrowed shirt with the 14 regulars for a team photograph that history happened to preserve. This may explain his omission from the Club war memorial – not strictly speaking a member of the Club.

Jackson's pal Major Ronald Gordon MC was one of at least eight London Scots to be killed serving in the Royal Field Artillery, but missed that team photograph, having played through the season before for the Club and for Scotland, because he was posted to India in late 1913. Born in Selangor, Malaya in 1893 and the son of a Colonial civil servant, Gordon joined the RMA at 18 in 1911, and after turning out for nearby Blackheath, switched to London Scottish and was picked three times in the centre for Scotland when only 20. But work – in this case the army – came first, and so his stellar rugby career was cut short even before the war. From India he was posted part-way home, to Mesopotamia in November 1914, was seriously wounded in the summer of 1915, and returned home to recuperate. Not that being wounded kept him from the rugby field: we find him coaching cadets and playing the odd game in 1916–17, before being posted to France once fully recovered. Wounded again in June 1917 and May 1918, he was awarded an MC and mentioned in despatches, before succumbing to his fourth set of wounds in August 1918.

Gordon was one of many Scots born overseas to play for club and country. In fact, of the four soldiers to play for Scotland and be remembered on the war memorials at both London Scottish and Blackheath FC, only Ronnie Simson was born in Scotland. In addition to Gordon, Walter Michael (W.M.) Dickson was a native of the Cape Colony, as was Stephen Sebastian Lombard Steyn. Picking up our 1913–14 team photograph again, we find the "Newfie" Jackson in the company of London Scottish regulars William Allan Stewart from Launceston, Tasmania and Calcutta-born Archibald William Symington.

We've met Robert Kyle, born in Ceylon. C.H. Abercrombie was also born in India and Logie Colin Leggatt in Bangalore. And for the avoidance of doubt, John Argentine Campbell was given the country of his birth as his middle name!

Lieutenant Archie Symington, MC, born on 20 March 1892, was one of our survivors, returning to play for the Club in 1919. A year later he scored two tries for the RAF against the Army for whom his team-mate from the Club photograph, Ronald Scobie, also scored a try. That was after. Before the war and after Fettes College he had typically for a London Scot managed to cram in a rugby blue while at Clare College Cambridge, and two caps for Scotland in the second row in 1914 before his 22nd birthday. After joining the King's Royal Rifle Corps, he was wounded at Béthune in December 1914 and invalided home for six months, but then returned to win the Military Cross in January 1916. After being gassed in the trenches and discharged, he again worked his way back to fitness and re-enlisted, this time with the Royal Flying Corps. He had found himself a career, surviving to the end of the First World War and rising between the wars to Squadron Leader. He had however retired by the time he died of heart failure in Ayrshire in 1941.

He wasn't the only capped clubman to be a "flyer" and survive. George Henry Hope Maxwell was selected among eight London Scots for the 1913 Ireland match, and seven years later was back in the national side, going on to win 13 caps in all. At over six feet and 16 stones he was noted at the time as one of Scotland's biggest ever forwards, but was also, like fellow forward Tanky Turner, a notable goal-kicker. Maxwell qualified as a doctor and was still serving in what was by now the RAF when promoted to Group Captain in 1941.

Maxwell wasn't picked for the 1st XV when our 1913–14 team photograph was taken, but a third future airman was – Ian McAllister Moffat-Pender made his Scotland debut in that last Calcutta Cup match, and served at the Front initially as a Captain in the Seaforth Highlanders, before switching to the Royal Flying Corps. Born in Ockham, Surrey on 18 August 1894, he eventually died in Glasgow in 1961. He very nearly did not make it. As the commanding officer of 45 Squadron reported at the time, Pender was almost lost a week before his 23rd birthday.

> While on north line patrol Lt O L McMaking and Capt I Mc A M Pender crossed the lines at 6.35pm (on the 11th instant) under the clouds at 4500 feet over Deulemont. While passing a gap in the cloud two Albatross scouts dived at them from the clouds, firing continuously. Cpl Alex (Lt McMaking's Observer) got in a full drum at the enemy scout from very close quarters. The EA [enemy aircraft] crashed in flames on the canal immediately to the left of Deulemont. The second EA attacked Capt Pender's machine from the side and one bullet passed through both the main petrol tanks and wounded Capt Pender seriously in the back. Pioneer W T Smith (Capt Pender's Observer) got in a full double drum at the EA from close quarters and it crashed four fields to the left of the first machine. Capt Pender then fainted and his machine got into a spin. As Pioneer Smith could not make him hear, he climbed over the side and forward along the plane to the pilot's cockpit and found the stick wedged between Capt Pender's legs. He pulled Capt Pender back and pushed the stick forward. The machine came out of the spin and Capt Pender almost immediately recovered. Capt Pender then brought the machine and landed his Observer safely near Poperinghe. Members of the 16th Divisional Ammunition Column, where Capt Pender came down, saw Pioneer Smith standing on the side of the machine and heard him encouraging Capt Pender, saying 'Pull her up, sir' as they were about to crash into some hop poles. Capt Pender did pull her up and landed on the other side with very little damage.
> (https://forums.ubi.com/showthread.php/481673-WW1-DCM-should-have-been-a-VC-I-think-!!!-what-a-hero-Forums)

The hop poles concerned probably belonged to the local Trappist monastery which was a billet for the British troops in the Ypres hinterland. The monks brewed throughout the war (it was decided the wisps of smoke were just beyond the range of German guns), and put the troops to work picking hops – then sold them the beer! The monks are still brewing; but without all that free labour. Twenty-year-old Pioneer Smith was awarded the DCM and later the MM as well, shot down four more enemy aircraft, and died in 1994 aged 98.

Whether Pender resumed playing at the Club is not known; certainly, he was not one of the returnees to pull on the Scotland jersey again. For a while he toyed with a political career, standing in 1929 as the Unionist candidate for the Western Isles seat in Parliament. In the 1930s Pender would be found in Australia. Most notably he wrote and translated works into Gaelic, and also wrote *A simple explanation of a conversational difficulty experienced by those learning the Gaelic language.*

Others though left "their Richmond turf" for the sea not the air. Lieutenant Cecil Halliday Abercrombie RN's father served with the Indian police. In 1902 aged 16, Abercrombie left Berkhamsted School for officer training at Royal Navy Dartmouth. He returned to London, married Cecily, settled in Kensington, and played for the Club in the mid-1900s, earning six caps between 1910 and 1913, scoring one try, while also playing first class cricket and scoring four centuries for Hampshire. The outbreak of war finding Abercrombie in the Mediterranean, he returned to England and transferred to HMS *Defence.*

The early part of the war at sea was characterised by the stand-off between the Royal Navy stationed at Scapa Flow and the German fleet safely berthed in Kiel and the other North Sea ports. The Battle of Jutland on 31 May/1 June 1916 was the climax to the game of cat and mouse when the two fleets emerged into the North Sea. HMS *Defence* was the flagship of Rear Admiral Sir Robert Arbuthnot – it was one of the ships where later inquests would show that Royal Navy policy of storing magazines on deck meant they were dangerously exposed to incoming fire. Thus it was that two salvoes caused a magazine to explode, and *Defence* went down with the loss of all but 10 of the ship's 903-man complement. Phil McGowan writes in his World Rugby Museum blog *Abercrombie, Wilson and the Battle of Jutland (May 2016)*: "She continued to fire on the German ships in defiance till the very last and several eye-witness accounts claim that it was Abercrombie's turret that remained active right up until the point she slipped beneath the waves."

Lieutenant Commander John Skinner Wilson, referred to in the same blog, died the same day, in the same battle, in pretty much the same way. HMS *Indefatigable* was peppered for 15 minutes when finally, shells pierced the ship's armour and the size of the explosions witnessed from nearby ships would suggest that here too, one or more of the magazines had gone up. A forward like Abercrombie, Wilson got his caps in 1908 and 1909. Yet another of our colonial sons, Wilson was born in Trinidad where his father Colonel Sir David Wilson worked for the Crown; Sir David would later go on to be Governor and Commander in Chief of British Honduras. Once again, we can only wonder what the son might have achieved.

We do not know where another of our sailors was born, and only vaguely do we know where he rests. Lieutenant Charles Arthur Campbell Russell was in a G Class Submarine of the type developed and launched in 1916. The G7's role was to patrol an area of the North Sea in search of German U-Boats. Communications stopped on 23 October 1918 and she was officially declared lost on 1 November. She was the last British boat to go down in the First World War. Lieutenant Russell is remembered on the Portsmouth Naval Memorial.

These Scotland internationalists, born all over the world, were mainly of course Scottish sons of colonial civil servants working where the maps showed the British Empire red. Boys would almost invariably be sent "home" to schools in Scotland.

The same was true of others in our 1913–14 photograph: Ronald Mackenzie Scobie first drew breath 8 June 1893 in Mandalay in what was then still British Burma. He would become a career soldier via Cheltenham College and Woolwich: he was commissioned into the Royal Engineers in 1914, and stayed on after the war, serving in a variety of posts during the interwar years.

The outbreak of war in 1939 found Brigadier Scobie, now aged 56, in a staff job at the War Office. He was soon back in the field and back at the Front, joining the Middle East Land Forces in 1940, then taking over the 70th Infantry Division at Tobruk, and in 1942, becoming General Officer Commanding the troops in besieged Malta. At the end of 1943 he took over III Corps and transferred to Greece, remaining in command of British forces there beyond the expulsion of the German army, and through the Greek Civil War. Lieutenant General Ronald Mackenzie Scobie KBE, CB, MC, finally retired in 1947, and lived out his last years in Aldershot. The last of his three caps was that 1914 Calcutta Cup match alongside Huggan, Pender, Symington and Usher from that club photograph, as well as five others from the Club's current or recent sides. Of his club team-mates in that Scotland side only Usher and Maxwell would pull on the national jersey again. But Scobie did, as we have seen, feature for the Army at least once after the war.

His military career was almost matched by Geoffrey Cathcart Gowlland, seated on the left of that team photograph with the military moustache he'd had for years. Gowlland was born on 27 May 1885 in Ealing; on his birth certificate his father Richard states his occupation as "Gentleman". He was sent to Fettes College and then the RMA; after being gazetted aged 20 as Second Lieutenant into the Royal Engineers, he was promoted to Lieutenant in 1908. He was in the London Scottish 1st XV by 1906–07, when he features in the first of many team photographs. His seven Scotland caps were all earned between 1908 and 1910. As a regular soldier he was one of the first to France in 1914 and like so many of his team-mates at London Scottish, would have seen action at the 1st Battle of Ypres in October/November of that year. He may have been wounded because by the end of 1914 the now Captain Gowlland was in Dorset in a staff post, but was soon back in the field with the army in Egypt, being mentioned in despatches from Sudan in October 1916 and December 1918. Meanwhile, in 1917 he wrote a monograph entitled *Construction of Bridges to Take Heavy Motor Transport* published by The Royal Engineers' Institute.

After a period of sick leave "on account of ill-health caused by wounds" (27 April to 27 August 1920) he was promoted to Major on his appointment as Chief Instructor in Workshops at the School of Military Engineering at Chatham. Promoted to

Lieutenant Colonel in 1931 and Colonel in 1937, he was Chief Engineer, Hong Kong during 1937–40 when he retired, then was redeployed and made a temporary Brigadier, as Chief Engineer in Northern Ireland. He finally retired again and saw out the remainder of the war commanding the home guard at Wimborne in Dorset.

Interestingly, research notes on the Gowlland family website suggest he had informed the London Scottish club he had been born in Scotland; when in fact he had merely been educated there. The Club would thus have validated his claim to be eligible to represent the country when in fact it seems perhaps he was not!

Stephen Steyn, Walter Dickson and William Stewart, though, were the pre-1914 equivalent of the modern day "kilted kiwis," recruited into the Scotland team. Steyn's mother was a Scot, but for the others, unless research turns up some Scottish grannies, it may be that their sole qualification was being members of London Scottish.

Lieutenant William Allan Stewart remains largely unknown, though he looks at us rather sternly from the right-hand edge of that 1913–14 team photograph. We can assume he was in London to study medicine, as he qualified as a surgeon in 1913 and was then commissioned into the RAMC nine days after war was declared. One of the Club's many outstanding wingers, he had already made a startling debut for Scotland with three tries against France on New Year's Day 1913 – the other two tries were grabbed by Ronald Gordon – and after Scotland failed to score against Wales a month later, Stewart crossed for four more against Ireland, and then another against Wales a year later. Four caps and eight tries was a pretty good return for Scotland's young Tasmanian. Reported missing in action, he in fact survived the duration of the war, but we know nothing of his achievements after that. Certainly, he did not reappear in a Scotland shirt and is not recorded as back at the Club – most likely he went back home to the other side of the world.

There had been no such scoring feats back in 1900 from Scotland's first Argentine-born cap, forward John Argentine Campbell's only appearance being in the 0–0 draw at Dublin's Lansdowne Road. Born at Las Flores, he was sent "home" to Fettes College, and Trinity College Cambridge, where he won his Blue at rugby three times, as well as at cricket and athletics, played for the Club and that once for country, then went back north for a spell as a teacher at Loretto. He eventually returned to the ranch, and played cricket for Argentina against England.

Lieutenant John Argentine Campbell, killed 1 December 1917 aged 40 in Honnechy, France; he played rugby for Scotland against Ireland, cricket for Argentina against England, and abandoned his polo team to sail back to Britain and enlist. (Image supplied by World Rugby Museum, Twickenham)

He was inevitably a top-class polo player and when war was declared, Campbell's strong sense of duty was exemplified by a letter to a polo-playing friend:

> Aug. 5, 14 Dear Lewis I have just heard that War is declared between England [sic] and Germany. Although possibly it may seem foolish, I would prefer not to play public polo while our people are at it over there; so I hope you will allow me to stand out. I feel that if one can go in for games at this time we shouldn't be here but should be on the way to the other side. What I do hope is that the Almighty, on whom that big German emperor is always calling, will give the Germans such a hiding that they won't rise up again for another 100 years! Yours …
>
> Quoted by Alistair McEwen, co-ordinator of Scotland's
> War Project at Edinburgh University

Campbell duly volunteered in 1915 and was commissioned into the Inniskilling Dragoons, incidentally, a polo-playing regiment. As a 40-year-old lieutenant, he died at a German dressing station in France as the consequence of wounds sustained on 2 December 1917.

Walter Dickson was particularly interesting. Despite the handicap of being stone deaf, he arrived in Oxford as a Rhodes Scholar and turned out for the university in the controversial 1912 Varsity match: Oxford selected five South Africans and an Australian … and Cambridge won for the first time since 1905. Dickson was soon on the books at London Scottish too, working as a surveyor, playing seven times at full back for Scotland including against South Africa in 1912, before returning home. He was renowned among his peers for racing cars at Brooklands and breeding bulldogs. Rugby historian and statistician John Griffiths has written that Dickson's hearing difficulties almost caused a diplomatic incident in the France match on New Year's Day 1913:

> There is an amusing story concerning the Scottish full-back Dickson who … was quite deaf and misinterpreted the French reaction [riotous heckling of English referee Baxter] to be a sporting appreciation of Scotland's play!

The Scots refused to play the French in 1914, and the series did not resume until 1920. Dickson meanwhile had returned from South Africa to Britain when war broke out, and was commissioned into the Argyll and

Lieutenant Stephen Sebastian Lombard "Beak" Steyn, South African with a Scottish mother, played rugby for London Scottish FC and Scotland, killed in Palestine, 8 December 1917, aged 28. (Image supplied by World Rugby Museum, Twickenham)

Sutherland Highlanders. Within weeks of getting to France, he was one of the seven London Scottish players killed at Loos on 25/26 September 1915.

Lieutenant Stephen Sebastian Lombard Steyn, nicknamed "Beak" for reasons clear from his photograph, was born in 1889. Five years younger than Dickson, he followed his fellow countryman from the Diocesan College at Rondebosch to University College, Oxford as a Rhodes Scholar, and into the dark blue shirts of the 1912 Oxford University side, London Scottish and Scotland too, though strangely he was picked for country in 1911, before his university thought he was worth a Blue.

Another of our Artillerymen, he had stayed in England after university. He had joined the King Edward's Horse as a private in 1910, began studying medicine at Guy's in 1913 but on the outbreak of war took a commission in the Royal Field Artillery (RFA), quite possibly because several of his club team-mates were already in the RFA. He was sent to France in September 1915 but soon moved on, first to Salonika and then to Egypt, where he was part of the British forces that drove the Ottoman Turks from Palestine, and was killed the day before General Allenby's troops entered Jerusalem to complete the three-year Palestine campaign made famous by the involvement of T.E. Lawrence. His body was reburied in Jerusalem's War Cemetery in 1920.

He wasn't the only one to be lost in that Palestine campaign. Two days earlier as Allenby advanced up from the Sinai, acting Lieutenant Colonel John Alexander Findlay was killed aged 33 or 34. He now lies in the Gaza War Cemetery. Mentioned in despatches three times, he was posthumously awarded a DSO.

Palestine wasn't the farthest posting for the London Scottish boys. Dr Maurice Burnett, who could walk to the Club on matchdays from his home in Richmond, Surrey, lies further still from home. Like his father a surgeon in the RAMC, he was made Captain in March 1915 and killed a month later in the Battle of Shaiba as the Turks tried to re-take Basra from the British.

Died Abroad …

These campaigns in far-flung foreign fields (and deserts and mountains) are often forgotten beside the near-at-hand horrors of the Western Front. France and Flanders of course dominate our thoughts now as they did then – it was by far the biggest theatre of the war and even without a Channel Tunnel was unnervingly easy to reach. In London, the Front seemed so very near and the threat from sea and – when the Zeppelin raids began – from the air was palpable.

The war had begun in the Balkans. It ended there for Maurice Adam Black. Born in 1878, educated at Rugby School and Christ's College Cambridge and a Blue in 1897 and 1898, he was one of many London Scots to go to war when well past the first flush of youth. Married to Ethel Maude Goldney on 15 February 1903, he played rugby for London Scottish and the Barbarians and polo at the Hurlingham Club. He was commissioned Lieutenant in the 5th Dragoon Guards in 1900 and served in the

Boer War during 1900–02. Major Black was wounded in France in October 1914, was then transferred to the Royal Flying Corps and was killed in a flying incident in Macedonia on 11 February 1917 aged 38.

The war in the Middle East and beyond had as much impact on the peace to come and the century that followed. And if the generals are often with hindsight accused of pursuing on the Western Front strategies that had been proven to fail, elsewhere, military strategy was shaped by experience.

Gallipoli involved not just the brand-new nations of Australia and New Zealand, whose soldiers were diverted in early 1915 to this initial campaign against the Ottoman allies of the Central Powers. London soldiers including London Scots fought and died there too.

Of all London Scots to die, perhaps the most renowned was David Revell "Darkie" Bedell-Sivright. Along with his brother he was an occasional for the Club in the 1900s while he studied medicine at Cambridge, and another who no doubt took advantage of – or recognised the necessity of – playing for the Club in order to be picked for country. He would merit a chapter on his own. The man was captured well by David Walmsley, writing in the *Daily Telegraph* in 2005:

> Added to his reputation as the toughest rugby player of his day, David Bedell-Sivright also enjoyed the status of Scottish heavyweight boxing champion. And, outside the sporting arena, he saved lives as a doctor and naval surgeon during World War I, but inside it was more likely to add to the casualty toll than reduce it. 'When I go on to that field I only see the ball,' the Rugby Football Internationals' Roll of Honour quoted him as saying, 'and should someone be in the road, that is his own lookout.'
>
> His boxing style was based on raw punching power rather than technique, and his reputation was such that no policeman felt like intervening when he blocked Princes Street for an hour while lying down on the tram rails to celebrate a famous victory. When he got up, he went to a cab rank and reportedly tackled a horse.
>
> Bedell-Sivright's aggression always remained confined within the touchlines and ropes. He captained both Cambridge and Edinburgh Universities and made his Scotland debut aged just 19. By the time he captained the British touring team to Australia and New Zealand four years later, he had already won 12 caps and played in the Lions side that visited South Africa in 1903.
>
> After his second tour, he spent a year stock-rearing in Australia before returning to medicine in the UK, having asked himself: 'What was I, with an average amount of brains and rather more of money, doing? Simply prostituting the one in order to increase the other. It wasn't good enough.'
>
> © Telegraph Media Group Limited)

Qualified now as a surgeon he was at Gallipoli with the Royal Navy in April 1915 when the man contemporaries viewed as indestructible succumbed to an insect bite and septicaemia.

Gallipoli claimed four others from the Club roster. Lieutenant Patrick Francis Considine (4th Battalion Royal Scots) fitted the pattern of Scottish public school and a brief spell at the Club just before the war as he trained in law and accountancy. Severely injured on 28 June 1915, when leading a bombing attack on the Turkish trenches, he was evacuated to Malta and died in Valletta two weeks later.

The weeks passed and another to die charging Turkish trenches, on 7 August 1915, was Lieutenant George Edward Forman Campbell, serving in the Gurkhas alongside the Auckland Mounted Rifles.

Already, on 28 June, the ill-fated Gallipoli campaign had claimed Captain Eric Templeton Young of the Cameronians (Scottish Rifles). Another to make his debut for Scotland in that last Calcutta Cup match, he was born 14 May 1892. Fettes College led to Magdalen College Oxford and though he turned out for the University he missed out on a Blue.

The same June day was also the last for Lieutenant Francis Wishart Thomson of the Royal Scots, an Edinburgh Academical who had had earned his Blue in 1912 while at University College Oxford. He was 24. His brother Eric was 22. They were killed on the same day in the same action. One day, two telegrams then, for Mrs Catherine Thomson, of 30, Drumsheugh Gardens, Edinburgh.

Though not recorded at the time, inscriptions on several memorials suggest Turkey's President Kemal Ataturk, addressed all the "Mrs Thomsons":

> There is no difference between the Johnnies and the Mehmets who lie side by side here in this country of ours. You, the mothers who sent your sons from far away countries, wipe away your tears. Your sons are now lying in our bosom and are at peace. Having lost their lives on this land they are our sons as well.

Age Had Begun to Wither

The variety of ages of the Gallipoli Five is indicative of the age range on the Club's war memorial. The likes of Tod and Russell were teenagers. At the other end of the scale, John Campbell was 40, Black 38, Captain Robert Kilgour Thom Catto 43, Captain Francis James Ogilvie MacKinnon 44 or 45, Captain Arthur Stanley Pringle 38, Lieutenant William Spens 40. These were men who did not need to join up, but they did so anyway. Two brothers who joined up in their 30s were William Pearson Cowper and Gordon W. Cowper from Hendon. William was a surgeon on HMS *Valiant*, having shelved his civilian career as an ophthalmologist to "do his bit." Both survived the horrors of the war itself only to die of illness in 1919. William was 38 when he died on 1 February. The next day Gordon, nearly 33, a Captain in the Gordon Highlanders on his way to Germany as part of the post-Armistice Army of Occupation, died of the Spanish flu – quite possibly the same illness that accounted for William. Another mother due to receive two telegrams and both three months after the armistice.

Captain Thomas Arthur Nelson, killed 9 April 1917, aged 40; played for London Scottish and won one cap for Scotland; John Buchan dedicated *The Thirty-Nine Steps* to his Oxford friend, who had become his publisher. (Image supplied by World Rugby Museum, Twickenham)

Another of the "oldies" was Captain Thomas Arthur Nelson, a 40-year-old intelligence officer with the 1st Lothians and Border Horse when he was killed by a shell at Arras on 9 April 1917. Far behind him lay a one-cap rugby career – against England in 1898. Ahead of him lay a career as a publisher – he was already working as a director of the family firm set up by his father, also Thomas.

His great friend from Oxford days, John Buchan, had dedicated *The Thirty-Nine Steps* to him.

> My Dear Tommy, You and I have long cherished an affection for that elemental type of tale which Americans call the 'dime novel' and which we know as the 'shocker' – the romance where the incidents defy the probabilities, and march just inside the borders of the possible. During an illness last winter I exhausted my store of those aids to cheerfulness, and was driven to write one for myself. This little volume is the result, and I should like to put your name on it in memory of our long friendship, in the days when the wildest fictions are so much less improbable than the facts. J.B.

Where They Fought and Fell

For London Scottish, as for everyone else, the dominant theatre was the Western Front. For four years and more, officers and soldiers alike criss-crossed the channel on leave, with London either the destination or the point of transit. Thus many of the London Scottish players who survived long enough to be granted leave will have returned periodically to friends and family in the home city; but the clubmen were not confined solely to France and Flanders – to visit the final resting place of all those who did not return, a pilgrim's travels would take him or her also to Gallipoli, Malta, Jerusalem, Gaza, Skopje, Kalamaria, Basra and India, to say nothing of the chilly waters of the North Sea, and not forgetting more prosaically, Hampstead, Grantham and Glasgow.

Indeed, the map of where London Scots fell encompasses some of the seminal events of the war: First Battle of the Aisne, 14–19 September 1914 (Simson, Huggan), Messines on Hallowe'en 1914 (Chapman, Farquharson, Kyle, J. Ross), Gallipoli in 1915 (Young, Bedell-Sivwright, Considine, F. Thomson, G. Campbell), Loos 25/26 September 1915 (Lieutenant Norman D.S. Bruce-Lockhart, Walter Dickson, Captain A.S. Pringle, Second Lieutenant K.M. Gaunt, Second Lieutenant W.G. Herbertson, Captain W.H. Robertson-Durham, J.M. Usher), Jutland on 31 May / 1 June 1916 (Abercrombie, Wilson) the first day of the Battle of the Somme on 1 July 1916 (Fraser, Captain R.W.H. Pringle among the 60,000 slaughtered in that fateful first assault, Begg and Captain C.E. Anderson in the days that followed), Passchendaele (3rd Ypres) on 31 July 1917 (Captain W.H.B. Baxter, Second Lieutenant L.C. Leggatt, Lieutenant H.B. Dickson). Were the Club a regiment, these would be its battle honours.

And Some Were Not Cut Down

When at last the conflict was over, and in the months following the Armistice, the survivors returned home. The last faces from our photograph were among them. We know little of Captain Alistair Buchanan Selkirk Legate, but Ernest Alexander Kinross is believed to be the only one of the XV not to be killed or wounded. Initially serving as a private in the London Scottish Regiment, he was another Messines survivor, and in 1916 he was commissioned as second lieutenant into the York and Lancasters. 1917 finds him promoted to lieutenant and acting captain. In April 1919, almost five months into the Armistice, he is in Cologne, presumably as part of the allied Army of Occupation – or rather he isn't … he's on a train back to Wimereux with a painful, sounding "deviation of nasal septum." In the 1920s, electoral registers record him living in Hampstead with his wife Dora, but in the '30s he seems to have moved into the City: in 1930 he visits New York; in 1934 is working as a broker at the London Corn Exchange.

Captain Charles Milne Usher was captured at Mons but unlike his team-mate R.D. Robertson released in 1915, he spent the next four and a half years as a POW. In 1919 he was back at the Club, and back in the Scotland side as captain in 1920, earning 16 caps altogether between 1912 and 1922. He also captained Scotland at fencing and sabre. He stayed in the army and from 1939 commanded the 1st Battalion of the Gordons. In 1946 C.M. Usher DSO OBE, Chevalier of the Légion d'Honneur, Croix de Guerre with Palm retired to Edinburgh as Director of PE at the University till 1959. He died aged 89 in 1981.

Finale

London Scottish FC survived the Great War, even if over a hundred members did not. The Club was rebuilt and thrived again, providing rugby for everyone from the ambitious international to the determinedly social player, including for another 52 who would die in the Second World War. Each year, on Remembrance Sunday, the boys and girls pause their Sunday rugby for a two minutes' silence. A wreath is laid at the Club's war memorial and the secretary recites *In Flanders Fields*. Then the whistle is blown and rugby resumes.

One hundred years after those first trenches were dug on the Western Front, on 14 September 2014, the anniversary of his death, the captains of London Scottish Under 15s and Under 18s teams laid a wreath on the grave of Ronnie Simson. They stood surrounded by their team-mates, being in France, fittingly, to play rugby in a commemorative tournament along with teams from Blackheath. Blackheath was the club of the first English international killed, Captain C.E. Wilson, two days after Simson; he lies buried in the churchyard at Paissy, the next-door village. The boys later played in shirts that each bore the name of a London Scottish player killed in the Great War. Had it been 1914, those 14- and 17-year-olds would instead have been awaiting their time.

Team captains of the London Scottish Under 15s and Under 18s laying a wreath on the grave of Lieutenant Ronnie Simson, on the centenary of his death in September 2014.
(© John Dennison, Francourt Events)

St Paul's Cathedral with search lights in 1916; watercolour by William Alister Macdonald; the Sutherland-born son of a Scottish Free Church minister, Macdonald exhibited his paintings in London between 1892 and 1936. (Reproduced courtesy of John Macdonald/ Guildhall Art Gallery, City of London)

The 2nd Battalion Scots Guards march out of the Tower of London on 16 September 1914 to join the 7th Division in the New Forest, Hampshire, before sailing for Belgium on 5 October. (Courtesy of Lord de Saumarez)

Hallowe'en, 1914, a painting by R Caton Woodville, depicting the attack on the German positions at Messines by the 1st Battalion London Scottish during the first Battle of Ypres, 31 October 1914. (Trustees of the London Scottish Regiment)

Colonel Douglas Lyall Grant MC TD played for the London Scottish Rugby Football Club and was its secretary 1913–39 and president 1939–63; he joined the London Scottish Regiment in 1909, won his MC at Neuve Chapelle in 1915, was shot down in 1916 and then spent almost two years in POW camps. (London Scottish Football Club)

The London Scottish Regiment disembark from a London omnibus at Ypres in October 1914, George Duncan MacDougald (1880–1945). (Trustees of the London Scottish Regiment)

The war memorial of the London Scottish Regiment in its Drill Hall at Horseferry Road, Victoria. (Trustees of the London Scottish Regiment)

v

The Return to the Front: Victoria Railway Station – Richard Jack (1866–1952). British-born, Jack was Canada's official war artist. (York Museums Trust (York Art Gallery), UK/Bridgeman Images)

Lieutenant (Acting Captain) G.H. Tatham ("Reggie") Paton VC MC 4th Battalion Grenadier Guards, sits (holding a puppy) with other members of his battalion and French officers; Paton was posthumously awarded the Victoria Cross for his actions at Gonnelieu during the Battle of Cambrai on 1 December 1917. (Courtesy of the Rennie family)

This stuffed ram's head, mounted with a silver snuff box was given to The Caledonian Club by J.A. Milne in memory of his son Captain Johnnie Milne MC, who died in Flanders while serving with the Royal Flying Corps on 24 October 1917. (The Caledonian Club)

A postcard embroidered in silk with the Star of the Scots Guards; such cards were made in France for many regiments serving there during 1914–15. (Private collection)

This beautifully illuminated and glazed war memorial lists the 209 members of The Caledonian Club who died in the Great War.

(The Caledonian Club)

5

The Oldest Kirk: Crown Court Church of Scotland

Sheena Tait

The Church of Scotland has had a presence in London since at least 1603 when James VI, King of Scots, became King James I of England. There is some evidence that courtiers who had followed the King from Scotland worshipped in a chapel in the precincts of the old Whitehall Palace. That site became known as "Scotland Yard" and subsequently housed the original offices of the Metropolitan Police.

Crown Court's roots go back to at least 1711 when a group of Scottish Protestants met in a meeting house in St Peter's Court off St Martin's Lane. The congregation grew steadily as the number of Scots in London increased and in 1719 this Scottish Kirk moved to a new location in Covent Garden, where it has remained ever since.

In 1914, the Crown Court congregation was enjoying worshiping in their new building, opened on Saturday 29 October 1909 by Lady Frances Balfour, who had done so much to raise the necessary funds, and dedicated by the Moderator of the General Assembly of the Church of Scotland, the Rev. Dr Robertson. Under their Minister, Alexander Macrae, the church had an active congregation with over 500 people on the communion roll. One commentator noted that "young lads and lassies" dominated the congregation which celebrated the centenary of the Sunday School on 25 May 1914. Church activities and organisations at that time included periodic Gaelic services, boy scouts, a reel and strathspey society, a mothers' meeting, church choir (with a paid leader), a rambling club and a night school which by 1914 had evolved into a social club for working girls.

During the war, Crown Court weddings reflected the broad range of social classes which comprised the congregation. Marriages of young, working class, men and women who had moved to London to find work and servicemen who had been posted to London and had then met their new wives were intermingled with "society weddings" of members of the families of the 1st Earl of Balfour and the Duke of Argyll both of whom had connections to Crown Court. While what passed as normal life was continuing the minister, Rev. Alexander Macrae, was also serving as chaplain to the Scots Guards, as Presbyterian chaplain to eight London hospitals and to

Wandsworth Prison. Such was the pressure of this work that, in May 1915, Crown Court granted him leave of absence to concentrate on his military duties.

Crown Court War Memorial

Alexander Macrae resigned from his ministry at Crown Court in May 1917, was appointed officiating chaplain to the forces and served overseas for the remainder of the war. In November 1917, he was succeeded by Rev. Joseph Moffett who had been on active service from September 1915 to September 1916 mainly with the 9th (Scottish) Division in France.

The church has always served Scots working or living in London and also serves Presbyterians from other countries working, visiting or living in London. This was also the case during the First World War and the names on the war memorial represent people from all corners of Scotland and elsewhere and different social classes. The migration of Scots to London at the end of the 19th century and early Edwardian era is reflected in the lives and careers of those recorded on the brass memorial.

The Roll of Honour of the names of the men from Crown Court who had served in the Great War was published in the church magazine for November 1919 and the following month this notice appeared:

> Permanent War Memorial
> It is time some effort was made towards the erection of some form of permanent memorial to those who fell in the War. In common with the churches throughout the length and breadth of the land – it might almost be said of the world – we, in Crown Court are desirous of perpetuating the memory of their heroic and self-forgetful sacrifice in the cause of Freedom and the Right. The particular form of the Memorial will naturally be determined in large measure by the amount of money received, and no doubt when this opportunity of subscribing to it is thus presented, the response will be such as to make it possible to give worthy, if necessarily inadequate expression to our appreciation of the valour of those who gave their all for us. Any suggestions as to the form it might take will be welcomed by the Kirk Session.

By July 1920, the Session was able to report

> We hope to be in a position very soon to proceed with the erection of the Memorial to our fallen heroes, and have under consideration a design for a brass tablet, which is greatly admired.

However, it appears that they had some difficulty in compiling the list of names to be honoured:

In spite of the oft repeated publication of the Roll of Honour, and the attendant request for names and particulars in the pages of this Magazine during the last year, it was only within the last few weeks that the names of two men who laid down their lives, finally reached us ... It would be a matter of reproach and enduring regret to all concerned if even one name should inadvertently be overlooked.

This was followed by the list of 23 men who had been identified as having died. The following year, in May 1921, the Session was ready to proceed:

The Kirk Session has decided that our War Memorial should take the form of a memorial brass. A design, submitted by Mr. Geo. W. Pridmore of Coventry, has, after careful consideration, been finally approved. It bears the words "To perpetuate the Memory of our Glorious Dead. The Men connected with the Session and Congregation of Crown Court Church, who gave their lives for Freedom and the Right." Thereafter follows the list of names, and beneath them the words from Scripture, "They jeoparded their lives unto the death in the high places of the field." The brass will be left plain, without decoration of any kind save the artistic lettering, which will be deeply engraved.

It is of course urgently necessary that the names with particulars of rank, Regiment and Honours, should be quite accurate before the work is finally put in hand ... but lest there should be any mistake, we print once more the list as we have it, and as it will be engraved ... Our readers, therefore, are asked to scrutinise the list most carefully, and notify the Minister ... if any error or omission is noted.

The names, rank and regiment of the 23 men who had been identified in July 1920 then followed.

This must have triggered some activity as when the memorial was unveiled on Sunday 15 January 1922, having cost £60; it held the 29 names we see today.

In the Crown Court *Church Magazine* of February 1922, the unveiling service was reported thus:

War Memorial Service
The Unveiling and Dedication Service of our War Memorial, which took place on Sunday, 18th January [sic], was of a deeply impressive and touching nature. It was marked by a simplicity and solemnity peculiarly appropriate to the occasion, and voiced the notes of proud, yet grateful remembrance and joyous peace, in one sweet harmony. "A dignified and beautiful service" were the words on everyone's lips as the congregation dispersed, and such indeed it was. None of us who were privileged to worship in Crown Court that morning will ever forget the "uplift," the atmosphere of stately joy and dignified peace, which prevailed throughout the service.

The praise list included the 23rd Psalm, and the second version of the 124th, as well as Alford's Hymn commencing:

"Ten thousand times then thousand,
In sparkling raiment bright,
The Armies of ransomed Saints
Throng up the steeps of Light."

General Lord Horne read the lessons: and the Rev. Alex. Macrae preached an eloquent and touching sermon, taking as his text the words inscribed on the Memorial, "They jeoparded their lives unto the Death in the high places of the field."

Thereafter, from high up in the Gallery there sounded the long drawn piercing notes of the bagpipes, as the pipers of the Scottish Clans Association of London played the Funeral March that is mournfully dear to the heart of every Scot: "The Flo'ers o' the Forest." To its slow music, Lord Horne followed by his Aide-de-Camp and the Clergy, proceeded slowly down the aisle to where the Memorial has been placed in the south wall of the Church, the congregation upstanding. Then when the last echo of the pipes had died away, Lord Horne unveiled the Memorial with the words "I unveil this Memorial to the Glory of God and to perpetuate the memory of the men connected with the Session and Congregation of the Church who gave their lives for Freedom and the Right, 1914–1918." He then read out the 29 names which are engraved upon the Memorial. One minute of Silent Prayer then followed, and then Mr Moffett offered the … Dedicatory Prayer …

The buglers of the Scots Guards then sounded the "Reveille," and the service concluded with singing of the 66th Paraphrase.

It has not been possible to track down details of all those named on the memorial but details of some can be recorded which give a flavour of the range of backgrounds of those attending Crown Court who then went on active service.

Albert Edward Stewart was born in 1878 in the Isle of Thanet in Kent. He was the youngest of eight children born to the Kent-born farm worker David Stewart and his wife Elizabeth. After school and working for a spell as a farm labourer, Albert joined the Royal Navy as a stoker. He initially signed up for a period of 12 years on 3 March 1896.

Albert sailed the world with the Royal Navy – in 1901 he was in Bermuda aboard HMS *Terror*. His initial 12 years' service expired in 1908 by which time he had been promoted leading stoker. Two years later, he signed up again and by April 1911 he was serving in HMS *Black Prince* as part of the Atlantic Fleet at Gibraltar.

When war broke out Albert was serving in HMS *Sutlej* which was then assigned to convoy escort duties off the French and Iberian coasts. In July 1914 Stewart was transferred briefly to HMS *Pembroke II* – the Royal Naval Air Station at Eastchurch in Kent. Finally, in August 1914, Albert was transferred to HMS *Lightning*. HMS *Lightning* was a torpedo boat destroyer allocated to the Nore Local Defence Flotilla.

On 30 June 1915 following the sighting of floating mines near the Kentish Knock Light Vessel, HMS *Lightning* and the destroyer HMS *Vulture* were sent out to deal with the mines. By 8:00 p.m. the ships had destroyed three mines and, as they searched for more, HMS *Lightning* struck another mine. The explosion lifted her out of the water and broke her in half killing 15 of her crew including Albert Edward Stewart. The bow section of HMS *Lightning* sank, while the stern was towed back to Sheerness and later broken up.

James Kennedy was born in Gollanfield, Inverness-shire in 1886, the son of Hugh Kennedy and his wife, Ann McCulloch. When James was a small boy, his father worked as a deer stalker and gamekeeper on the Coignascalan estate in Moy. By the time James was a teenager, the family had moved to Mealigie near Boleskine and his father was working as a shepherd.

James became an electrician and builder, eventually moving to New Malden in Surrey where he had his own business as a house decorator. In 1909 he married Mary Ann Grant, the Edinburgh-born daughter of William Campbell Grant. The couple had two children, Margaret and Ian, both born in England.

James joined the London Scottish Regiment as a private just after the outbreak of war and was sent to France in March 1915. He served with the London Scottish in France until July 1915 when his commanding officer recommended him for a commission.

James was commissioned as a Second Lieutenant in the 1st Battalion the Cameron Highlanders in August 1915 and fought at the Battle of Loos where he was badly wounded. James died of his wounds the following day, on 26 September 1915 and was buried in Noeux-Les-Mines Communal Cemetery, south of Béthune in France. His service medals were sent to his widow Mary Ann after the war.

William Young was born in 1884 in Marnoch, Banffshire the third of five children born to farm servant George Young and his wife Agnes. William stayed in Banffshire, working as a farm labourer throughout his teens. Later he became a baker and moved to London to work in a hotel, lodging in Camden Town. In 1915 he married a fellow Scot, Mary Fairlie, from Stirlingshire who had been working as a cook for a wealthy family in Cadogan Square.

William joined the 14th Battalion the London Regiment (London Scottish) in 1916 and was killed at Gommecourt, about eight miles north of Albert and the site of a "supplementary" operation, on 1 July 1916, the first day of the Battle of the Somme.

John Smith Melville, eldest child of commercial traveller Alexander Melville and his wife Agnes, was born in Cults, Fife in 1883. After school, John became a lithographer working for the printing firm of Paul and Matthew in Dundee, he also joined the Fifeshire Artillery Volunteers. He enlisted in the Royal Field Artillery in Glasgow on 11 May 1901 and then transferred to the Royal Horse Artillery (RHA) in February 1902. John was transferred to the reserve in 1909 and discharged in 1913. During his 12 years in the RHA, John spent three years in India and the remainder of his time in the UK.

John married Cecil Baptie in Farnham in the spring of 1915 and they settled in Waltham Abbey. When John enlisted during the war, he joined the Mounted Branch of the Corps of Military Police landing in the Balkans on 16 June 1915. Unfortunately, John caught malaria and died at sea on 30 September 1916. John is commemorated on the Chatby Memorial in Egypt.

Arthur James Edgar Butler, the eldest son of leather worker Arthur W. Butler and his wife Florence Finnigan, was born in the London parish of St Olave Southwark at the start of 1889. By 1911 Arthur, with his family, was living in Rotherhithe and working as a warehouseman for a walking stick manufacturer.

Arthur enlisted in the 1/6th Battalion the London Regiment (City of London Rifles) and landed with his regiment in France on 18 March 1915. He fought with his regiment in the Battles of Aubers Ridge, Festubert, Loos and the subsequent actions of the Hohenzollern Redoubt in 1915. Arthur was still with his regiment in 1916 during the Battles of the Somme, for the German attack at Vimy Ridge and the Battle of Flers-Courcelette in which the Division captured High Wood. His division was successful in capturing Eaucourt l'Abbaye during the Battle of the Transloy Ridges; however, during the attack on Eaucourt l'Abbaye the front-line trench occupied by Arthur's regiment was heavily shelled on 8 October and Arthur was one of the 20 other ranks who were killed that day.

Arthur is commemorated on the Thiepval Memorial.

James William McHattie was born on 28 December 1892 and was baptised in St Marks Church, Enfield on 23 January 1893. He was the second child of 10 born to Banffshire-born baker James McHattie and his wife Margaret Jane Gillespie.

After leaving school, James started work as an optician's assistant. He enlisted as a Private with the London Scottish Regiment and was in France with his regiment on 15 September 1914. He was commissioned as a Second Lieutenant in the York and Lancaster Regiment in December 1915 and was promoted Lieutenant with the same regiment in July 1917.

In January 1918, James transferred to the Royal Flying Corps. James returned to France to join 20 Squadron, flying Bristol Fighters. On 1 April 1918, James became one of the founding members of the new Royal Air Force. But he and his pilot were killed on 25 April 1918 when their aircraft overshot St Marie Cappel aerodrome on return from patrol, stalled and crashed.

James was buried at Longuenesse (St Omer) Souvenir Cemetery, Pas de Calais where his headstone reads:

> *A Silent Thought*
> *A Hidden Tear*
> *Keep His Memory Ever Dear*

Family Groups

In common with many memorials across the country, the Crown Court War Memorial bears several names from the same family or household.

John Alexander was a Huntly-born baker who had moved to London at the end of the 19th century and lived at 117 Kings Road, Camden Town. In 1911, he had two lodgers:

James Stewart Gordon was the third child born to tailor Alexander Gordon and his wife Jane Stewart, in Fochabers on 8 January 1877. When he grew up, James trained as a baker and moved to London to find work. James moved out of the Alexander household to marry Catherine Mackie Anderson in Chelsea in the spring of 1917 and the couple set up home at 74 Portland Place. James enlisted in the London Scottish Regiment on 1 May 1917 and served with them in France where he was killed in action at St Eloi on 29 March 1918. James was buried at Albuera Cemetery, Bailleul-Sire-Berthoult, Pas de Calais, where his gravestone reads, "Till we meet again."

William Beveridge was born in Perth in 1885 the third of five children born to plumber William Beveridge and his wife Jessie. Towards the end of the 1890s, the family moved from Perth to Cullen in Banffshire where William senior set up his own business in which William junior was employed. However, William did not stay with the family business; he trained as a baker and moved to London, also lodging with the Alexander family. William enlisted with the London Scottish Regiment and landed in France on 22 June 1916. He then served in the Balkans from 29 November 1916 and in Egypt until April 1918. William was killed in action in Palestine on 20 April 1918 and was buried at Jerusalem War Cemetery in Israel.

Another Scottish family represented on the War Memorial is the Percy family. Robert Percy was a Dumfriesshire hairdresser who with his wife, Josephine Clark, had two sons, William and George. When the children were young, Robert and Josephine moved to the Baillieston area of Glasgow where Robert set up his own business.

The Percys' eldest son, William John Percy, was born in Dumfries in 1892. After William left school, he started work as an apprentice in a drapery warehouse. He then moved to London where he enlisted in the army. William appears to have served with the London Regiment and the Royal Sussex Regiment then moved to the 2/10th Battalion The Royal Scots eventually reaching the rank of Lance Sergeant. William served with The Royal Scots in north Russia in August 1918 as part of the Archangel Force – part of the Allied intervention in Russia after the Russian Revolution. William died of wounds on 28 October 1918 and is commemorated on the Archangel Memorial in Russia.

Their second son, George Clark Percy MC was born in Dumfries on 4 January 1895. After attending an elementary school in Glasgow, George won a scholarship to Allan Glen's School where, during his final year, he acted as secretary to the headmaster, Dr Kerr. George joined Glasgow University in 1913 studying English, Mathematics and Natural Philosophy in his first year. He went on to study Logic & Metaphysics and Moral Philosophy in his second year but his studies were cut short when he was commissioned as a Second Lieutenant with the 1st Battalion the Cameronians (Scottish Rifles) in February 1915. George landed in France in July 1915 and fought with his regiment at the Battle of Loos where the British used poison gas for the first time. During localised fighting around Ypres in April 1916, the Germans exploded a mine creating a crater 30 yards wide just 10 yards from the lip of the British trenches. The following evening, 20 April, Lieutenant Percy led a raid of 15 men on one of the German saps which they found evacuated with the exception of one man "with whom Lieutenant Percy had an encounter at close quarters, the German unfortunately escaping" *(The National Archives (TNA) WO95/2422/2: 1 Battalion Cameronians War Diary)*. George's battalion received news of the start of the offensive on the Somme on 1 July 1916 and on Sunday 16 July relieved the Glasgow Highlanders at High Wood. They attacked High Wood at dawn on 20 July and George was wounded in the right shoulder during the fighting. A report dated 13 November 1916 from General Haig was published in the Second Supplement to *The London Gazette* of 2 January 1917 reading:

Captain George Clark Percy MC of the Scottish Rifles; both he and his brother William are named on the Crown Court War Memorial. (University of Glasgow Archives & Special Collections, University collection, GB 248 CH4/4/2/2/219)

> I have the honour to submit a list of names of those officers, ladies, non-commissioned officers and men, serving, or who have served, under my command, whose distinguished and gallant serviced and devotion to duty I consider deserving of special mention.
>
> Supplement to *The London Gazette*, 4 January 1917, p. 191

Among these names was that of "Percy, Lieutenant G.C. serving in the Scottish Rifles." George was awarded a Military Cross for his actions on 21 June 1917. The Supplement to *The London Gazette* of 25 August describes his actions:

> For conspicuous gallantry and devotion to duty. With his platoon he formed part of a working party in front of our line. Although subjected to heavy artillery fire, he showed complete disregard of danger, attending to the wounded and encouraging the men. When finally ordered to withdraw, it was due to his great coolness and good leadership that his platoon got safely back to our lines, and having seen the last man in, he returned and remained with a badly wounded officer under heavy fire until assistance reached him.
>
> Supplement to *The London Gazette*, 25 August 1917, p. 8814

George was killed by a shell burst on 31 July 1917 while leading his company out of their trench. The *Dumfries and Galloway Standard* of 25 August 1917 quotes his commanding officer:

> I expect you have heard by now from the War Office that Captain Percy was killed in action during the recent great battle [Somme]. We are all so terribly sorry. He was a fine man, and loved by all, and is a great loss to me now. He was killed in the very act of leading his men out of their trench to attack the enemy, and it was a great grief to us all when we heard that he had fallen. He died the noblest death man can die, and though he made the supreme sacrifice, I know he gave his life freely.
>
> *Dumfries and Galloway Standard*, 25 August 1917, p. 3

George is commemorated on the Ypres (Menin Gate) Memorial.

One family represented on the memorial lost their three eldest sons. Thomas Kerr was born in Edinburgh and had been a career soldier in the Seaforth Highlanders. Thomas had been born a Delworth but his step-father was George Kerr and Thomas appears to have used the two surnames interchangeably.

Thomas married Annie Thomson in Edinburgh on 9 November 1886. Their eldest son Thomas was born as Charles Thomas Delworth in Glasgow on 25 February 1889. Their second son, Alexander John Kerr, was born in 1892 in Fermoy, Cork, Ireland and their third son, Arthur, was born in 1894 in Tipperary.

Thomas Kerr senior retired from the army in 1899 and by 1901 was working as a commissionaire and living in Deptford where his family grew up.

Arthur Kerr, was working as a dispatch clerk and cyclist in a publishing company by the age of 16. Arthur signed up to the Duke of Cornwall's Light Infantry in London and arrived in France on 27 December 1914 aged 20. He fought with his regiment through the second Battle of Ypres in 1915, the Battles of the Somme in 1916, Battle of Vimy and the attack on La Coulotte in 1917 but was killed in action on 2 October 1917 during the Battle of Polygon Wood. Arthur is commemorated at Tyne Cot Memorial in Belgium.

Alexander John Kerr, was employed as a junior clerk and typist with a firm of wholesale furnishers when he was 18. However, Alexander left this job and moved to Parkstone in Dorset, where his older brother Thomas was already living, and found a job as a chauffeur. Alexander enlisted in the Mechanical Transport Corps of the Army Service Corps in Bournemouth on 2 September 1915 and landed at Rouen on 4 October the same year where he was attached to the 15th Motor Ambulance Convoy. Alexander was granted home leave from 9 to 23 December 1917 and while on leave, he married Mary Katherine Trissler in St Bartholomew's Church East Ham on 15 December 1917 where Mary settled after their marriage. When he returned to the Front, Alexander was posted to 87 Field Ambulance and was later attached to the 1st Warwick Field Ambulance. Alexander died of wounds he received while in action in the field in Belgium on 8 March 1918 and was buried in the Menin Road South Military Cemetery.

When he was old enough Charles Thomas (known as Thomas), found a job as a chauffeur and fitter in Poole, Dorset. While he was in Dorset, Thomas married Minnie Elizabeth Stacey and they had two children Thomas Reginald Blair Kerr Delworth, born in 1915, and Charles Arthur Benjamin Kerr-Delworth, born in 1918. Thomas enlisted in the Mechanical Transport Corps of the Army Service Corps on 17 January 1916 and landed in France with his regiment on 28 April 1916. Thomas served with his regiment through the war and was eventually appointed lance corporal. By the start of 1919, Thomas was working at the MT School of Instruction and his family must have been expecting him home soon. Unfortunately, on the night of 25 February 1919, a fire broke out in the canteen where Thomas was sleeping and Thomas died of the burns he sustained. Thomas was buried at Les Baraques Military Cemetery, Sangatte, France.

Bankers

A Scot, William Paterson, famously founded the Bank of England in 1688. Continuing the tradition of Scottish bankers in England, three of the names on the Crown Court memorial worked in banks.

The Honourable Arthur Middleton Kinnaird MC was born in 1885, his birth being registered in the St George Hanover Square registration district in London. He was the fifth son of Arthur Fitzgerald Kinnaird, 11th Lord Kinnaird, and his wife Lady Mary Agnew. After attending Eton, he worked in Barclays Bank in Pall Mall of which his father was a director.

Arthur M. Kinnaird was an elder at Crown Court Church where he had served as representative elder to the Presbytery of England from 1913 to 1915. His father, the 11th Lord, was a key figure in the development of association football having learned to play as a schoolboy at Eton. He was one of the founders of the Football Association (FA) and arranged the first Scotland-England international match, which ended in a 0–0 draw. Arthur senior played in nine FA Cup finals (still a record) and was president of the FA for 33 years. Such was his fame that he was presented with the FA Cup in 1911 and it remained in the family until 2005 when it was sold for nearly £500,000. Arthur senior also taught in ragged schools in the poorer parts of London and succeeded his father as president of the Young Women's Christian Association (founded by his mother Lady Mary Jane Kinnaird) in 1887.

Arthur junior originally enlisted as a private in the Royal Fusiliers (City of London Regiment) and was commissioned as a temporary second lieutenant in April 1915. He was appointed Aide de Camp to Major General Rycroft, commander of the 32nd Division, and served with him in France until July 1916. He was then transferred to the 1st Battalion the Scots Guards and his commission as second lieutenant was confirmed in December 1916. He was then promoted to Lieutenant in July 1917.

Arthur was killed in action on 27 November 1917 and is buried at Ruyaulcourt Military Cemetery, France, his older brother, Douglas having been killed three years earlier. Arthur's Military Cross was gazetted posthumously on 23 April 1918 and the citation reads:

> For conspicuous gallantry and devotion to duty in forming up his company in most trying circumstances and conditions of weather, maintaining direction and capturing and consolidating the first objective.
>
> Supplement to *The London Gazette*, 23 April 1918, p. 4873

Alexander Macdonald was born in 1885 in Kenmore in Perthshire. He was the eldest of seven children born to Daniel Macdonald and his wife Ann. Shortly after Alexander's birth the family moved to the hamlet of Dull, near Aberfeldy where Alexander attended school and then went on to join the Union Bank. Alexander must have done well at the bank as by 1911 he was living in Hampstead and working as a bank clerk in the Bank of Montreal (now BMO) in the City.

Alexander joined the London Scottish Regiment at the start of the war and landed in France in November 1914. Over the next two years, Alexander took part in many battles and was wounded twice.

He was declared "presumed dead" on 1 July 1916. A comrade described the events writing:

> On the 1st of July the platoon were in the British front line trench when he gallantly volunteered to go over to the German lines, which our comrades were occupying, with ammunition which they were in great need of. He left the trench, and since then nothing has been seen or heard of him, and I am afraid that the worst must have happened.
>
> *Perthshire Advertiser*, 19 July 1916, p. 5

Andrew Ganson was born in Lerwick, Shetland the oldest child of farmer Thomas Ganson and his wife Elizabeth Slater. Andrew attended the Anderson Institute in Lerwick and then took a job as an accountant with the Union Bank of Scotland in Ellon, Aberdeenshire where he lodged with the Cowe family in The Square, Ellon. In 1902, he was appointed as an accountant at the New Pitsligo branch and in 1903 he moved to the London office of the bank in Cornhill and lodged with his aunt Helen Slater in Brixton.

Andrew married Ethel Maud Archer in the spring of 1915 and on 12 July he enlisted as a Private in the Inns of Court Officers' Training Corps. He went to No 9 Officer

2nd Lt Andrew Ganson, Highland Light Infantry, killed in France 1916 – on the Crown Court War Memorial. (Reproduced by permission of the National Library of Scotland)

Cadet Battalion on 8 March 1916 and was commissioned as a Second Lieutenant in the Highland Light Infantry on 6 July the same year. Andrew joined his regiment in France in September and was involved in the fighting at Flers-Courcelette, where the British used tanks for the first time.

On 14 December, Andrew's battalion was ordered to the front line to relieve the 1/6th Gloucester Regiment and Andrew was killed in Martinpuich on the way up. Andrew was buried in Martinpuich British Cemetery, Pas de Calais where his headstone reads:

> *Of The*
> *Union Bank Of Scotland*
> *Shetland And London*

Scottish drapers in London

Whether or not there was an association of drapers in London at the start of the 20th century who made a practice of recruiting young men from Scotland, there appears to be a disproportionate number of drapers on the Crown Court War Memorial. In addition to William John Percy, there are a further eight drapers represented.

George Cruickshank Morrison was born in 1890 in the small Aberdeenshire village of Gamrie or Gardenstown. He was the youngest of seven children born to mason Robert Morrison and his wife Isabella Wilson. George grew up in Gamrie and served his apprenticeship with the local Macduff draper James Sim. In 1908, he moved to London to work for the wholesale drapers Foster Porter & Co Ltd and, by 1911, was lodging in their premises at 47 Wood Street E.C.

In 1914, George enlisted in the 8th Battalion of the Gordon Highlanders in Aberdeen. The battalion moved to Aldershot and then, in February 1915, were sent to Bordon in Hampshire. On Sunday 9 May, the battalion took the train from Bordon to Folkestone from where they sailed to France, landing at Boulogne on 10 May 1915. According to the unit war diaries, the 8th Gordon Highlanders were the first unit of Kitchener's New Armies (wartime volunteers who agreed to serve for the duration of the war, wherever the army sent them) to arrive at the Front on 11 May 1915.

On 24 May the battalion moved to Armentières for instruction in trench warfare and in the afternoon marched the two miles to the trenches, where they stayed until 5:30 p.m. the following day. Just before the battalion left the trenches it came under fire from rifle grenades, one of which hit George Morrison and killed him instantly.

George Eric Edwards DSO, the fifth of six children of shoemaker Eric Edwards and his wife, Margaret, was born in Lossiemouth in Moray on 23 February 1889. When he grew up he became a draper and moved to London about 1910 to work for the firm of Foster, Porter & Co wholesale drapers and, by 1911, was a drapery assistant lodging in their premises at 47 Wood Street E.C. George was both a work colleague and shared lodgings with George Cruickshank Morrison who is also commemorated on the Crown Court War Memorial.

George Edwards enlisted in the Seaforth Highlanders in Elgin in September 1914 and was sent to France, landing there on 1 May 1915. He reached the rank of Lance Sergeant, and was commissioned Second Lieutenant on 22 July 1916. George fought with his division at Ypres, Festubert, The Second Action of Givenchy, the attacks on High Wood and the Battle of the Ancre in which the Division captured Beaumont Hamel and took more than 2,000 prisoners. It was during this action that George won his DSO on 13 November 1916. The story is told in the *Morayshire Roll of Honour*:

> At Beaumont Hamel the 51st Division scored a conspicuous success as pioneers of the "leap frog" system of attack. Beaumont Hamel was reckoned to be impregnable. Second Lieut. Edwards, Lossiemouth (afterwards killed) won the D.S.O., captured a German Regimental Commander and his Staff, and some 400 men. Details of his exploits were recorded in "The Times" and other newspapers about this date ... as one of the most singular instances of courage and coolness that had been known in the War. It was not then stated who was the hero of this episode, but afterwards it became known that the young officer was a Morayshire man and a native of Lossiemouth – Lieut. George E. Edwards of the 6th Seaforths. This officer was awarded the D.S.O. on 13th February 1917, for "conspicuous gallantry in action." Accompanied by a few men he advanced through our barrage and held the entrance of a cave in which there were about 400 Germans. With rare effrontery and courage he called in a loud voice for their instant surrender, and the enemy, thinking he was well-supported, regarded themselves as his prisoners. But after a little while it became evident to the German officers that this young fellow was acting on his own account and had no supports, so they turned the tables upon him and suggested that he should become their prisoner instead! So Edwards seeing no help near was compelled to surrender to them. Later on, however, supports appeared when the tables were turned again and Lieut. Edwards secured his prisoners and he himself proudly marched twelve of them, including their battalion commander, back to Battalion Headquarters. This cool and daring action reads like a page of romantic history and well might the official notice state "he set a splendid example of courage and determination throughout."
>
> *The Morayshire Roll of Honour. A biographical record of the men and women connected with the county who took part in the Great War, 1914–1918*, p. ix & pp. xiv-xv

This was not the only brave act George carried out. He was mentioned in Haig's despatch of 9 April 1917. George continued to fight with his battalion in the Arras Offensive and the Third Battle of Ypres and was promoted to Acting Captain on 20 July 1917. However, his luck eventually ran out and he was killed during capture of Bourlon Wood at the Battle of Cambrai on 20 November 1917.

After the war, Lieutenant Colonel Graham, MC, former commander of the Seaforths said:

> but for the bravery of Lieut. G. E. Edwards, Lossiemouth, the 51st Division would probably have failed in November, 1916, to take Beaumont Hamel. In the whole of the records of the late war, where acts of great bravery were so common, he did not believe there was a braver action than that of the late Lieut. Edwards. He had been recommended for the Victoria Cross, but for some reason unknown to him the lesser honour of the D.S.O. was all that was conferred, an honour which he regretted to say that brave officer did not live to enjoy.
>
> *The Morayshire Roll of Honour, 1914–1918*, p. ix & pp. xiv-xv

George was commemorated in his home town long after the war. On Sunday 23 August 1931:

> The home green of the Moray Golf Club was, on Sunday, the scene of a simple, yet heart-stirring ceremony, such as remembrance of the glorious dead must always be. The occasion was the unveiling and dedication of a memorial sundial in honour of Captain George Eric Edwards DSO, and Sergeant Alexander Edwards VC, two Lossiemouth loons, and former caddies on the Moray golf course, who were killed in the Great War. Those who were present can never forget the dignity and simplicity of the proceedings. In the centre of the green, with its velvety smoothness and verdant greenness, stood the beautiful little sundial draped in the Union Jack, the flag those soldiers served so nobly. Standing around erect and with bared heads were the officers and soldiers of the battalion, while a large crowd of visitors and townspeople gathered in the background. The relatives of the two soldiers stood a little apart on the green, and one could not but expect to see them visibly affected as they thought with pride of those loved ones who had given their lives for their country.
>
> *The Northern Scot*, 29 August 1931, http://www.northern-scot.co.uk/Features/75-Years-Ago-472.htm, accessed 28 May 2014

George was buried at Orival Wood Cemetery, Flesquières, France.

William Cowie was born early in 1892 in the parish of Logie Pert, Angus to William Cowie and his wife Isabella Wishart. William senior was a forester's labourer and by the time young William was nine years old, the family had moved to Addicate Cottage in Stracathro. William was the eldest of five children born to William and Isabella and after leaving school, he served his apprenticeship as a draper with the firm of Mitchell Brothers in Swan Street, Brechin. He then found a job with the large London drapers Marshall and Snelgrove and by 1911 was an assistant in the store, and living in the staff hostel at 16 Marylebone Lane. While in London, William joined the London *Camanachd* (Shinty) Club.

William enlisted as Private 2783 in the London Scottish Regiment and landed in France on 8 March 1915. He joined his regiment, together with 127 other men, on 14 March. Two months later, William was with his regiment at the Battle of Aubers. The regiment spent the first two weeks of June recuperating and training in the rear trenches and, on 13 June, returned to the front line as relief for the Cameron Highlanders. The routine of rotating through the front line and reserve trenches followed by a period of rest lifted slightly in July when the battalion was gifted tin baths and water-heating apparatus. A bath house was established and the men were able to have a hot bath. At the start of September, the men were issued with Tam O'Shanter bonnets described as "a more serviceable article than the Glengarry" as "the bonnets could be pulled down over the ears when sleeping at night." (The National Archives (TNA) WO95/1266/2: 1/14 Battalion London Regiment, *London Scottish War Diary*).

On 21 September the battalion moved to a bivouac in Le Marequet Wood and then, on the night of 23 September, they marched to another temporary camp near Verquin in preparation for the "big push" – the Battle of Loos. At 7:22 a.m. on 25 September the battalion advanced and immediately came under heavy machine gun and rifle fire. The fighting on the first day was a success from the Allies' point of view but three officers and 350 men from the battalion were killed or wounded. Over the following two days, the battalion made little progress and remained under heavy fire until, on the afternoon of 27 September, the London Scottish moved back to the trenches they had originally occupied on 25 September. Although he is not named individually, William Cowie may have been one of the 350 men injured on 25 September as he died of his wounds in No 6 London Field Ambulance on 28 September 1915, aged 23.

William was buried at Noeux-Les-Mines Communal Cemetery, Pas de Calais and is also commemorated on the Stracathro War Memorial, in Brechin Cemetery and on the London *Camanachd* Club memorial in Crown Court.

Alexander Shaw, second of five children of sailor Alexander Shaw and his wife Annie, was born in Nairn parish in 1890. Alexander's father died when he was a child and by the age of ten, he was the eldest in the family headed by his widowed mother, as his older brother had died as a child. Alexander later moved to London to work for Marshall and Snelgrove.

Alexander enlisted in the Lovat Scouts in Nairn and landed at Gallipoli with his regiment on 7 September 1915. He later transferred to the 1st Battalion the Cameron Highlanders and then the 7th Battalion the Gordon Highlanders.

Alexander was killed on 23 April 1917 at the Battle of Arras when he was part of a party of two officers and 100 men who acted as a forward evacuation stretcher bearing party. Alexander is commemorated at Brown's Copse Cemetery, Roeux.

Gordon Donaldson MM was born at the start of 1883 in Penzance, Cornwall where his father Thomas, a travelling draper, was living with his wife Emma. Gordon was the fourth child in the family who had settled in Cornwall. Gordon also became a draper and appears to have travelled the length of the country to learn his trade; in 1901 Gordon was working as a draper's assistant in Dumfries while by 1911 he had moved to London where he was a draper's assistant with Marshall and Snelgrove and living in their premises on Oxford Street.

Gordon married Margaret Andrew Turnbull in St John the Evangelist Church, Wembley on 3 April 1915. He joined the Middlesex Regiment and was later transferred to the East Surrey Regiment.

Gordon spent the war in France where he died of gunshot wounds in the abdomen on 2 October 1918. He was awarded the Military Medal posthumously; it was not gazetted until February 1919. Gordon was buried at Haringhe (Bandaghem) Military Cemetery, West Flanders, Belgium.

James Robert Stevenson was born in Oban on 9 November 1893, the only son of builder, and later bailie of Oban, James Stevenson and his third wife Katherine Waddell. James attended Oban High School and then, in his late teens, moved to London to work as a draper for the department store Debenham & Freebody, living at 11 Endsleigh Gardens NW.

James signed up at St Pancras on 3 September 1914 (just four weeks after Britain had declared war on Germany) as Private 3599 in the 11th Battalion of the Argyll and Sutherland Highlanders. The tall red-head must have done well in his basic training at home, as he was appointed Lance Corporal at the start of October and was promoted to Corporal on 26 October 1914.

James had almost a year with his regiment before they landed at Boulogne on 9 July 1915, then travelling on to Noyelles in northern France. James was promoted to Sergeant on 10 August and survived the Battle of Loos, notable for being the first time the British used poison gas during the war, in September.

After a short period of rest in the town of Allouagne, the battalion was again sent to the front line to relieve the 11th Middlesex Regiment. While there, James received a shrapnel wound to his head on 24 October. He died of his wounds at No 1 General Hospital Etretat on 17 November 1915 and was buried at Etretat Churchyard aged 22.

Andrew Ballantyne, second child and oldest son of Andrew Ballantyne and Maggie Dobson, was born on 31 July 1895 in Galashiels, Selkirkshire. After attending school at Gala Park Public School in Galashiels and Wilton Public School in Hawick, he started work with J & A Burnett a draper's shop in Hawick's High Street. In his late teens, he then moved to London to work as a wholesale drapery warehouseman for Cook Son & Co Ltd of St Paul's Churchyard, one of the largest British wholesale clothing traders and drapers of the late 19th century and early 20th century.

While he was in London, Andrew enlisted in the 2nd Battalion the Gordon Highlanders on 26 October 1915 and arrived in France on 1 June 1916. Andrew fought through the notorious first day of the Somme where the 7th Division was part of the early success taking the villages of Mametz and Fricourt on the southern part of the British Front. After a short period of rest and re-training, the battalion was in action again in the fighting for Guillemont and Ginchy where Andrew was shot in the head by a sniper and killed on 6 September 1916. One of his officers was quoted as saying:

He with several of his company was well forward, some 80 yards from the enemy front; shelling was very heavy, and the whole company was endeavouring to establish a position by entrenching from shell-hole to shell-hole. An officer, since killed, shouted some orders to a small party (one of which was Andrew): he apparently put his head up just a little above the small cover they had, when a sniper's bullet killed him. Personally, I miss poor Andrew more as time goes on. ... He was a thorough young gentleman. ... He did his duty to the very last, and died in one of the most desperate efforts in the great battles of the Somme.

De Ruvigny, Vol. 3, p. 14

Andrew is commemorated on Thiepval Memorial.

George Henderson, the second of 10 children of farmer James Henderson and his wife Mary Ingram, was born at Towie, Aberdeenshire early in 1879. When he was old enough, George secured a job as an assistant to a local general merchant and then moved to London to work as a draper's assistant in the firm of Thomas Wallis & Co where he lived in their staff accommodation at 7 Holborn Circus.

George enlisted in the 103rd Company the Machine Gun Corps in Paddington and went out to France in April 1916. He was involved in the Somme offensive, fighting at the Battles of Albert, Bazentin Ridge and Pozieres Ridge. In 1917, George fought at the start of the Arras offensive when he was wounded and died of his wounds on 29 April 1917. George was buried in Aubigny Communal Cemetery Extension in Pas de Calais.

Samuel Small and his Grand-daughter

One of the most intriguing stories of Crown Court and the First World War involves a soldier who lost his life but is not among the names on the War Memorial. Samuel Small does not appear in any lists of members but he does have a connection to Crown Court.

Samuel John Small was born in Walsall in 1876 to labourer Samuel Small and his wife Betsy Meers and was baptised in St John's Church on 13 December 1876. By the time he was 14, Samuel was working as a carpenter and 10 years later, he was working as a painter and lodging in Liverpool.

A Canadian-Scottish connection for Crown Court: Private Samuel Small of the 26th New Brunswick Battalion was killed in France on 28 September 1916 and is commemorated on the Canadian Memorial at Vimy Ridge. (Courtesy of Carolyn Small)

When Samuel's father died at the start of 1906 Samuel and his mother Betsey decided to emigrate to Canada. They travelled on the Allan Line ship *Virginian* from Liverpool arriving in Montreal on 29 June 1906 and planned to live in St John County, New Brunswick. Samuel married Scottish-born Catherine Hardie Macdonald on 22 October 1910 in St John, New Brunswick. Samuel and Catherine had three children, Annie (born 1911), William (1913) and Alexander (1914). Samuel enlisted with the Canadian Expeditionary Force on 25 November 1914. He joined the 26th New Brunswick Battalion, part of the 2nd Canadian Division which took part in the Battle of the Somme in 1916. On 15 September that year, the Canadians took part in the Battle of Flers-Courcelette which saw the first introduction of tanks on the Somme battlefield. From 26–28 September the 26th New Brunswick Battalion fought in the battle for Thiepval Ridge.

Private Small was killed on 28 September 1916 just outside the village of Courcelette. He is commemorated on the Canadian Memorial on Vimy Ridge.

Samuel Small's story might have ended there but for a strange series of coincidences which started over 90 years later …

On Christmas morning 2009 the Session Clerk of Crown Court Church, Alan Imrie, was in the church safe collecting the communion vessels when he noticed a small collection of books lying on one of the shelves. As he hadn't noticed these particular books before Alan picked them up to have a look and a small, grubby copy of St John's Gospel caught his attention. It had a grubby white cover with an unfamiliar coat of arms which seemed to consist of a mixture of flags, surrounded by laurel leaves and surmounted by a crown. When he opened the book, Alan found a pencilled inscription:

Pte S J Small
26 Batt CEF
New Brun
Canada
Reg No 69879

Obviously, Private Small had attended a service at Crown Court at some point and had left his bible behind.

Private Samuel Small's St John's Gospel found at Crown Court in 2009. (Courtesy of Sheena Tait/ Crown Court Church of Scotland)

His curiosity piqued, Alan enlisted the help of Sheena Tait and together they set out to find out more about Private Small and how his copy of the gospel came to be at Crown Court.

In addition to the basic information above, Sheena discovered that Catherine Hardie Macdonald had been born in the parish of Balfron, Stirlingshire on 18 June 1883. She was the second of six children born to farm worker John Macdonald and his wife Margaret Paterson. The family had moved from Stirlingshire to Perthshire around 1884–1889 as John took a variety of jobs on the big estates in the area – in 1891 he was a gamekeeper on the Achray estate and by 1901 he was an estate manager for the Glenbruich estate. In 1906 the whole family emigrated to New Brunswick intending to buy a farm.

Samuel and Catherine's children had all married in the 1930s and 1940s in New Brunswick and the youngest, Alexander, had died as recently as 1995. Alan and Sheena hoped that they would be able to trace a descendant to whom they could pass Samuel's bible.

In the meantime, Alan had discovered that the 26th Battalion of the Canadian Expeditionary Force had sailed from St Johns, New Brunswick on board SS *Caledonia* on the 13th June 1915 arriving at Plymouth on 1 July. The men were based at Shorncliffe Camp in Kent until they left for France on 2 September 1915. It is a reasonable assumption that Private Small came to London with some friends on a weekend pass. Whether one of the group knew Crown Court or whether it was an accident that they chose that church we shall probably never know, but Private Small left his bible behind.

By summer 2010, Alan and Sheena knew more about the background of the man and his bible but were no further forward in their quest to find a relative to pass it on to. Then Alan went on holiday to France.

While in France, Alan and his wife visited the Canadian Memorial at Vimy Ridge near Arras and saw Private Small's name carved on the monument. They also talked to one of the young members of Canadian Veteran Affairs who serve as guides, explained their interest and that the church was looking for ways to contact the family. "Where was Private Small from?" asked the guide, "St John, New Brunswick," "but I'm from St John, New Brunswick!" Once everyone had recovered from the shock, the guide suggested that the quickest way to trace relatives would be to write a letter to the local newspaper *The Telegraph-Journal* to see if anyone would respond.

Once home Alan wrote to the City Editor asking if he would print his letter. Two days later, the City Editor phoned Alan. He wanted to turn Alan's letter into a full feature with the help of local historians and using military records which were not available online. With Alan's co-operation, the article eventually appeared in the paper on 13 October 2010.

The response was overwhelming. Many people knew the family or were family members but the most striking reply was from Caroline who was one of Private Small's grand-daughters. Caroline sent a photo of Private Small and asked if the church could send her the bible, as she wanted to show it to her auntie Annie. "Auntie Annie" turned out to be Mrs Annie Andrews, Private Small's eldest child who was now living in a nursing home in St John, aged 99. Clearly the church wanted to return her father's bible, but posting it felt rather impersonal.

In the meantime, the article in *The Telegraph-Journal* continued to generate interest locally. So much so, that it was possible to arrange for a formal presentation to be made. On Saturday 23 October 2010 local MP, Rodney Weston, formally presented the bible to Annie Andrews on behalf of the Government of Canada – exactly 47 years to the day after Samuel's wife, Catherine, had died.

Annie Andrews née Small died eight months later on 2 June 2011 at Embassy Hall, Quispamsis, New Brunswick.

Annie Andrews, daughter of Samuel Small, being presented with Small's newly discovered St John's Gospel by Canadian MP Rodney Weston in October 2010. (© Telegraph-Journal Brunswick News Inc., Canada)

6

"For Scottish Gentlemen": The Caledonian Club

David Coughtrie

The Caledonian Club is often styled as "a little bit of Scotland in the heart of London" and it remains a thriving presence in the 21st century world of clubs in the capital. Members and eminent Scots visiting London are well entertained and traditions such as Burns Suppers continue to thrive with style. Its history is recognised at the Clubhouse in Belgravia, where reminders of the First World War and the toll it took on its members are not hard to find. The Club's artwork and artefacts tell a story of courage and tragic loss amongst London Scots who fought in Scottish and Canadian regiments and who were members of The Caledonian Club during the First World War.

During the Great War however, the Club faced two major existential threats: its proprietary owner, Robertson Lawson, who held the majority equity, had died bringing into sharp focus the long running debate about members owning the Club; and the increase of Club Member casualties on the Western Front and the other theatres of conflict left the Club vulnerable to collapse. On 1 February 1917, the club secretary reported that 140 Club members had fallen. This was set to rise much further in 1917 and 1918.

The Founding of a Caledonian Club in London

The Caledonian Club was originally founded in St James in 1891 by Neville Campbell as a proprietary club. Campbell was born at Birnam, near Dunkeld in Perthshire in 1860. Both his parents had been born in India, his father, General Napier George Campbell of the Royal Regiment of Artillery in Agra and his mother, Catherine Virginia D'Este in Bengal. His family moved to Devon and then to London, where his mother died in Lordship Lane, Dulwich.

After his marriage to Mary Smith from Philadelphia he became a wine merchant in 1883, joining with Alexander Wood to form Wood Campbell and Co, described at

This 1933 watercolour shows the Club's home during the Great War. On the left is 33 St James's Square, formerly Derby House, where the Club occupied the upper floors from 1911. Next door (centre), is No. 32, London House, leased from 1919. The St James's Square premises were destroyed by a bomb in 1940 and after temporary homes with other clubs, The Caledonian Club acquired its present home in Halkin St in 1945. (The Caledonian Club)

the time as, "one of the best known …. whose operations as importers and agents have been developed with marked enterprise and success over a 15-year period." Wood Campbell was also renowned for its own-brand "Glen" whiskies. It is thought that Neville Campbell's intent in setting up a club for Scottish gentlemen was to provide premises to promote his company's wines and whiskies in St James's Square at the heart of London's traditional gentlemen's club country.

Neville and his wife seem to have moved around various homes in London. The 1891 census records them living in Hammersmith with their two children. However, the newly-formed club had its first premises in Waterpark House, 30 Charles II Street opposite the Campbells' home. The qualification for membership was being a "Gentleman of Scottish descent."

After three years, Campbell converted the ownership of the Club to a limited liability company. The Club continued to prosper and in 1901, the majority ownership passed to Robertson Lawson, a chartered accountant, who served on the committee in various capacities along with other elected members. As membership grew the Club moved to new premises in Derby House at 33 St James's Square, previously the home of Lord Derby. A considerable sum, raised by members, was spent in renovating the premises and, as a result, it was described as "one of the finest clubs in London." The increasing membership and success of the Club led to several attempts from 1905 by some members to buy a majority interest and so establish a Club owned by members. However, no conclusion was reached but the membership continued to grow.

At the outbreak of war, the subscription was eight guineas for Town Members, six guineas for Country Members and five guineas for Members on active service. The Committee took the decision to reduce the subscription for those members on active service overseas from five guineas to one guinea. However, the Secretary, Frank E. Stanley wrote to all members on 1 February 1915 to remind them that:

> In response to enquiries in regard to the subscription payable by members on Active Service abroad, the Committee have now considered the matter and decided that:
>
> The amount of the Annual Subscription for members on Active Service at the Front be One Guinea (£1 1s). Members returning to this Country on the customary 5 or 7 days leave will not be liable for additional Subscription.
>
> If a Member is in this country for periods, which collectively amount to more than two months, he will kindly remit to the Secretary the balance of his Service Membership Subscription.

Use of the Club continued unabated and served as a welcome place of respite for those serving abroad when they passed through London going to the Western Front and other theatres or returning for well-earned leave. The Committee was already sensitive to the needs of the servicemen and at the 10th Annual General Meeting of members of the Club held on Wednesday 10 June 1914 at 5:15 p.m. precisely, as the notice indicates, the Committee were able to report the following proposal:

> Having regard to the large proportion of Service Members in the Membership of the Club, it was decided last year to invite the following Regiments to nominate representatives to serve on the Committee, viz.:

Cameron Highlanders	Highland Light Infantry
The Black Watch	Gordon Highlanders
Seaforth Highlanders	Royal Scots Fusiliers
The Kings Own Scottish Borderers	Royal Scots
Argyll And Sutherland Highlanders	Scottish Rifles

Nominations were received from each of these Regiments and elections made, which were duly confirmed by members of the Club at the last Annual Meeting.

However, despite the hardships and fairly strict "Gentlemen Club Rules", consideration was given to entertaining the Ladies, albeit in a modest fashion. A notice to this effect, dated 18 April 1916, was sent to all members with the 1916 Report by the Secretary.

By August 1917, the toll on the membership of the Caledonian Club from casualties in the Battles of Arras and Cambrai had risen significantly to 159, adding to the earlier losses on the Western Front from the Somme through three hard fought years.

At a recent event in the Club a few years ago, the late Alastair Stewart, a distinguished former chairman of the Club and vice-president, recalled one of his own early recollections of a retired Brigadier who always sat on a stool at the end of the members' bar and would indulge younger members with recollections of his time during the First World War.

He had joined the Black Watch as a young subaltern on the Western Front in late 1917 to be asked by his Colonel if he was a member of the Caledonian Club. If not, the Colonel who expected his officers to join the Club, would be happy to propose him. The subaltern replied that he would be much obliged but felt prudence dictated he should await the end of hostilities before taking advantage of the Colonel's offer. He survived, became a Member in January 1920, and was still lunching regularly in the Club when he died more than 60 years later.

The Formation of the Members' Club

Lawson's death in 1917 brought matters to a head. John Stewart-Murray, Marquess of Tullibardine, but from 1917 8th Duke of Atholl, spearheaded the appeal for funds to acquire ownership of The Club from Lawson's estate, so creating a wholly-owned Members' Club.

In a poignant letter to members, dated 18 June 1917, Atholl, writing from the family home at Blair Castle, addressed the appeal for funds to purchase the Club not just to members but to other prominent Scots,

> I make no apology for approaching non-members as I do feel it is a duty for us to do what we can to maintain a Scottish centre for gentlemen of Scotland in London and at this moment especially so. The Club is at present the "rendezvous" for a very large number of Scottish officers and in peace-time it is almost home for them. Therefore, even if they should never have occasion to use it, Scotsmen of means will be doing their countrymen a good turn by joining the club and by helping me to raise the guarantee fund.

BLAIR CASTLE,
BLAIR ATHOLL.

18 June 1914

Dear Sir,

I feel that it is incumbent upon me as Chairman of the Caledonian Club, London, to make an earnest appeal not only to it's members, but also to other prominent Scotsmen, to assist the committee to reorganise the Club as a members' one —

Mr. Robertson Lawson who has just died was in effect the proprietor of the Club; unless the members can take over his interests and provide a further sum besides the Club is bound to collapse —

If at this juncture, a particularly favourable one, the members, and other Scotsmen of good position & not yet members, will come forward generously and sign the attached guarantee form I have not a doubt but that it will be a success —

I make no apology for approaching non members, as I do feel it is a duty for us to do what we can to maintain a Scottish centre for gentlemen of Scotland in London, and at this moment especially so. The Club is at present the "rendezvous" for a very large number of Scottish Officers, & in peace time is almost a home for them. Therefore, even if they should never have occasion to use it, Scotsmen of means will be doing their countrymen a good turn by joining the club and by helping me to raise the guarantee fund —

I remain yours v. truly

Atholl

The letter from Club chairman "Bardie," now 8th Duke of Atholl, urging members to acquire the Club (The Caledonian Club)

On 1 January 1918, the Club secretary, Frank E. Stanley, wrote to all members as follows:

> With reference to the committee's previous circulars of 26th June and 3rd August last, they now have the pleasure to inform Members that the response thereto was so satisfactory, (the amount so far received or promised exceeding £16,000) that they felt justified in proceeding with the negotiations for the acquisition of the Club Company's assets, and the Re-organisation as a Members Club. ...
>
> As previously indicated, a Company limited by guarantee, and without any Share Capital, now has been formed under the name of 'The Caledonian Club Trust Limited', which all Members will be required to join, and under which their liability as guarantors, under any circumstances, is limited to £1 each, only payable in the event of the Club ever being wound up.

After many years, the Club was finally a fully-fledged members club, thanks to the tireless efforts of the chairman Atholl, members of the committee and the secretary. Despite the continuing loss of members in the ongoing conflict, particularly at the Battles of Arras and Cambrai (Vimy Ridge), the Club survived with Bardie as chairman until 1919.

The first General Meeting of the new Club was held on 8 March 1918 and the declared aim of the Club was, "to be the representative national Club and headquarters for the Scots in London." A hundred years later the Club is today still maintaining its objective "to be the home from home of Scots in, or visiting, London."

Bardie

John Stewart-Murray was born on 15 December 1871 at Blair Castle, the family home in Perthshire, to the 7th Duke of Atholl and his wife Louisa Moncrieffe and given the title Marquess of Tullibardine, traditionally bestowed upon the eldest son, or in this case, the eldest surviving son. He was known as "Bardie" for the rest of his life. He had a charmed childhood and only two early disappointments are recorded; the first when he accepted the gift of a live bear, only for his mother to intercept the arrival of the animal and, not unreasonably, send it straight home, secondly when he was refused permission to learn the bagpipes!

Bardie grew up to be a military man who in 1892 was commissioned into the Royal Horse Guards and took part in Kitchener's expedition to the Sudan, as the Staff Officer to the Colonel commanding the Egyptian Calvary. He took part in the fighting at the Battle of Omdurman, outside Khartoum, where heavily outnumbered forces commanded by Kitchener defeated the marauding Dervishes. Bardie was mentioned in dispatches and awarded the DSO and, no doubt, he also encountered another Scot, Douglas Haig, who also took part in this battle as the leader of a squadron of Egyptian Cavalry. It is highly likely that Bardie would have heard from Haig that he, along with other commanders had been offered a young subaltern to join his squadron but decided to turn him down. His name was Winston Churchill! However, Lieutenant Churchill was to go down in history as part of the 21st Lancers' last great cavalry charges at Omdurman, much to the chagrin of Haig, who had a less engaged battle.

Bardie married his fiancée Katherine Ramsay at St Margaret's Church Westminster on 20 July 1899. When, a few months later, the Second Boer War broke out, Bardie volunteered for service in South Africa in the 1st Royal Dragoons and was involved in the fighting to relieve Ladysmith. The Boers had by now been driven from their entrenched positions and Kitchener wanted new mounted regiments to counter the Boer guerrilla campaign and so, building on an initiative by the Caledonian Society of Johannesburg, he asked Bardie to raise a regiment of Scottish Horse comprising

Known as "Bardie", John Stewart-Murray, Marquess of Tullibardine and later the 8th Duke of Atholl, instigated the purchase of the Caledonian Club by its members in 1917. (From the collection at Blair Castle, Perthshire)

Scots in South Africa. These were joined by Scots enlisting in London through the support of the Highland Society of London of which Bardie was president and two regiments were eventually formed.

In South Africa Bardie had become friendly with Colonel John Capper, who on his return to England was put in charge of a balloon factory at Farnborough. Among those on site was Lieutenant John Dunne who was working on the design of an aeroplane and Capper asked if they could carry out tests on the prototype at Blair well away from intrusive publicity. As initial experiments were not very successful the War Office withdrew funding and Bardie formed a company to finance continued work on the project. A second prototype was built in 1910 whose performance exceeded Dunne's hopes, achieving unexpected speed and showing unusual stability in flight. Unfortunately, in 1912 Dunne became seriously ill. He was unable to monitor development of the design and production and so in the spring of 1914 rights were handed to the Armstrong Whitworth Company but any further progress was overtaken by the outbreak of war. In 1912 Bardie was elected chairman of the Royal Aero Club; he continued as chairman for eight years and then as president until his death.

Bardie had a profound sense of public duty and was greatly supported by his wife, Katherine, who had trained at the Royal College of Music and was keen to encourage him politically, speaking on his behalf at public meetings. In the general election of 1910 he was elected as the Unionist MP for West Perthshire. In this role he spoke often on matters of land management and military affairs. In 1912 he took a sensitive stance in the dockers' strike, aware of the suffering of men who refused to desert the cause and return to work even though their families were destitute and starving. He told the House of Commons of families of "eight and ten whom he had found struggling to live on 1d. or 2d. per day." After the conclusion of the strike he launched an appeal to raise funds to enable the strikers to reclaim possessions they had been forced to pawn in order to survive. He continued to represent West Perthshire until 1917 when on the death of his father he took his seat in the House of Lords.

Bardie was appointed Brigadier General in command of the Scottish Horse, with seven regiments eventually raised "fully manned and horsed." In August 1915 three regiments embarked – without their horses – for Gallipoli to reinforce the Suvla landing. Conditions at Suvla were appalling with a desperate shortage of water as the men took over trenches from the Anzac brigade and sheltered behind parapets which "consisted of human bodies covered with earth." Dysentery was rife. In November there was a massive storm which flooded the trenches and then the rain turned to snow. In December the evacuation commenced with Bardie in charge of the withdrawal of the Scottish Horse. After some months in Egypt the three regiments of Scottish Horse were to Bardie's intense disappointment disbanded and the men re-allocated. The Scottish Horse would fight with distinction in France notably in October at Le Cateau in the last month of the war.

In 1917 the 7th Duke died and Bardie returned to Perthshire as 8th Duke of Atholl. He became Lord Lieutenant of the county and in 1918 was appointed Lord High Commissioner to the General Assembly of the Church of Scotland, a position he held until 1920, and also made a Knight of the Order of the Thistle. In 1919 he headed the committee to establish the Scottish National War Memorial at Edinburgh Castle, saying that "the rebel spirit which lies dormant in every Scot" had roused itself within him at the thought that the Scottish regiments which had suffered so badly in the Great War should not be commemorated in their own country. The Memorial was opened in July 1927 by the Prince of Wales. Bardie died at Blair Castle on 16 March 1942 after a short illness.

Members of the Club in The Great War

Although the Club was not strictly a Service Club there was a strong military influence, as reflected by the numbers lost in the Great War. At the outset of war, there were just over 1,200 members with roughly half serving in the Forces. Two hundred and nine officers are listed as killed in action on the Club War Memorial. Their names and regiments, together with the regimental coats of arms are emblazoned on vellum on a Roll of Honour. It was illuminated by Miss Jessie Bayes and is enclosed in a wooden triptych. Today this hangs in the Club's premises in Halkin Street.

The now retired Field Marshal Earl Haig, in his role as a vice-president of the Club, commented on the Roll of Honour that "such a record is most eloquent testimony to

Lieutenant, later Major Edward McCosh MC of the Highland Light Infantry, pictured (left) alongside his friend Captain Alexander Reid, was a Caledonian Club stalwart and a rugby player with the London Scottish; he was killed near Calais on 26 September 1918. (Courtesy of the McCosh family)

the spontaneous devotion with which the gentlemen of Scotland, as represented in this Club, did their duty in the War."

Major Edward McCosh MC, born on 14 December 1890 near Airdrie, was the youngest son of a family of eight. Edward's paternal grandfather James McCosh had founded the law firm J&J McCosh of Dalry, which is still in existence today, and became the lawyer for Bairds of Gartsherrie, starting a relationship between the McCosh family, Bairds and pig iron and steel processing that lasted 120 years.

Edward, followed his three older brothers to Fettes and then to Cambridge University. Edward excelled at sport and was a Rugby Blue in 1910 playing opposite Ronnie Poulton, one of the great pre-First War England backs and captain in the Calcutta Cup match against Scotland in March 1914.

After graduating from Cambridge, he followed his older brothers again in joining clubs and associations including The Caledonian Club in London and London Scottish FC. With Edward at this rugby club were five others from that 1910 Varsity match who would not survive the war.

A life of commerce beckoned but then the Great War started. With his background and education, he clearly believed in doing the best he could for his team, be that team a sporting one, his battalion or his country. When the call to arms came Edward volunteered for and enlisted in the 9th Highland Light Infantry, Glasgow Highlanders, and on embarkation to France in late 1914 was the most junior officer.

Doing the right thing in the context of the war was to try and help the battalion help shorten the war. In late 1915, when after a year of front-line duties, the Glasgow Highlanders were to be given an extended period of back up duties, Edward and other Junior Officers were "little short of mutinous" not wanting to be associated with "the highly paid consumers of strawberry jam and marmalade" i.e. the senior officers who stayed in relative safety and comfort way behind enemy lines.

Until September 1918, it could be said that McCosh "had a good war." There were periods of intense action, raids on enemy lines and manning forward positions under intense fire, actions for which he received the MC and was mentioned in despatches twice. He also commanded the battalion for one month in 1917, a period of intense action around the Menin Road, during a changeover of Commanding Officer. His belief in doing the right thing and helping his country endured for he refused any offer of a staff position, preferring to be with his men. As a result, by mid-1917 he was the only officer in his regiment, of those who started in 1914, that still had front-line duties, the others having been killed, invalided out or transferred to non-active roles.

When not on the front line it was critical to keep up the morale of the battalion and Edward was a major organiser of sporting events and concerts to occupy the men. One such rugby match involved playing a representative French Army side.

> The result was three tries to nothing in our favour, the French playing with more vigour than knowledge of the game. One particularly stout forward in corduroy breeches, hob-nailed boots and a beard, evoked equal admiration for the good-natured ferocity of his play and the unblushing way he continually picked up the ball in the scrum. An understanding was made with the referee that the Frenchmen were not to be penalized too strictly; otherwise we would never have got on with the game.

Another example evokes the London musical hall traditions which inspired much ad hoc entertainment at the Front:

> Towards the end of our rest, we gave our second big concert. Lieutenants McCosh, Alexander and Todd appeared as girls, somewhat tall and broad, but wonderfully pretty in their make-up nonetheless. When they came on to sing, the audience nearly took the roof off the house. Very few recognized them and one member of the battalion went so far as to state that he was in the habit of 'walking out' with one of them.

But on 26 September 1918, Edward McCosh's luck ran out. He was wounded in the arm and leg by a German rifle grenade during the Allies' final great offensive of the war. The Glasgow Highlanders' Chaplain, Reverend Arthur J. Glossop, wrote to his mother:

> I was with your boy after he was wounded just before the stretcher started from the line. He then spoke quite strongly and gripped my hand when he went off.

We all, including the doctors, thought he would do well. I am now sorry I didn't ask him for a message for you, but I did not want to alarm him, and we thought all was to be well.

Brigadier General Baird observed: "He was quite the best young officer of his rank and service in my Brigade." *Shoulder to Shoulder* stated of McCosh:

His death was felt as a personal loss by every officer and man of the battalion in which he had served since 1914. He had been offered tempting staff appointments on several occasions but had always insisted on remaining with the battalion he loved. Always cheery, always fearless, his popularity extended beyond the battalion through the brigade and division.

Subsequently, it was learnt that Edward may have died because there were no blood supplies at the Field Hospital. On arrival there he was in good spirits and chatted freely to the medical staff. Loss of blood eventually took its toll and he went into shock and died because of this and not because of the injuries he had received per se.

Major McCosh was one of four Club members to lose their lives in the Great War, who had also played rugby for London Scottish – perhaps a surprisingly small number given that both clubs recruited members from among the middle-class Scots in London.

McCosh would surely have known William Spens. Spens was 16 years his senior but had re-joined McCosh's battalion, the 9th Highland Light Infantry, Glasgow Highlanders, in 1914, having been a volunteer during 1895–1904. Born in 1874, the son of William George Spens and the Hon. Mary Catherine Spens (née Borthwick) of Edinburgh, he was employed as a chartered accountant in Edinburgh until 1900, then became Secretary of the Stock Conversion and Investment Trust Ltd in London from 1900 to 1914. Lieutenant Spens was killed on 17 May 1915 at Festubert and now lies in Mont-Bernanchon Churchyard, in northern France.

Charles Edward Anderson was a professional soldier, educated at Bedford School, and the Royal Military College, Sandhurst. He was commissioned into the Gordon Highlanders in 1910, rising to Lieutenant in 1912 and finally to Captain. The son of Anne Rose Anderson, of Flore House, Weedon, Northants, and the late William Henry Anderson, Captain Anderson was a casualty on the Somme on 20 July 1916, and is buried in the little Dernancourt Communal Cemetery.

The Club's fourth rugby player was Alan William Mather who had initially joined the London Scottish Regiment as a bugler. A survivor of the Regiment's first action at Messines on Hallowe'en in 1914, Mather transferred with a commission as second lieutenant into the Black Watch in 1916. In 1917 or 1918 the by now Lieutenant Mather transferred again into the Royal Flying Corps and was attached to the 40th Training Depot Station. Tragically, having survived the horrors of the Western Front, he died in a flying accident over Lincolnshire just 13 days before Armistice was declared.

All four men are thus commemorated on the war memorials at the Caledonian Club and London Scottish FC.

Works of Art

Works of art donated to the Club became an important aspect of the Club's environment after the First World War, perhaps reflecting loss and nostalgia but ultimately providing solace and a sense of peace.

One outstanding benefactor to the Club was Brigadier General Sir William Alexander KBE CB CMG DSO TD (1874–1954). Sir William, who joined in 1935, donated four paintings. *Through the Dunes* by Johan Frederik Cornelis Scherrewitz and *Turf Leaders, Clonare,* by Erskine Nicol RSA ARA are the most valuable in the Club's collection. The other paintings are *The Waif* and *The Night of Trafalgar.*

Sir William, born in Glasgow, was educated at Kelvinside Academy, Glasgow University and in Gottingen where he specialised in chemistry and chemical engineering. He joined Charles Tennant & Co, St Rollox Chemical Works, Glasgow, and served an apprenticeship in acid and heavy chemical production. Sir William ultimately became Managing Director. He played rugby for the west of Scotland, cricket for Stirling County and had considerable success as a horse breeder. From 1899 until the First World War he served as a Captain in the 6th Battalion of the Black Watch Territorial Force. In 1911 he married Beatrice Ritchie of Paramatta, New South Wales with whom he had two sons.

After volunteering Captain Alexander, aged 40, served in France from 1915 with the Black Watch as part of the 51st (Highland) Division. He was involved in severe fighting and was promoted to major in the field, awarded a DSO and the Légion d'Honneur for distinguished service. Because of his specialist knowledge of chemicals, he was recalled from France in 1916 to become Director of Administration at the National Explosive Factories. He brought them to a state of efficient production in a remarkably short space of time.

Now Lieutenant Colonel, he was transferred in 1917 to the Aircraft Supply and

Brigadier General Sir William Alexander KBE CB CMG DSO TD and Caledonian Club benefactor. (Commerce & Industry, British Sports and Sportsmen, 1930)

Production Department, Ministry of Munitions as Controller, and raised output of aeroplanes from 200 to a peak of 4,000 per month, complete with all requirements in aero engines, accessories and spares. Alexander was awarded the CMG in 1918 and the CB in 1919. He was promoted to Brigadier General and was appointed to the Air Council also in 1919. At this time the Italian Government conferred on him the order of St Maurice and St Lazarus. Sir William, knighted in 1920, was later Unionist MP for Glasgow Central from 1923 until 1945.

The portrait of Colonel Douglas Lyall Grant MC TD (see separate colour plate) graces the Club's library, here he sits in three-quarter profile looking straight at the viewer. He wears a tweed jacket and waistcoat and a kilt in Grant tartan together with the London Scottish Football Club tie. At the top right of the canvas are two coats of arms, the lower one is the badge of the London Scottish Regiment and the one above the arms of Glenalmond College. On the top left is the badge of the London Scottish Football Club, whose members paid for this portrait. He played for the Club before the war, became secretary in 1913, continued in that post until 1939 and then became president until 1963 – a quite extraordinary 50-year record of service to the rugby club, holding the top two volunteer posts one after the other.

In 1909 Lyall Grant enlisted in the London Scottish Regiment and was appointed piper to G Company. At the outbreak of war in 1914, Second Lieutenant Lyall Grant went to France with the 1st Battalion London Scottish and was present at the Battle of Messines He was Mentioned in Dispatches, probably for actions at the Battle of Givenchy. In 1915, he participated in the Battle of Neuve Chapelle where he earned his MC. Subsequently Lyall Grant was returning from leave in England in 1916 when the aircraft was shot down and he spent most of the rest of the war as a POW. His diary of his time in captivity is deposited at the Imperial War Museum. As Lieutenant Colonel he was the Commanding Officer of the London Scottish Regiment 1926–30.

Another key work is the portrait by James Gunn, PRP RA of Andrew McTaggart. Sir Andrew McCormick MacTaggart retired as chairman of international construction company, Balfour Beatty, in 1966 having spent 54 years with the company, only interrupted by his service in France in the Great War with the Royal Engineers. A pioneer of hydro-electricity, he was responsible for the company's development and construction of the Lochaber hydro-electric scheme. Born on 13 July 1888 in Kirkmichael and knighted in 1951, Sir Andrew designed and supervised projects in India, Italy and East Africa as well as irrigation works on the River Tigris and railways in other parts of Iraq. Balfour Beatty still hold their Board Dinners in the Caledonian Club. MacTaggart died on 20 June 1978. The achievements of those who survived offer glimpses of what might have been achieved by the comrades who died.

Captain John Theobald "Johnnie" Milne MC of the 46th Squadron, Royal Flying Corps was shot down and declared missing in action in Flanders in 1917, and presumed dead on 24 October. No trace was found and he is commemorated on the Flying Service Memorial at Arras. His father, J. A. Milne, a member of the Club from 1899, was chairman from 1920 to 1924 and again from 1927 to 1932.

Milne senior donated the Club's large, silver-mounted ram's head snuff mull by Henry Tatton (see separate colour plate) and said to his fellow members at the unveiling of the club memorial to the Great War in 1923, "most of us have lost valued friends, some of us beloved relatives." In his case the latter was certainly true and this snuff mull bears testament to his strength of feeling.

J. A. Milne, chairman of The Club 1920–24 and 1927–32 (artist unknown) (The Caledonian Club)

The mull, with its memory and purpose, remains a centre of attention in the Club today. Snuff is powdered tobacco that is sniffed up the nose from the back of the hand a pinch at a time. This type of ram's head mull, the word derived from a Scottish dialect term for "mill" referring to the grinding of the tobacco, originated in Scotland in the Victorian era. It was a way of passing a quantity of snuff around at large social occasions and mulls, some with receptacles in the head for cheroots, might have casters to enable them to be sent down the table. The design gained popularity in clubs, officers' messes and fraternal organisations at a time when snuff was the most popular medium of tobacco consumption in Europe and the Glasgow tobacco lords were the major importers.

The large curly horns terminate in citrine set thistles, the high-domed snuff holder and cover has a faceted citrine and is embossed with thistles, with four chains to which are attached tools, a rake, duster, spoon and pricker with inscribed on a shield-shaped plaque "To the Caledonian Club in Proud Memory of Capt. 'Johnnie' Milne, Flanders May 24th 1917," the whole supported on three turned brass supports. The hallmarks on the horns give the maker but behind the lid the hallmark has been over-stamped "Scott AD, Regent Street London," possibly indicating a repair. The pendant spoon, rake, pricker and brush have English hallmarks. The spoon was for scooping the snuff from the mull to the hand, the rake for smoothing snuff, the pricker for loosening it and the brush for the tidying of the moustache or clothes.

Courage and Sacrifice War Memorial

This War Memorial by Sir Edgar Bertram Mackennal KCVO RA (1863–1931) is a symbolic bronze statue in which a mother and son are seen together. He embodies the eager courage of those about to submit to the ordeal of battle and she the poignant spirit of a mother's sacrifice in the hour of the country's need.

An Australian sculptor, Bertram Mackennal came to Britain to study at the Royal Academy Schools and worked briefly in Paris under Rodin. He created sculpture for public buildings here and in Australia as architects deemed his confident baroque style suited their work. Mackennal famously designed medals, coins and stamps for George V. Other Mackennal war memorials are in the Houses of Parliament, Eton College and Cliveden. His *Diana Wounded* is in the Tate Gallery. With Mackennal present, Haig, unveiled the memorial at Derby House.

Major Dr Archibald Stodart-Walker MBE FRCPE MB CM (1870–1934) was a Fellow of the Royal College of Physicians of Edinburgh. After doing considerable research in psychology and neurology he abandoned medicine for literature in 1898. He served in the RAMC during the First World War and was mentioned in dispatches.

He wrote several books and his *Occasional Verse* was published in 1920; he also wrote the following lines for the unveiling of the War Memorial at the Club, 26 July 1923

By this small act of grace, we who remain
May take in one fleet moment of our time
A sacrament of memory sublime,
And call the migrant spirits home again.

They come by faith in our remembrance led
By Lowland wynds, o'er silent Norland hills,
To stir our pulses, dedicate our wills;
'Twere mockery to think of them as dead

Though pain our resignation oft surprise
With old regrets; be constant as we dwell
Upon their honour; the requiem bell
No longer tolls, but banners blaze the skies

Let us speak proudly and without a tear
Of their high valour and each brave resolve,
Seeing at last, as grief in pride dissolve,
The cup of consolation shining clear.

Let us rejoice that their surrendered lives
Are as a beacon whose inspiring rays
Will keep us steadfast in the doubting days;
In each strong heart a fallen one survives

The Courage and Sacrifice War Memorial By Sir Edgar Bertram Mackennal KCVO RA (1863-1931) (The Caledonian Club)

7

Canadian Scots in Great War London

Malcolm Noble

On 1 July 1867 the colonies of British North America, together with the territories of New Brunswick and Nova Scotia formed the Dominion of Canada. This legislation defined precisely the degree of autonomy accorded to Canada. Great Britain declared war on the central powers in 1914. This automatically involved Canada. The Canadian government was empowered to determine the scale of their involvement.

A Canadian Expeditionary Force (CEF) was raised with "drive, efficiency and enthusiasm, in a well-ordered mobilisation." The mustering point was at the Valcartier Camp, constructed for the purpose in the province of Quebec. Canada, with a population at the time of some seven million, contributed an impressive 620,000 to the allied armies in Flanders and France. Of these, just under 10 percent, almost 61,000 died, and 173,000 were wounded. At first, British generals, Edward Alderson and Sir Julian Byng, commanded Canadian troops. In June 1917 a Canadian general Sir Arthur Currie, became the first non-British Commander of the now re-named Canadian Corps.

Out of a total of 69 battalions, 11 were specifically Scottish. Many of them had longstanding links with Scottish regiments. The following section summarises the history and involvement in the Great War of the Canadian Scottish battalions. The CEF was conveyed successfully from Canada across the Atlantic to England and to the Western Front. There would be significant numbers of Canadian troops in London at any time. They could be in training, transit or recuperating from wounds. Various kinds of social facilities were made available for them from 1915 onwards. These comprised the National Liberal Club for officers, Canadians-only social clubs funded through private initiative for other ranks, and churches for all.

Canadian Scottish

In 1622 King James VI of Scotland and I of England and Ireland permitted one Sir William Alexander to establish Scottish settlements in what became Nova Scotia.

Further migration came from Scotland to Eastern Canada following the failed Jacobite uprisings in 1715 and 1745. Following the American War of Independence some 40,000 Empire Loyalists, including many Scots, moved to Canada, mainly to New Brunswick, Quebec and Nova Scotia. Scots now formed one of the three ethnic groups that would dominate Canada: the others being English and French. The emigration of whole Highland communities gained pace from the middle of the 18th century: wholesale clearances emptied Highland glens, destroyed communities and sent hundreds of families at a time to Canada. In the 2011 census, 4.7 million or 15 percent of the total population claimed Scottish ancestry, the largest number, over two million living in the province of Ontario.

By 1914 the Scots, though fully assimilated into Canadian society, had retained the outward symbols of a distinctive Scottish identity. The Presbyterian religion, highland games, clan associations and their tartans, Burns Clubs, and scotch whisky were all part of Canadian life. Gaelic was still spoken in areas such as Cape Breton. Canadian Scots were prominent in supporting Canadian participation in the First World War. When war was declared on 4 August, the Governor General of Canada (Queen Victoria's third son, Prince Arthur, Duke of Connaught) informed London that there was "great exhibition of enthusiasm here." The emotional connection to their Scottish origins was reflected in the formation of specifically Canadian Scottish regiments. They wore the same tartans as their British Army counterparts, and attached great

Scottish mothers and their children on a train in Quebec, Canada, 1911; the Royal Scottish Corporation provided grants for passages across the Atlantic. (William James Topley/Library and Archives Canada, C-0007758)

importance to their pipe bands. The pipers of the Argyll and Sutherland Highlanders of Canada (Princess Louise's), were proud to have been chosen to play the Canadian Corps across the Rhine into Germany, in December 1918.

The 16th Battalion Canadian Scottish was formed in September 1914. Recruits came from the militia units of the Canadian Argyll and Sutherland Highlanders, Queen's Own Cameron Highlanders, Seaforth Highlanders and Gordon Highlanders. The battalion first saw action at the Second Battle of Ypres in May 1915.

A famous action by the battalion at the Ancre Heights, involved an advance through heavy machine-gun fire on 16 October 1916. The attack faltered but 18-year-old Piper James Richardson struck up his pipes and, playing the regimental march *Blue Bonnets*, led his comrades across no man's land. Thus inspired, about one hundred of the Canadian Scottish soldiers rushed forward, to reach their objective and capture the Regina trench. On returning to the Canadian lines Richardson picked up a wounded soldier and carried him to safety. However, he then returned to where he had left his pipes, disappearing in shell fire never to be seen again. Private Richardson was awarded a posthumous Victoria Cross. The battalion took part in the occupation of the Rhineland after the Armistice, returning to England on 27 March 1919 and eventually reaching Canada on 4 May 1919. The battalion was demobilised four days later but reconstituted as the Canadian Scottish Regiment (Princess Mary's).

There was a strong tradition of forming regiments named after their Scottish equivalents. One such, was the Argyll and Sutherland Highlanders of Canada (Princess Louise's). This regiment was founded in Hamilton, Ontario, in 1903. The connection with Argyll in Scotland, was reinforced by the regimental march *The Campbells are Coming*. They first saw action in late September 1915. Lieutenant Hugh McKenzie of the Regiment, was awarded the Croix de Guerre and a posthumous Victoria Cross in 1917. The Black Watch of Canada (Royal Highland) Regiment was founded in 1862, in Montreal. Their regimental march was *Highland Laddie*. This was the oldest of the Canadian Scottish regiments. They arrived in France in July 1915 but were disbanded after the Battle of Vimy Ridge in April 1917. Two members of the regiment were awarded the Victoria Cross. They were Lance Corporal Frederick Fisher and Corporal Jack Good. The awards were given for valour at the Battle of Amiens on 8 August 1918.

The Calgary Highlanders were formed just before the start of the war, as the 43rd Calgary rifles. They never left Canada as a single unit but contributed recruits to many CEF battalions. The Queen's Own Cameron Highlanders (QOCH) of Canada were also founded just before the start of the war, in Winnipeg, Manitoba. Initially, the regiment remained in Canada but embarked for England in June 1915. They took up positions on the Western Front in early 1916. Sergeant Robert Shankland of the QOCH received a battlefield commission following the action at Sanctuary Wood in 1916. He was awarded the Victoria Cross in 1917 for gallantry at Passchendaele. The Cape Breton Highlanders were founded in 1881. They embarked for England on 12 October 1916. The regiment was disbanded in 1920, subsequently forming part of the Nova Scotia Highlanders.

The Essex Scottish dated from 1885. They were a militia regiment based at Windsor, Ontario. Their British links were with the Essex Regiment, previously the 44th East Essex, known for their part in the burning of the White House and other public buildings in Washington DC during the War of 1812. The regiment first saw action at the Second Battle of Ypres in 1915.

The Cameron Highlanders of Ottawa were a militia regiment dating from 1806; in 1870 they had played a part in the suppression of Fenian raids. The regiment was not sent to France as a unit, but served instead to recruit and train troops for the CEF. They had links with the Highland Light Infantry (City of Glasgow). Their base was Galt, Ontario.

The Lorne Scottish (Peel, Dufferin and Halton) Regiment was founded in 1886. Some embarked for England in March 1915 and the rest in March 1916. Their regimental march was *Do you ken John Peel*. They were based in Brampton, Ontario, and the name was derived from a review of the Halton unit taken by the Marquis of Lorne in 1879.

The Royal Highlanders of Canada were a militia regiment which embarked for England in September 1914 and for France in April 1915.

The Stormont, Dundas and Glengarry Highlanders were based at Cornel, Ontario. They were the successors to loyalist regiments fighting for the British during the American War of Independence. They embarked for England in October 1917 as a militia regiment.

The Seaforth Highlanders were based at Vancouver, British Columbia. They were a militia regiment that had embarked for England in April 1916. Their first action was at the Battle of the Somme and they remained at the Western Front until the end of the war. Like the Essex Scottish, the Calgary Highlanders and the Royal Highlanders of Canada their regimental march was *Highland Laddie*.

The Toronto Scottish did not exist in name until 1921. They had adopted a Canadian name, the 75th (Mississauga) Battalion of the CEF. Entering the line in August 1916, the battalion saw action at the St Eloi craters, the Somme, Vimy Ridge, Canal du Nord, Bourlon Wood, the road towards Cambrai and Valenciennes. They took part in every major engagement involving the CEF and were awarded 16 battle honours, 10 of them emblazoned on the regimental flag.

They had three recommendations for the Victoria Cross. The commanding officer, Lieutenant Colonel Colin Harbottle led a frontal attack into the village of Le Quesnel in August 1918. He was awarded bar to his DSO. Sergeant Ernest Jeffrey received the DSM for his bravery at the taking of the sunken road beyond Dury Ridge on 2 September 1918. The third recommendation was accepted: medical officer, Captain Bellenden S. Hutcheson, an American citizen who had joined the Canadian Army while his own country remained neutral, was awarded the Victoria Cross for looking after the wounded out in the open, at Dury Ridge on 2 September 1918.

There were nine Sikh soldiers serving overseas in the Canadian Army during the Great War. Two of them served in the 75th and one, Lashman Singh, was killed in action in the last weeks of the war. The other, Hari Singh, survived and volunteered for the newly constituted Toronto Scottish in 1921.

Caledonian London

On 14 October 1914, 10,000 Canadian soldiers arrived at Southampton and were encamped on Salisbury Plain. By December 1916, total Canadian strength had reached 131,029. Large numbers of Canadian soldiers were to be stationed in London until 1919. These included newly disembarked recruits, and soldiers in training, or recuperating from wounds, or on leave. On first arrival, all recruits were given six days leave. Afterwards, no more than 10 percent of soldiers in any unit might be absent from camp at any one time. Those on leave departed at 1300 hours on Saturday and had to return by midnight on Sunday. Prior to departure for France, soldiers were granted four days embarkation leave. Those serving at the Front could expect 10 days leave each year, although officers were entitled to 10 days after every three months. If they so wished, soldiers could spend their leave time in London.

London's Gentlemen's Clubs had lost members and staff because of the war. Older members of staff had to cope on their own without those younger colleagues who had volunteered for Kitchener's Army. Moreover, many clubs were concerned that the loss of younger members to the forces might cause a serious loss of revenue. Many of them were, therefore, keen to recruit Canadian officers as temporary members, and were prepared to offer a discount on fees to encourage them to join for the duration of the war. However, only officers would be welcome in these clubs. Class distinctions were strong at that time and it is unlikely that private soldiers would have felt comfortable in the atmosphere of a gentlemen's club.

On 11 September 1916, the National Liberal Club was requisitioned by the British government for unspecified War Office purposes. The Club responded by taking out a lease on the nearby Westminster Palace Hotel. They were to remain there right through to 1920. The War Office then decided to allocate the National Liberal Club to the CEF. The location was perfect as the premises were close to the Canadian High Commission, government departments in Whitehall and to railway stations serving the channel ports. The club premises offered spaces suitable for recreation, offices, catering facilities and accommodation for officers.

Nothing was done officially for non-commissioned officers and other ranks. Most soldiers, therefore, were left with the choice of remaining in camp or drinking in London. Sir Sam Hughes, Canadian Minister for Militia and National Defence, banned alcohol in Canadian army camps. This decision was treated with contempt by ordinary soldiers, leading to even larger numbers frequenting London's public houses.

Lady Julia Drummond was a Canadian Scot, born of Scottish parents in Montreal. She was a prominent member of many women's organisations in her native city. This included the position of Chairman of the National Council of Women. Shortly after the outbreak of war, Lady Julia moved to London as head of the Canadian Red Cross. Her son, Guy Drummond was killed at Ypres in July 1916. Lady Drummond's experience with the Red Cross led to a concern over the well-being of the men stationed in and around London.

She therefore took a leading role in establishing the King George and Queen Mary Maple Leaf Club in London's Berkeley Square. Membership was limited to Canadian non-commissioned officers and other ranks. Its stated purpose was to "keep the boys out of trouble." She was inspired with a sense of "wartime duty, patriotism and nobility." Lady Drummond and other philanthropists also arranged for Canadian citizens to donate funds for comforts and other necessities, for the soldiers. Other Canadians-only social clubs were established in London over the course of the war.

The magazine of St Columba's Church of Scotland in Pont Street, Knightsbridge, details visits by Canadian soldiers during the war. The Very Reverend John Neil DD, Moderator of the Canadian Church, worshipped there on his way to visit his countrymen both in England and serving on the Western Front. He wrote to the Minister at St Columba's on his return to Toronto. The letter dated 21 June 1918, details the steps that he planned to take to assist returning soldiers in adapting to civilian life at the end of the war. Dr Neil described how he had opened the general assembly of the Church in Toronto and had preached a sermon. Following this, as he put it "he was set free and only an ex-moderator." His intention now was to work with every presbytery in Canada, together with other Protestant churches in providing chaplains in England and France to assist returning soldiers. His hope was that "if we can win these men to the church they will be a mighty power of good, have great influence with the young life of our land." He felt that the resultant "spirit of brotherliness, optimism and self-sacrifice will do much to enrich our Church."

A Canadian soldier visiting St Columba's in October 1918, brought unmistakable evidence that trench warfare had given way to a sustained advance towards San Quentin and the Hindenburg Line. He had taken part in the liberation of a village that had been under enemy occupation since 1914. On entering a house that had suffered serious damage, leaving only one room intact, he found a large family bible and in it a prayer card with a poignant message: roughly translated from the French as "Lord, do your best. Despite the enormity of my mistake, I am still hoping for your goodness. My hope, my Lord is that your fidelity will fulfil the promises you made to me." A villager had returned for the first time since the German advance in 1914. He had buried 20,000 Francs in the garden, hurriedly. To his surprise and delight he found the money intact, exactly where he had left it. The soldier went on to explain how this had now become a war of almost continuous movement.

Four Canadian soldiers including the officers of the Army Medical Corps arranged to be married at St Columba's on the same day. Major John McMillan, MC, from Finch, Ontario married Edith Leslie from Montreal. Major Russell Robertson from Vancouver married Charlotte Jack from Quebec. Major Alexander Scrymgeour came from Montreal. He had been the first Canadian to have been awarded a Victoria Cross in the First World War. Major Scrymgeour married Ellen Carpenter a nursing sister from Montreal.

Private Frederick McClellan Fancher, of the 49th Canadian Regiment, was also married at St Columba's on that day. He came from Edmonton and married Annie Baxter from Edinburgh. Neither they nor their wives were to know that the war would end in a matter of weeks. For the newly-wed Fanchers that was no relief, and there was no happy ending: they were back in Canada in early October, he with a gun-shot wound to the head and a depressed fracture of the skull in a military hospital. He was buried on 31 December 1918. His record describes the fatal wound as self-inflicted.

An unusual account was published from a Canadian soldier of a connection with the Gaelic Society of London. He had served with the Nova Scotia Highland Brigade. They had, it appeared, created "something of a sensation," with the Balmoral head-gear and kilts, as they marched through London. Ian Sinclair, of the Gaelic Society had met several soldiers from the regiment and he had inquired of them if any had an acquaintance with Gaelic language. In this way, therefore the writer of the letter found himself preaching in Gaelic at the Crown Court Church of Scotland on 10 December 1917. Two Scottish members of Lloyd George's Coalition Government were present for the occasion. These were Robert Munro KC, Secretary of State for Scotland, and Ian MacPherson, Under-Secretary of State for War.

Lieutenant General Sir Alistair Irwin KCB CBE, and a vice-president of the Royal Caledonian Education Trust relates the story of his Canadian great grandfather, Colonel William Hendrie and his wife travelling separately to England in 1915.

William Hendrie was co-founder of the 48th Highlanders of Canada. His family had emigrated from Edinburgh to Canada in the middle 1800s. On the outbreak of war, he was considered too old to go to France with his regiment. But he went anyway and was put in command of the 1st CEF's Remount Centre. He took with him as batman his personal piper, a former Gordon Highlander called Charles Dunbar. They spent time on Salisbury Plain before deploying in early 1915 to France. He was considered somewhat eccentric, insisting that Dunbar played the pipes every morning for the horses.

The nature of his duties well out of the firing line made it possible for his wife to plan to travel from Canada with her children to visit him. She booked a passage on the *Lusitania* but received a letter from William telling her, because of the potential dangers of the voyage from German U-Boats, mines and surface raiders, not to travel unless she could secure cabins on the boat deck. There were no spare cabins, so the family sailed later on the *Mauretania*. Mrs Hendrie's sister-in-law, Dorothy Braithwaite, a nurse, decided to go anyway. The *Lusitania* was torpedoed by a German U-Boat on 7th May 1915 with the loss of 1,198 lives, amongst whom was Dorothy who gave up her place in a lifeboat to someone else.

Battlefields

After a brief period of service in the trenches a little south of Armentières, the CEF made ready to engage in the second Battle of Ypres. The Allied lines formed a curve 17 miles long. This became known as the Ypres Salient and at the centre of it was the walled town of Ypres itself. The Canadians arrived here for the first time in April 1915. The Germans had bombarded the town, damaging the Gothic Cloth Hall and Cathedral which dated from the 13th and 14th centuries. Most of the residential quarters remained undamaged at this point, and the inhabitants were generally still living in the town.

On 22 April at five o'clock in the morning the Germans opened the valves of gas cylinders for about eight minutes, thereby releasing 160 tons of chlorine into a light north-easterly wind. The Canadians reported a cloud of green vapour several hundred yards in length between the French trenches and the enemy's front line. Those involved were half suffocated and, with eyes streaming and nose and throat burning, many abandoned their positions and fled, leaving behind large numbers of dead. The Canadians though had escaped the gas attack. This was the first use of gas in the First World War. It was also the first battle that engaged the CEF. The danger that had to be averted was that the enemy might overrun the Ypres Salient, and seize the channel ports. If that happened, it would not be possible to deliver supplies and reinforcements through the Pas de Calais. The Canadian forces had prevented a breakthrough over the first three days of the German offensive. After this, British and French reinforcements had arrived, ensuring that the Ypres Salient would remain in Allied hands.

Following this, British and French forces began their offensive in Artois. On 15 May the Canadians engaged in the Battle of Festubert. Initially the Canadian attacks were not successful. Overall, according to the official history, the Battle of Festubert had been a "frustrating experience for the Canadians." On 15 June, the 1st Canadian division was deployed from the La Bassée Canal northward to the right of the British line. From this position the 48th Highlanders of Canada captured a critical strongpoint known subsequently as the "Canadian Orchard." Until mid-September 1915 the Canadian front was largely quiet and just before the end of September a second Canadian division arrived in France. Canada now had a full Army Corps in the field.

The Battle of the Somme lasted from 1 July into November 1916. The aim of the British offensive was primarily to relieve the French who were under heavy attack at Verdun. The Canadian Corps began to take up position in August under the command of British General Julian Byng. The Canadian Corps attacked with two divisions on a 2,200-yard front against the German defences at Courcellete. The first tanks in the history of warfare were brought into use with seven out of 49 available to the Canadians. However, the tanks allocated to the Canadians were soon put out of action by shellfire and through getting stuck in the mud. Of the 32 tanks in the battle only 10 managed to assist the infantry effectively. The Canadians were to suffer 24,000 casualties in the Battle of the Somme.

In 1914, Newfoundland was still a separate dominion of the British Empire, and not part of Canada. The Royal Newfoundland Regiment took part in the Battle of the Somme offensive at Beaumont Hamel on 1 July 1916. The attack failed. Only 68 Newfoundland and Labrador soldiers answered the roll call at the end of that day. There had been 324 killed and 386 wounded.

Sir Douglas Haig, as commander-in-chief of British and Empire forces, launched a further offensive on 12 October. This led to the Battle of the Ancre Heights. The Canadian Corps were given the task of capturing the German strong point known as the Regina Trench. This was achieved on 16 October.

Efforts to capture Vimy Ridge, strategically important as a high point near Arras, had all ended in failure. However, on Easter Monday 9 April, following a bombardment from 983 heavy guns, the Canadian Corps assaulted the Germans positions on the ridge. King George V sent a message of congratulation, noting that "the people of Canada will be forever proud that the taking of the coveted Vimy Ridge had fallen to the lot of their nation". For the first time a Canadian Army had gone into battle as a separate entity, winning one of the few clear-cut victories of the war.

Following Sir Julian Byng's promotion in June 1917, Sir Arthur Currie became the first Canadian national serving as Commander of the Canadian Corps. The Official History notes that the achievements of his command had been largely responsible for creating an atmosphere that "led towards nationhood and fostered a sense of Canadian identity."

Currie objected to the deployment of the Canadian Corps at the Third Battle of Ypres, better known as Passchendaele. He considered that there was no great strategic advantage to be gained from straightening the line at the Ypres Salient. Moreover, he predicted that his forces would suffer 16,000 casualties. The Canadians succeeded in taking the ridge and capturing what remained of Passchendaele village on 10 November. Currie's prediction proved remarkably accurate. The Canadian Corps sustained 15,654 casualties during the Battle of Passchendaele. Accounts vary on casualty rates at Passchendaele. However, the Canadian Official History suggests that

Pipers of the Canadian Black Watch lead the Canadian Corps into Mons, Belgium, on 10 November 1918, the day before the Armistice. (Reproduced by permission of the National Library of Scotland)

the total British and Empire casualties amounted to 260,000. The estimate of German losses was 202,000. The territory taken at such a high cost was overrun during the German offensive in March 1918.

On 8 August 1918, there was a clear British victory at Amiens. Soon afterwards the advancing Allied forces overran the Hindenburg line. During October 1918 they were advancing across the whole Western Front. On 10 November the Belgian army had liberated the town of Ghent. The French Sixth Army, together with the British Second and Fifth armies had crossed the river Scheldt. The Third Army captured Maubeuge. The information that the Armistice would come into effect at 11:00 a.m. on 11 November, reached Canadian Corps headquarters at 6:30 a.m.

Currie's Canadian Corps entered the town of Mons at 11:00 p.m. on the night of 10 November, facing machine-gun fire from the German defenders. The Canadians cleared the town of remaining German soldiers shortly after first light. At 10:00 a.m. pipers of the Black Watch led the Canadian Corps into Mons. As the guns fell silent all along the Western Front, the war ended near where it had begun just over four years earlier.

Aftermath

German General Ludendorff may have described the British Army on the Western Front as "Lions led by Donkeys," but that charge cannot be levelled at the Canadians. The Canadian casualty rate overall was 37.5 percent and even higher, 42 percent, or 28 out of 69 for the general staff. Sir Arthur Currie, as commander of the Canadian Corps led by example, in visiting the front lines regularly.

The Canadian Army had performed with distinction from 1915 until the end of the war. Canada sought to follow Britain's example by establishing ex-servicemen's associations to look after the welfare of those returning from the battlefronts. There were 14 separate organisations created for this purpose in Canada. They were too fragmented to be able to cope with the demands for help during the 1920s. In 1925 the now Earl and Countess Haig were invited to tour Canada and visit these ex-servicemen's associations. Haig resolved to secure a merger to create a single association. And thus in 1925 the Canadian Legion of the British Empire Services League was formed in the capital, Ottawa. It was incorporated by a special Act of Parliament and in 1960 Her Majesty the Queen consented to the formation of what became the Royal Canadian Legion. The Legion's mission is to support veterans, members of the Canadian Armed Forces, Royal Canadian Mounted Police (RCMP) and their families.

Canada had no choice but to go to war on the side of Great Britain in 1914. The constitution of 1867 required Canada to support Britain in the event of war: though the Canadian Government might determine the level of involvement. However, in December 1931, the Statute of Westminster granted to Canada, and the other Dominions full legal freedom, including the power to declare war. Today, Canada's Armed Forces have a high profile in peacekeeping and humanitarian interventions.

Retired General John de Chastelain, who advised on the IRA placing weapons beyond use, has observed that the qualities of leadership required today are: "the ability to lead effectively and manage resources carefully." They are not so very different from those required in Flanders and France between 1914 and 1918.

Two Canadian Scots in London served in the British Cabinet during the First World War. William Maxwell "Max" Aitken was a Canadian businessman who moved to Britain and in 1916 bought the mass circulation *Daily Express* which would become the most successful newspaper in the world. He had already been elected to Parliament as a Conservative in the second election of 1910, and Lloyd George brought him into his Coalition Cabinet as Minister of Information and Chancellor of the Duchy of Lancaster in 1918. Aitken was elevated to the peerage as Lord Beaverbrook, and would later serve also in Winston Churchill's wartime cabinet.

Andrew Bonar Law was known as Britain's Canadian Prime Minister. Strictly speaking, this was not the case. Bonar Law was born in New Brunswick in 1858. New Brunswick was still a separate colony prior to confederation in 1867. His father was a Minister of the Free Church of Scotland. Shortly after the death of his mother, Law was sent to Scotland to live with an aunt. Despite leaving school at the age of 16 and not going to university, Law was to be successful in business and later in politics. He was elected as Conservative and Unionist Member of Parliament for Glasgow Blackfriars in the "Khaki election" of 1900, towards the end of the Boer War. He was to serve in Parliament subsequently, for the constituencies of Dulwich, Bootle and Glasgow Central. In 1902 he was appointed Parliamentary Secretary to the Board of Trade. In 1911 he was elected leader of the Conservative opposition. In May 1915, the Liberal Government of H.H. Asquith brought the Conservative and Labour Parties into Government, and Law was appointed Secretary of State for the Colonies. However, in December 1916 Asquith fell from office and David Lloyd George took over as Prime Minister. Law then served successfully as Chancellor of the Exchequer, Lord Privy Seal and Leader of the House of Commons, and as leader of the Conservative Party duly became Prime Minister when his party voted to withdraw from coalition government and forced Lloyd George to resign in 1922. At the subsequent general election, he won an outright victory for the Conservatives but he was seriously ill with throat cancer, resigned in May, and died in October 1923. He was Britain's shortest-serving Prime Minister of the 20th century and the only one born outside Great Britain.

It was a Canadian doctor, Lieutenant Colonel John McCrae, whose poem inspired the adoption of the poppy as the symbol of remembrance:

"In Flanders Fields the poppies blow
Between the crosses row on row
That mark our place, and in the sky
The larks still bravely fly
Scarce heard amid the guns below

We are the dead, short days ago
We lived, felt dawn, saw sunset glow
Loved and were loved, and now we lie
In Flanders Fields

Take up our quarrel with the foe
To you, from failing hands we throw
The torch, be yours to raise up high
If ye break faith with us who die
We shall not sleep, though poppies grow
In Flanders fields."

John McCrae, 1915

Before that, though *In Flanders Fields* had already during the war become the poem that soldiers recited and memorised and copied into letters home, and it was an inspiration to recruitment among Canadian Scots and beyond, throughout Britain's empire and dominions.

McCrae had written the poem in May 1915, during the Second Battle of Ypres, sitting in the back of an ambulance and surveying the scene after the emotional burial of a close friend. The scrap of paper was then thrust into a pocket as McCrae went about his duties as a front-line medical officer. But later in the year it was submitted first to the *Spectator*, which rejected it, and then to that quintessential London magazine *Punch*, which published it in December 1915. McCrae was no stranger to London. A regular visitor before the war, and coincidentally there when war broke out, he returned frequently when on leave from France, the last time for a few days in London and Kent with his brother and fellow doctor Tom, near the end of 1917. John McCrae would die of pneumonia and meningitis the following January.

8

Traditional Entertainment and Comradeship: The Caledonian Society

Hugh Cowan

The migration of Scots to London in the 19th Century had created a demand for traditional entertainment and comradeship amongst the exiles. The evolution of Scottish clubs and societies in the capital meant that by the turn of the century the diaspora could be linked socially and there was no shortage of opportunities to join traditional festivities. The onset of war saw these groups set aside their formal dinners and celebrations and focus efforts on supporting Scottish troops.

The Caledonian Society of London had been instituted in 1839 after preliminary action over the previous couple of years. At that time there were two well-established Scottish societies in London, the Highland Society and the Society of True Highlanders, but both were geographically prescriptive in their nature. The founders of the newcomer felt that there was a need for a society that would be more attractive to all the growing number of professional Scots in the metropolis regardless of the part of Scotland from which they came. The new society flourished strongly for the first few years but then experienced a difficult period from which it had emerged by the mid-1850s to establish itself as an association of Scotsmen which had as its objects the advancement of Scottish national, philanthropic interests and the promotion of good fellowship among Scotsmen in London. Its annual programme included a festival dinner in January, at which the life of Robert Burns was celebrated and a charitable ball, both of which became features of the London social calendar. An element of exclusiveness was sought by limiting the number of ordinary members to one hundred.

Relations with the Highland Society had always been cordial and in 1859 the two societies came together to form the London Scottish Rifle Volunteers that later became the London Scottish Regiment. The ball was abandoned towards the end of the 19th century but by then the festival dinner had been joined in the annual programme by informal dinners. All dinners featured piping and other musical entertainment and keynote speeches were to be heard on many of the informal evenings. Guests were always welcome and included ladies at the Festival.

Thomas Reid Moncrieff, secretary and lynchpin of the Royal Scottish Corporation and a Caledonian Society president. (Caledonian Society of London)

The quarter century leading up to the First World War had been a particularly successful time for the Society. Although records for the period are incomplete, due to a major loss of archives during the later war, available evidence suggests that the membership was drawn from a cross section of successful professional and business men in London and it is clear that some of its presidents, who normally held office for a single year, were self-made men of considerable means. The pre-war annual programme centred round six informal dinners, each preceded by business meetings, and the Festival dinner. In the final peace-time session of 1913–1914, all the dinners were held in the Holborn Restaurant in Kingsway with speakers on the informal occasions addressing James Watt of steam engine fame, lantern slide illustrated thoughts on the Scottish hills, Queen Margaret of Scotland and the Scot of the Future, with the final evening of the season dedicated to singing and recitations by members, the last two events perhaps particularly poignant in view of what was about to come. The participation by members in musical entertainment was a notable reflection of a generation brought up before the era of the gramophone, talking cinema or radio and many had their special party pieces for which they were well known. Philanthropic support included that provided to the Society's two main charities, the Royal Scottish Corporation and the Royal Caledonian Asylum, and was discharged by donations from surplus Society funds, annual subscription lists to which members contributed and by encouraging members to become involved in charity governance.

The annual programme of the time had a long summer recess starting after the April dinner and running through until a pre-season business meeting in October leading to the Annual General Meeting and first dinner in November. The nation declared war on Germany on 4 August 1914, deep in this recess. A conference of Scottish associations in London was held and a message from its convener asking for an opinion on whether entertainment should be suspended while the war lasted was among items considered at special meeting of the Society's Council on 17 September.

Five decisions were made: all social events were to be suspended for the time being, the full programme of routine business meetings was to continue to enable charitable and other service activities, the current Society officials were to continue in post for the following session, the usual subscriptions to the main charities were to continue and funding was approved to provide temporary premises for a recreational club for the recently formed 2nd Battalion of the London Scottish Regiment if this were to be appropriate. The reason for ceasing social functions is not recorded but may have reflected an aversion to apparent frivolity at a time of national endeavour and sacrifice. There was clearly a risk that if the war was prolonged, impetus might reduce to the point that charitable support would suffer, but in the event this did not happen. We know that the business meetings were held on the premises of the Royal Scottish Corporation courtesy of that organisation. However, the published Chronicles of the Society tended to concentrate on social activity and, without the business meeting minutes, our sources for the war-time period remain somewhat thin.

By late November 1914 contributions to welfare provisions had been made for a number of Scottish regiments and, that month, the decision was made to "work in harmony" with the Federated Council of Scottish Associations in London in order to channel the Society's charitable war work in an efficient manner; the Society's honorary secretary John Douglas became chairman of the Council and members provided strong support including the provision of two further members of its Executive Committee. This was clearly most successful and the work was reported at subsequent Society meetings. These arrangements were to continue until the end of the war. As well as the provision of comforts for the troops, food parcels were sent to prisoners of war, both well supported by contributions in cash and kind from members and their ladies. By the war's end, the Society had adopted 10 individual prisoners in an extension of the earlier system. In 1917, the president and the honorary secretary accepted office as trustees of the Church of Scotland's St Andrew's Soldiers' Club in Aldershot. All this was done without diminishing support for the two traditional charities.

An unusual event early in the war had witnessed an appeal from a past president of the Society for assistance in his initiative in raising a body of 500 men to assist in the defence of the east coast of England. Privately raised units of this type were perhaps redolent of an earlier age and the Society may have been relieved to have been able to offer the excuse of full commitment in London for non-participation in this case.

Throughout the war, business meetings were well attended, more than £1,000, in addition to many gifts in kind, was donated for the work of the Federated Council and the Society's subscription lists for the Royal Scottish Corporation realised over £6,000 as part of Corporation's annual appeals of 1913 to 1918 inclusive. Similar details for the Royal Caledonian Schools (as the Asylum had become in 1916) seem not to have been available but we do know that 40 copies of a book on the Highland Regiments were presented to the Schools. The book had been published by a Society member with profits committed to a military charity. It was also noted that many members were active in war work led by other organisations.

The Society maintained contact with the London Scottish Regiment by sending telegrams after notable events and, largely, through a Society past president, Bernard Green, senior major of the 1st Battalion when it deployed to France in November 1914. He was wounded in 1914 but was subsequently promoted to lieutenant colonel and commanded the battalion during two periods in 1915 and 1916, and would do so again after the war. He had been made a Companion of the Order of Saint Michael and Saint George (CMG) in 1915.

A second member to be recognised for service during the period of the war was James Cantlie FRCS. A Banffshire man, he completed his medical training in London and held the appointment of Demonstrator in Anatomy at Charing Cross Hospital for 16 years while also surgeon to the Hospital. In 1887, he moved to Hong Kong where he remained for nearly 10 years, founding the College of Medicine for Chinese and being its Dean from 1889 to 1896. On returning to London, his positions included Lecturer in Anatomy at Charing Cross Hospital, Surgeon to the West End Hospital for Nervous Diseases and Surgeon to the Seamen's Hospital at the Royal Albert Docks. He also pioneered teaching ambulance work to the public, was a founder of what later became the Territorial Army element of the Royal Army Medical Corps, founded the first Volunteer Aid Detachment and became chief surgeon of the St John's Ambulance Brigade of the Metropolitan District. Cantlie was known in the Society for his fluency in the Doric (the original dialect of north-east Scotland) and for his party piece, the song the *Tinker's Waddin*. During the war, he led a major programme of emergency first aid and nursing training and for this, and other work, he was created Knight Commander of the British Empire.

Largely due to its age profile, and it seems likely that the number of persons who served in the war-time forces while members was very small, the Society suffered no direct war losses and even relatively few such losses among its families. Nevertheless, at least five sons of members fell. Of these, the late Captain G.H. Tatham Paton MC, of the Grenadier Guards and only son of the then president George Paton, was awarded a posthumous Victoria Cross following an action at Gonnelieu, France in December 1917. The citation read:

> Lieut. (A/Capt.) George Henry Tatham Paton, M.C., late G. Gds.
>
> For conspicuous bravery and self-sacrifice. When a unit on his left was driven back thus leaving his flank in the air and his company practically surrounded, he fearlessly exposed himself to re-adjust the line, walking up and down within 50 yards of the enemy under a withering fire. He personally removed several wounded men and was the last to leave the village. Later, he again re-adjusted the line, exposing himself regardless of all danger the whole time, and when the enemy four times counter-attacked he sprang each time upon the parapet, deliberately risking his life, and being eventually mortally wounded, in order to stimulate his command.
>
> After the enemy had broken through on his left, he again mounted the parapet, and with a few men – who were inspired by his great example – forced them once more to withdraw, thereby undoubtedly saving the left flank.

Paton who was 22 when he died had been born in Innellan, Argyllshire and is buried at Metz-en-Couture Communal Cemetery, France. His medals are held in the Grenadier Guards Regimental Headquarters at Wellington Barracks in London.

One member died as a result of injuries sustained in the Gretna (Quintin's Hill) railway disaster in 1915. A less visible but still significant effect of the war on the Society lay in the war service of those who became members later.

The Armistice on 11 November 1918 came too late to allow an orderly transition to a peace-time programme that winter and session 1918–1919 was a transition year with the war-time president remaining in post once more. There was no dinner following the November meeting at which telegrams of congratulation were authorised to be sent to the Admiralty, the headquarters of the Army in France, the headquarters of the still new Royal Air Force and the 1st Battalion of the London Scottish Regiment in France. The first post-war dinner was held in December and was unusual in being only for members who heard a report from the president on the war-time activities of the Society. Most of these have already been described but one further highlight was the continuing intake of new members that would shortly lead to the creation of a waiting list. There is no record of the Festival dinner having been held that year but we are told that the customary date could not be accommodated at the Holborn Restaurant the following year in January 1920 and it was moved to the end of the season in April. With this change, the annual Burns celebration ceased after more than 60 years and it would not be restored until 1947 – perhaps a final casualty of the Society's war.

The Armistice did not mark the end of the Society's war-time involvement. Douglas, in his capacity as chairman, reported on the work of the Federated Council at a dinner in December 1919 and donations and assistance to various war related charities continued. Two major examples were the well supported appeal for the Scottish National War Memorial now part of the historic fabric of Edinburgh Castle, and the Saint Barnabas Pilgrimages whereby Scottish relatives were enabled to visit the graves of their kin who had been laid to rest in France and Flanders. Funds were raised and a trip took place in the summer of 1924. Every Scottish regiment was represented and four members of the Society took part as stewards. Over 130 cemeteries were visited and the care devoted to their layout and maintenance clearly made a very great impression. The tour started and finished at Ypres in Belgium and was accompanied by the pipes and drums of the London Scottish.

As we have seen the same president and honorary secretary led the Society throughout the war-time years and it perhaps appropriate to record their biographies as an illustration of the Society's membership of the time.

George William Paton was born in Greenock in 1859 and was educated at Greenock Academy and at a private school in Roxburghshire. He started his business career in shipbuilding in Greenock and later moved into sugar importing. He served as a member of Argyllshire County Council in the mid-1890s until he moved to Liverpool to become managing director of a match company. The company subsequently amalgamated with the well-known match company Bryant and May and Paton eventually became the latter's managing director, and later the chairman. He was also the chairman of the (wartime) Match Control Board. He would become a vice-president of the Royal Scottish Corporation, a life managing director of the Royal Caledonian Schools, chairman of Trustees of the St Andrew's Scottish Soldiers Home at Aldershot, an elder at St Columba's and patron of the Borough of Poplar Children's Carnival Fund. He went on to hold a number of Ministry of Labour appointments and was a member of Council of the Industrial Welfare Society and also of the Council of the Empire Forestry Association. He was knighted in 1930 in recognition of his public services. His unique Society record of six consecutive years in the chair was recognised by the award of the Society's Gold Badge with five bars, also unique.

George William Paton was president of the Caledonian Society and chairman of the Royal Scottish Corporation's committee of management throughout the war; his son, G.H.T. Paton VC MC was a governor of the Corporation until he was killed in action in 1917. (Caledonian Society of London)

John Douglas would become the Society's president in 1920 having previously been honorary secretary for 12 years and before later going on to serve as honorary historian for a further seven sessions. He was described as a leading participant in almost every branch of Scottish life in London. A native of Edinburgh, he was a governing director of William Douglas and Sons Limited of Edinburgh and London, manufacturers of plant and equipment for meat processing, and had moved to the latter city in 1891. Pre-war, he had established the *Douglas Year Book of Scottish Associations* and was always ready to lecture or talk on Scottish subjects. He had been joint honorary secretary of the London Committee for the 1911 Glasgow Exhibition. His parts in the wartime Federated Council, the St Andrew's Soldiers' Club at Aldershot and the Saint Barnabas Pilgrimages have already been described and he also acted as Military Representative for the Borough of Wandsworth, responsible for adjudicating on claims for exemption from military service. He was active in the governance of the Royal Scottish Corporation, a Life Managing Director of the Royal Caledonian Schools and would become chairman of Putney Hospital and a member of committee for the London Scottish Regimental War Memorial Fund. Among his many other interests, he had been chairman of the Vernacular Circle, of the Burns Club of London and later the Club's president, Chief of the Scottish Clans' Association of London and vice-president of the London Scottish Choir. He was also a Fellow of the Society of Antiquaries of Scotland and an officer of the London and Middlesex Archaeological Society.

The opening dinner of the first wholly post-war session, that of 1919–1920, is co-incidentally the earliest Society evening for which a full programme is still held. It was clearly a nostalgic event. After the loyal toasts and the welcome to the new president, the main speech or Sentiment as it is known, was "Our Glorious Sea Songs" given by a long-time member with key extracts sung by himself. Two Scots songs were sung solo by members, the pipe major played his selection and gave his toast and the evening finished with the company singing Auld Lang Syne with the four verses again sung solo by members. This may have been a fitting introduction to the interwar years when the Society flourished but perhaps with not quite the full energy, enthusiasm and reflected entrepreneurism that it had enjoyed in the immediate pre-war years.

Federated Council of Scottish Associations in London

It was soon apparent that the volunteers in the various Scottish groups all seeking ways to support Scots at the Front or otherwise involved in war effort risked duplicating their efforts and that pooling of resources and activities would make much more sense.

The Federated Council of Scottish Associations in London was therefore formed early on in the war and used the premises of the Royal Scottish Corporation for many of its meetings. Its stated aims were to coordinate the voluntary war work while maintaining its Scottish character, and to assist with recruitment for the Scottish regiments. The exact circumstances of the formation are now lost to us but its Committee included officers from the Caledonian Society, the Royal Scottish Corporation and the Royal Caledonian Schools.

What is clear from The Chronicles is that the Council worked effectively throughout the war years and continued to operate for a few years post-war. In doing so, they quote verbatim the Council's fifth annual report delivered by its chairman John Douglas on 25 November 1920 which summarises its wartime and early post-war activities, and a slightly abridged version of this fascinating account is reproduced in the Appendix.

The same entry in the Chronicles includes a short summary of the Treasurer's report that indicates that from its inception in 1914 until the close of 1919 the Council collected £5,013 and spent £4,720. The cost value of goods distributed was estimated to have been approximately £10,000. One pound then would be worth about £80 today.

Despite the positive approach to the Council's future expressed in late 1920, it does not seem to have survived much further into that decade. An attempt to revive it at the start of the Second World War was unsuccessful.

9

To the Immortal Memory: Burns Clubs in London

Jim Henderson

What we now know as The Burns Club of London was formed under its original name of the London Robert Burns Club in 1868. In 1901 a newer club, known as the London Burns Club (Scots) was formed and throughout the war years the two clubs co-existed, with broadly similar aims and both pursuing some of their regular activities scaled down due to the national situation. Each made special efforts to increase their donations to the charities then known as Royal Caledonian Schools and Royal Scottish Corporation and now operating as Royal Caledonian Education Trust and ScotsCare. The present club name was adopted three years after the end of the First World War when the younger club merged with London Robert Burns Club.

Having been in existence for nearly 46 years at the outbreak of the Great War, the London Robert Burns Club had grown and prospered and had great plans for the rest of the second decade of the 20th century, including arrangements in place for big events in September of that year and preparing for the celebration of the club's golden jubilee in October 1918. Towards the end of July 1914, it became obvious that the events of that autumn would have to be postponed although just how long that postponement would last did not become clear for some time.

The founder of the London Robert Burns Club and for many years the driving force behind it was Colin Rae Brown (1821–1897). A native of Greenock who combined great energy with a love of literature, he had become a very successful businessman with his pioneering work on development of mass circulation newspapers. By the time he moved to London in 1862 to further his business interests he was recognised as an authoritative and distinguished Burnsian, having already been president of Greenock Burns Club (known as the Mother Club because it was the first Burns club to be set up) three times in the 1840s and secretary of the committee organising the Burns Centenary Festival in 1859, marking 100 years since the poet's birth. After his arrival in London he hosted a dinner each year to celebrate the birthday of Robert Burns to which he invited many guests and it was always he who proposed the principal toast to "The Immortal Memory of Robert Burns." The transition from a gathering of friends to a club was gradual but the foundation of the London Robert Burns Club is considered to be the Grand Inaugural Dinner organised by Colin Rae Brown at Hallowe'en 1868 in the Bedford Head Tavern, Maiden Lane, Covent Garden.

For many years thereafter, the club held a Hallowe'en dinner at which the president-elect was installed and then subsequently, in place of the dinner, the season was marked by a series of very impressive Hallowe'en concerts which raised substantial sums of money for London-based Scottish Charities.

Through the energy and enthusiasm of Colin Rae Brown the club was to play a central part in the formation of the Burns Federation, the worldwide federation of Burns Clubs. After attending the unveiling of the bust of Burns in Poets' Corner in Westminster Abbey on 7 March 1885 he and two friends from Kilmarnock Burns Club, Provost Mackay and Captain Sneddon, developed an idea they had discussed a few years earlier and resolved to take the necessary steps to form an international federation of Burns clubs and that it should be based in Kilmarnock. Brown argued successfully to have the London club placed as number one on the membership roll.

The London Robert Burns Club's offer to host the annual conference and general meeting of the Burns Federation (later the Robert Burns World Federation) in September 1914 had been accepted some two years earlier and by early summer 1914 plans were well advanced. Permission had been obtained to hold the business meeting in the council chamber of the Guildhall. When Britain declared war on Germany on 4 August 1914 it was immediately apparent that holding the planned event in London was not only inappropriate but also practically impossible because the War Office had taken possession of the railways. The following day the club's secretary, James Thomson, wrote to the Burns Federation, "I suggest that under the terrible circumstances the 29th annual meeting be held pro forma at Kilmarnock or Glasgow simply to elect officers, minutes, etc, and to arrange that all being well the 30th annual conference be held in London in 1915." Whilst writing the letter he received one sent the previous day by Lord Rosebery in his capacity as Honorary President of the Burns Federation saying, "Lord Rosebery presents his compliments to Mr James Thomson, and fears that until the heavy cloud of war now hanging over us is dispersed, it would be a mistake to hold any such festive meetings as those mentioned in Mr Thomson's letter." He was, of course, referring to an earlier letter setting out the plans for the conference. Sadly, James Thomson's hope that life would have sufficiently returned to normal in time for the meeting to be held in September 1915 proved to be wildly optimistic and it was not until September 1920 that the London Robert Burns Club would eventually host the conference of the Burns Federation.

Another plan which had been made was the proposed visit of Mr John Gribbel of Philadelphia, USA, to these shores, first to London for the 1914 conference of the Burns Federation and then to Scotland. Mr Gribbel was a wealthy businessman and Burns enthusiast and had earned the gratitude of all admirers of Robert Burns and the whole Scottish nation when he had bought the Glenriddell Manuscripts after they had controversially been offered for sale in order to return them to Scotland where he felt strongly they belonged. A great welcome had been prepared for him in London and other cities across the UK by Burnsians who wished to show their appreciation of his philanthropic gesture.

The original manuscripts consisted of two leather bound volumes in which the poet had written copies of many of his poems and letters for his friend and neighbour Captain Robert Riddell of Glenriddell. After the death of Captain Riddell and then of Burns they had been given by the poet's widow, Jean Armour, to Dr James Currie, the first biographer of Burns, and in 1853 were placed by the Currie family in the library of The Athenaeum, a private members club in Liverpool. Great consternation was expressed when The Athenaeum needed to raise funds and decided in 1913 to sell these important documents as it was feared they were likely to leave these shores forever. Before handing over the original manuscripts, which are now housed in The National Library of Scotland, Mr Gribbel had authorised the production of 150 facsimile editions and the London Robert Burns Club was honoured to have received one of them, which is now on display in The Caledonian Club where The Burns Club of London holds its meetings.

Although the event which triggered the war happened on 28 June, Mr Gribbel wrote a letter to the London Robert Burns Club on 1 August saying, "It will be a privilege to be present at the conference in London. I will sail on the Mauretania on September 2nd." It seems surprising to us in this age of instant access to international news that he does not seem to consider his transatlantic trip to be in any danger of cancellation. He was eventually able to make his visit to the UK in the summer of 1920 and received the warmest of welcomes.

With the conference and Mr Gribbel's visit postponed the club began to consider what to do about its more routine activities now the country was at war. It was quite clear that these would have to be severely curtailed and in October the committee resolved to reduce the annual subscription to five shillings instead of a guinea for the year 1914–15 in recognition of this. The only events held were a small private meeting at Hallowe'en for the installation of the president-elect, J. Garioch Whyte, and the annual Anniversary Festival on 25 January 1915. In April the club advised the Burns Federation that it would be impossible to hold the postponed conference in September of that year and recommended that the London conference should be again postponed until 1918 when the club would celebrate the completion of its golden jubilee. This provides a further example of the poignant optimism about the duration of the war held by the committee in common with many of their fellow citizens.

At the London Robert Burns Club's annual general meeting in May 1915 the officers and committee were re-elected en bloc. Having no premises they could put at the disposal of the war effort they deliberated on how to strike a balance between keeping up morale by retaining some aspects of normal life in the capital while recognising the dire situation facing the country. They advised members:

> With respect to social gatherings it has been decided meantime to carry on, and keep the members in friendly touch with one another, by holding the two gatherings which justify the Club's name and existence; the Halloween dinner

and installation of the new president at the end of October, and the Birthday Anniversary celebration in January.

They went on to offer to allow any member who so wished to borrow for a few days the facsimile copy of the Glenriddell Manuscripts which Mr Gribbel had presented to the club, something that would never be countenanced today. The club proposed to ask the City of London Corporation to give safe custody to the "precious relics" in the Guildhall Library after members had had the opportunity to borrow and study them.

Quite understandably, the decision to continue with even a reduced programme of social events did not meet with the approval of all members. One returned his booking form for the Hallowe'en dinner with the message, "I very certainly shall not be present. There is a war on though the committee seems unaware of the fact. I shall shortly send remittance for two annual subscriptions and my resignation to show what I think of 'jollification as usual.'" However, 61 people did attend the Hallowe'en dinner and a collection was held and the proceeds distributed with one guinea going to the Veterans' Club tobacco fund for wounded soldiers, two guineas to the Red Cross and £2 being given to Private Donald McLeod of Queensland to enable him to visit his family in the Hebrides. That appears to be the only donation made by the club to an individual so it is likely that a club member met Private McLeod while he was stationed in London and successfully pleaded his case. The 1916 January celebration also went ahead and included a toast to the Imperial Forces with responses from a Captain Chaplain for the Army and an Engineer Commander for the Navy. A collection for the wounded raised more than £8 (equivalent to roughly £575 today).

As the war dragged on the club kept its resolve to carry on functioning but it responded to changing circumstances by varying the nature of the meetings it organised. At the 1916 AGM the officers and committee were once again re-elected en bloc and those present resolved to carry on and endeavour to find some opportunities to help in the war. It did not take long for the first of these opportunities to emerge. The following month a circular to members said:

> It has been brought to the notice of the London Robert Burns Club that the Scots Guards stationed at Wellington Barracks have had very little attention paid to them by the various organizations that exist to entertain the wounded and help to brighten their lot. Mr Neil Turner, Past President, has kindly placed his garden at Finsbury Park at the service of the club for a Garden Party.

That garden party took place on 1 July 1916 and was followed by another in Heston on the 28th at which 160 men were entertained. The following summer two further garden parties were held, one at Sutton Hall at which nearly 250 Scots Guards and Canadians were entertained and another at Finsbury Park for Scots Guards, Canadians and local wounded soldiers.

In August 1916 the committee decided that the Hallowe'en gathering that year should take the form of a tea and entertainment for the Scots Guards. A few days

Officers of the 3rd Battalion Scots Guards and others enjoy a dinner at a London restaurant.
(Courtesy of the Regimental Trustees Scots Guards)

before the event took place special instructions were issued by the War Office that during winter months all soldiers in London, whether in barracks or hospital, must be indoors by dusk. In normal times the club's meetings went on much later into the evening and special permission was obtained for the soldiers attending to stay out until 8:30 p.m. After tea, served at 5:30 p.m., a concert was held which included an impromptu turn by Captain Bruce Bairnsfather whose *Fragments from France* had earned him world-wide fame. He drew a sketch embodying his famous characters *Old Bill* and *Our Bert*.

In January 1917, in place of the customary banquet to celebrate the birthday of Robert Burns, the club held a "Grand Patriotic Gathering and Burns Concert to Colonial Soldiers" in Queen's Hall and guests were welcomed by The Right Honourable Andrew Bonar Law, the Colonial Secretary. Artistes included the London Scottish Choir, pipers and dancers of the Royal Caledonian Schools, Matheson Lang (a well-known Canadian-Scottish actor and playwright) and Harry Lauder (who went on to play a very important role in the fusion of the two clubs). The event raised £288 which was donated to the Schools.

At the AGM in May 1917 the great William Will was elected president, an office he would hold until 1920. He said he was strongly opposed to the Hallowe'en meeting taking the form of the customary dinner and concert that year. In its place a luncheon attended by 73 members and friends was held at the Holborn Restaurant.

With the help of Lieutenant Colonel John Buchan, who had already made his name as an author alongside his diplomatic career and was a member of the club, the new president ensured that the 1918 January celebration was an international gathering. It was attended by the American ambassador and representatives of the French, Italian and Russian governments and Buchan was one of the speakers.

On 28 June of that year the London Robert Burns Club gave a welcome home luncheon to another of its most distinguished members, Harry Lauder, on his return from his most recent charity tour of Canada and the USA which had raised 130,000 dollars. Although his act was not popular with all Scots, Lauder had earned great respect for his tireless touring and fundraising, including the fact that he took only a few days off from these activities when his only son John was killed at the Front in December 1916.

The event at Café Monaco attracted an attendance of 201 and the main toast was proposed by Ian Macpherson (later Lord Strathcarron), Under-Secretary of State for War. Others present included Lord Balfour, Lord Glenconner, Andrew Fisher (former Prime Minister of Australia) and Sir Thomas Lipton. The annual Hallowe'en celebration took the form of a matinée, the profits of which were donated to The Harry Lauder Fund, which later became The Harry Lauder Million Pound Fund for maimed Scottish soldiers and sailors.

Ruhleben internment camp seems to have been considered as nearly equivalent to a prisoner of war camp. Male citizens of the Allied Powers who had the misfortune to be in Germany at the outbreak of war were detained there, including the son of L.G. Sloan JP who went on to succeed William Will as president of London Robert Burns Club in 1920. One of the many clubs started by the internees as a way of getting through their incarceration was a Burns club and during the war numerous discussions took place in London on ways of sending them haggis and whisky, although it is not recorded whether any reached them. Young Sloan died in internment in 1918.

After the Armistice was declared and peace was now a reality, the club lost no time in organising for January 1919 an especially grand Birthday Festival to honour Scotland's Bard to make up for the more subdued events held during the previous four years and to combine it with a joyful celebration of the end of the war. All the allied embassies were represented, and the toast list was impressive. The toast to the London Robert Burns Club was proposed by Robert Munro KC (later Lord Alness), Secretary of State for Scotland. The British Imperial Forces were toasted by Lord Morris KCMG KC LLD (former Prime Minister of Newfoundland) and responses were given by Admiral Sir Rosslyn Wemyss GCB CMG MVO, First Sea Lord, Major General Sir Newton Moore KCMG MP, Major the Rev. Charles W. Gordon (novelist Ralph Connor) and Captain Bruce Bairnsfather. The toast to the Immortal Memory of Robert Burns was proposed by General Sir Ian Hamilton GCB DSO ADC, and finally Scottish Literature was proposed by John Murray CVO DL

FSA, to which Buchan (later Lord Tweedsmuir) and Lieutenant Colonel E.A. Ewart (author Boyd Cable) replied.

The London Burns Club (Scots) was pursuing a broadly similar course of action to that of its sister club during the war years. The two clubs had similar aims, with the key difference between the two being that the newer club restricted its membership to "gentlemen of Scottish nationality by direct male descent" whereas the older club was open to all regardless of nationality or gender. Both clubs made regular visits to the Royal Caledonian Schools in Bushey and donated frequently to the Schools and the Royal Scottish Corporation. It is interesting to note that London Burns Club (Scots) also regularly marked Hallowe'en. Its Hallowe'en concert was not held in 1915 because of the war but was again the following year and deemed a great success although substitute artistes had to be found for the pipers and dancers of the Royal Caledonian Schools who were unable to perform because of an outbreak of diphtheria in the Schools. On the night of the 1917 concert there was an air raid before midnight and it was reported that many of the audience did not reach home until early next morning. The journey home for the audience at the 1918 concert was uneventful and the surplus from the event resulted in donations of £150 to the Royal Caledonian Schools and £52 to the Royal Scottish Corporation.

In addition to the January and October events the London Burns Club (Scots) held occasional concerts, talks and socials at other times of year. Despite the issue of an air raid warning shortly before the start of the social in September 1917, over 100 members and friends attended and the entertainment commenced. When the antici-pated raid began the programme of song and dance continued to the accompaniment of heavy gunfire. The club's whist drives were very popular social events as well as a means of generating income for their soldiers' comfort fund and charitable dona-tions. A record attendance of 240 was achieved at a whist drive in 1918. In a depar-ture from tradition the club held a Burns Commemoration Service in Romford Road Congregational Church, Forest Gate, in January 1917 instead of its customary dinner. The service included solos sung by Harry Lauder who was one of their honorary vice-presidents. The following January they again held a service in place of the dinner, this time in City Temple.

By continuing to hold some of their regular events throughout the war each of the Burns clubs in London was able to maintain morale among their members while raising money for Scottish charities, entertaining troops passing through London and sending parcels of comforts to troops at the Front. For example, in the final year of the war London Burns Club (Scots) sent 63 parcels to Scottish soldiers on various fronts overseas, made up from: 87 pairs of socks, 22 mufflers, 12 suits of underclothing, six dozen handkerchiefs, 36 tins of boracic powder, 58 tins of Vermistraafe, 26 sticks of shaving soap, one hundredweight of Lifebuoy soap, 60 volumes of light literature, writing pads, 9,000 cigarettes and 102 ounces of tobacco.

These two Burns clubs in London had similar aims and from 1910 onwards several proposals to unite the two clubs had been put forward. They were all unsuccessful with the main obstacle to a merger being the difference in their criteria for membership.

In 1916 William Will made a very strong effort to achieve fusion, pointing out how wrong it was that rivalry should exist between two clubs which both espoused the wish expressed by Burns "That man to man the warld o'er, Shall brithers be for a' that." In an effort to move things forward Will also offered to stand aside from becoming president of London Robert Burns Club the following year if the clubs combined so that someone nominated by the other club could lead united clubs. Harry Lauder was a member of both clubs and had urged fusion of the two on several occasions. He wrote a letter supporting William Will's appeal for fusion and was asked to chair a meeting of the two clubs to discuss the matter. Despite Lauder's advocacy in favour of fusion the proposal could not be agreed at that stage.

In the three years after peace was restored, each club resumed a full programme of events which mainly attracted larger attendances than in the war years. This enabled them to increase the donations they made to their chosen charities, which included The Royal Caledonian Schools, The Royal Scottish Corporation and the London Scottish Regiment.

During these three post-war years efforts to unite the two clubs continued and a merger was eventually achieved in 1921, thanks largely to the efforts of Lauder (Sir Harry from 1919) and Will, who played a major role in the merged club throughout the first half of the 20th century. The united club continues to honour him each year by inviting a distinguished speaker to deliver The William Will Memorial Lecture. The name of the club formed by this marriage was agreed to be The Burns Club of London, with membership open to all admirers of the poetry and genius of Robert Burns without reference to nationality.

10

Caring for the Children: The Royal Caledonian Education Trust

Malcolm Noble

This is the story of a charity, originally founded in London, with a proud history of supporting Scottish armed forces children for over 200 years. It is a history which commenced with the outbreak of the Napoleonic Wars, encompasses the Great War and takes us right up to the present-day conflicts in Iraq, Afghanistan and Syria, which are still shaping the context for the British military and therefore influencing the lives of children and young people who have a parent who serves or has served in the British armed forces.

Boys at the newly opened Royal Caledonian Schools' site at Bushey in 1903.
(Royal Caledonian Education Trust)

The charity, was originally named *The Caledonian Asylum*. It was formed in 1815 to support the education of armed forces children, together though in much smaller numbers, with the education of poor Scots in London. In the first phase of its existence, the Caledonian Asylum was based initially in rented premises and then in a purpose built boarding school in what is now the Caledonian Road in London. The premises were quickly outgrown and the children were relocated in 1903 to new purpose-built schools at Bushey, in Watford. A name change would eventually follow. The word *Asylum* was increasingly used only for institutions for the insane (as they were known at the time) and for political refugees. Accordingly, the Board of Guardians decided on 7 December 1916 to rename the *Royal Caledonian Asylum* as the *Royal Caledonian Schools*, or the *Schools* for short.

The Caledonian Asylum 1815

The period of the Great War was one of immense difficulty for any institution responsible for children with a parent serving in the forces or the merchant marines. Most of the children resident in the Bushey premises were from armed forces families and had parents serving on one of the battle fronts, or at sea in the Royal Navy. Therefore, many of the children would have experienced the anxieties of having a parent who served a long way from home and for lengthy periods. During this period, the Committee of Directors, headmaster and staff frequently organised commemorative services, entertained wounded soldiers and welcomed visitors from allied countries. The Schools' pipe band and Scottish dancers performed locally as well as attending formal events in London. Historical accounts show much was done by the Schools both with the children and wider afield to boost morale and support the war effort.

On 14 June 1815 an Act of Parliament established a Corporation:

> for the well governing of an establishment an Asylum or House for the Reception, Maintenance, Education and Employment of the Children of Soldiers, Sailors and Marines, Natives of Scotland, who have died or been disabled in the Service of their Country, and of the children of indigent Scotch Parents resident in London, not entitled to Parochial Relief.

A Charter of Incorporation set out the objects of what became known as the Caledonian Asylum. The Charter set out the names of 96 nobleman and gentlemen who had responded to the initial appeal for funds and thereby appointed Guardians for Life of the Asylum, contributing a minimum sum of 10 guineas per year.

The initiative for setting up the Caledonian Asylum had been taken by the Highland Society of London in the year 1808. As the Charter of Incorporation noted, at the end of the Napoleonic wars, there were large numbers of children "in a desolate and forlorn state as a result of a parent suffering death or disablement, and of Scotch parents in the greatest poverty and want." In 1814 the Highland Society of London passed over responsibility for the Asylum to the subscribers of funds.

Subscribers paying at least 10 guineas a year would be Guardians for Life. Anyone paying at least five guineas a year would be Guardians as long as they continued to do so. The Guardians, together with president, vice-presidents and treasurer, constituted the body corporate. This Court of Guardians appointed a Committee of Directors charged with the running of the Asylum. The first set of Guardians for Life included the Royal Princes, the Duke of Marlborough, the Duke of Buccleuch the Duke of Argyll, the Duke of Montrose, the Duke of Roxburgh, and the Duke of Wellington. There were also 21 Earls, and three Marquises. The list of Lords, Knights and other gentlemen, included the Lord Provosts of Edinburgh and Glasgow.

The first president of the Caledonian Asylum was Edward, Duke of Kent and Strathearn, the father of Queen Victoria. Following the incorporation of the institution, strenuous efforts were made to raise money in Scotland. The Duke of Kent and Strathearn, for example, wrote to the ministers in every parish in Scotland. His letter referred to

> it not being on the ground of humanity and national feeling only, that your parishioners may be earnestly solicited to give homes to the Caledonian Asylum; but also on the principle of right and justice which entitles the poor and helpless of all nations to claim the parental relief of their native country.

One subscriber was John Galt, the Scottish author and founder of the town of Guelph in Canada. He became the first secretary of the Caledonian Asylum. The intention had been to raise sufficient funds to provide a purpose built boarding school in Scotland. However, Galt explained to the Duke of Kent and Strathearn that there would be enough money to fund the capital but not the running costs. Galt was then charged with organising an "Institutionary Dinner of the Caledonian Asylum." The guests were the Asylum's subscribers and the function was held in London's Freemason's Tavern. It proved to be quite an occasion, with 23 toasts; music provided by a Military Orchestra, the Scottish Orchestra and Highland pipers; as well as a poem commissioned for the occasion by James Hogg, the Ettrick Shepherd.

At a suitable point in the proceedings, the Duke of Kent and Strathearn rose to speak. He said that he considered that

> what claim has not Scotland on the whole empire, in that debt of gratitude to the Army and Navy which can only be acknowledged by supporting the children of those who have so gallantly shed their blood for us. I have to share with you the very judicious observations made by Mr Galt: 'It may be said that London is not the proper place for directing Caledonian Asylum and that the National Institution of the Scottish Nation should be in Edinburgh.' This objection presented itself in great force to the members of the Highland Society or rather in their affections when pointed out to them the propriety of raising the

establishment in their native country but on reflection they considered that although funds for erecting suitable edifice might be collected in Scotland, permanent income would only be obtained from the opulence and liberality of the London public.

The Caledonian Asylum would, therefore, be established in London. After a period in temporary accommodation, grounds were acquired in the Copenhagen Fields in Islington. The new Caledonian Asylum opened with accommodation for 100 boys and girls in 1828. Queen Victoria became the Asylum's patron in 1852. However, the growth of London in the middle part of the century soon led to the Asylum being surrounded by buildings and next-door to the new Pentonville Prison.

An insight into life at the Caledonian Asylum was provided by the son of the first headmaster. The Reverend John Lees lived on the island of North Uist in the Outer Hebrides. He responded to an advertisement in the *Inverness Courier* newspaper. The Asylum's Committee of Directors were looking to appoint a headmaster. The successful candidate would have to be an experienced schoolmaster, a Minister in the Church of Scotland and a Scot, Rev. Lees met these requirements and was appointed to the post, at a salary of £130 a year. He commenced his duties in February 1824 and in 1828 managed the move into the first purpose built Caledonian Asylum in what is today the Caledonian Road in Islington.

Before too long the pleasant semi-rural location of Copenhagen Fields in Islington was converted into a cattle market and Pentonville Prison erected right next door to the Asylum. The staff of the Asylum were all Scots including the caretaker, an ex-drill sergeant called Young. He was a Peninsular War veteran and suffered still from a leg wound obtained at the field of Waterloo. He played the pipes to entertain the children. It was rumoured that he had eloped with his wife and that as a consequence both had been cut off from their respective families. He and his wife were popular with the children, particularly after rescuing one of the boys who appeared to be drowning in a local pond. The accounts by Rev. Lees and his son James, suggest that lessons were overall well taught and that the children were kept in order with little recourse to the cane.

Time to Move

At the current school premises, there was no prospect of expansion and the Committee of Directors decided to acquire a new site on the outer edge of London. Just under 10 acres of land was purchased in Bushey and plans for a new building were prepared by Sir William Emerson, President of the Royal Institute of British Architects. Construction began in 1901 and the buildings were completed in 1903. The children left the old Asylum on 2 May and, following a three-week holiday, they entered their new premises on 23 May 1903.

A Festival Dinner had been held each year since the founding of the original Caledonian Asylum in 1815. The 98th Annual Festival of the Schools was held in the

Whitehall Room of London's Metropole Hotel on Wednesday 11 June 1913. The event raised £1,268 for the Schools. Attendees were subscribers to the Schools and their guests. The funding for the Schools came from voluntary subscriptions. There were three categories of supporters: Guardians, Donors and the 882 Annual Subscribers, depending on the amount paid. The Committee of Directors was appointed by the Court of Guardians. The Annual Report for 1913, presented to the Annual General Meeting on 11 June 1914, noted that 14 boys and 11 girls had left for employment and there were 109 boys and 63 girls on roll. The Schools sought to maintain a distinctly Scottish ethos. This was reinforced through the school uniform, piping and Scottish dancing.

At the start of the Great War, discussions arose over the appropriate use of the term "Asylum," and eventually "Royal Caledonian Schools," or the "Schools" for short, was approved by King George V, and adopted.

Kaiser Wilhelm II referred to the opening of the Baltic and North Sea Canal in 1895 as an important event "related to foreign policy." He invited "squadrons or individual ships representing countries all over the world." This was an early indication of German intentions to challenge the existing balance of power at sea. Nevertheless, the British Government accepted the invitation to attend. Sir Donald Currie MP, owner of the Union Castle shipping line, agreed to convey the British representatives on his ship, the *Tantallon Castle* and William Gladstone, Prime Minister until the previous year, would lead the official party.

A girls' callisthenics class in September 1898; The Caledonian Asylum uniform maintained a distinctly Scottish ethos. (Royal Caledonian Education Trust)

Sir Donald was a director of the Royal Caledonian Schools in Bushey. In that role he arranged for five boys from the Schools, two of them pipers and the others Scottish dancers, to accompany them on the voyage. The ceremonies were scheduled to commence on 19 June 1895, also coincidentally Queen Victoria's birthday. The Kaiser had arranged for a 21-gun salute in her honour. This was preceded by the boy pipers playing Scottish airs, cheered by lines of sailors on the decks of the ships of the international fleets.

At the outset of the Great War, the Committee of Directors agreed that any children eligible for entry to the Schools would be offered automatic admission in event of a father being killed in battle. During the war, parties of wounded soldiers would be sent by London hospitals to enjoy musical entertainment and refreshments at the Schools.

A great number of children were affected by the loss or deployment, even if temporary, of a parent in the forces. Most of the children resident in the Bushey premises were from armed forces families and had parents serving on one of the battle fronts, or at sea with the Royal Navy. Therefore, the Royal Caledonian Schools were particularly exposed to the difficulties experienced by children, who had a parent serving a long way from home and for lengthy periods. The Committee of Directors, headmaster and staff organised commemorative Services and welcomed visitors from allied countries. The Schools' pipe band and Scottish dancers regularly performed onsite at Bushey, as well as at events held locally and in London.

The Schools published a monthly magazine called *The Old Caledonian*. Copies were sent to Old Caleys serving in the forces. One, joining the London Scottish Regiment on 2 September 1914, sent his diary to the magazine. This details somewhat drawn out preparations for joining the British Expeditionary Force between his enlisting on 3 September 1914 and embarking for France on 21 November. His service in the Caledonian Schools Cadet Force appears to have been instrumental in his securing a place in the first draft. Just before departure, he notes that "all our equipment is condemned and we are issued with fresh." Another, Daniel Johnson, wrote to the magazine in 1915, saying "We are all looking forward to a speedy finish to the War, but still it is as well to see it through so that the enemy can never be in a fit state to strike us again; there is no point in leaving a job half done." He points out the fact he is unable to give any news as the letter must pass the censor. Writing from a casualty clearing station on 8 May 1915, one Old Caley described the effects of the then new and unexpected use of mustard gas, which he sees as "a terrible death for its victims, they appearing ghastly when taken to our hospitals."

By the middle of 1915, Old Caleys were to be found in battle fronts across the globe, as the European conflict became a world war. Tom Jardine was wounded in the attack on Hill 60 in Flanders and was convalescing near Loch Lomond. J.H. Morrison was on his way to the Dardanelles. James Vass was stationed in Egypt along with his brother Andrew. In 1914 we find them taking part in the South African invasion of neighbouring German South West Africa (what is now Namibia). Bernard Rennie had left the Schools in 1910. He emigrated to Canada, first finding work as a farm hand and then becoming a news reporter for a church newspaper. Dissatisfied with his lot, he enlisted in the American Army. On the outbreak of war in 1914, Bernard bought himself out for £60 and joined the Canadian Expeditionary Force. Lance Corporal John Blair, of the 6th Royal Fusiliers, sought to provide the Schools with a "plain and unvarnished tale of my doings during the past two years of the war." He had been wounded four times and on visiting the Schools during a period of convalescence, presented the children with a German belt, which he described as a "trophy of war." William McFall, of the Gordon Highlanders, was killed while retreating under "terrible shell fire and struck in the head by a piece of shell and instantaneously killed." The obituary for Harry Graham, killed at Givenchy 22 December 1915, included the first verse of a poem written by home shortly before his death:

Royal Caledonians! He was one of you
Keen to serve his country, for a gallant lad was he
Kindest son and brother, and a comrade tried and true
Pure in life and brave in death, Could
Better record be.

A visit to the Caledonian Schools by nearly 100 wounded Scots soldiers was a great success. All staff and children were involved in the preparation of this event. The soldiers were piped into the building where they were given refreshments. There was an exhibition of work, piping displays, a swimming competition, Highland dancing. They were given a talk on the history of the Schools and after tea, viewed various artefacts including a collection of medals and a set of bagpipes played before the "Thin Red Line" at Balaclava during the Crimean War. Before departing, a disabled veteran remarked that this had been "one of the happiest afternoons in his life." The visit enabled the children to feel that they could play some part in supporting Scottish soldiers. As winter approached, Caley girls suggested that they might knit mittens for the troops. A subscriber, W.H. Thompson provided the wool and 120 pairs of mittens were soon on their way to Lady Tullibardine, for the Scottish Horse, commanded by Lord Tullibardine.

The December 1916 edition of the *Old Caledonian* magazine contained an article written by the headmaster, John Newcater. His purpose was to explain to Old Caleys and the children themselves, how things changed for those leaving civilian life for active service in the forces. He listed some of the lifestyle changes that would face new recruits. These included living among 32 men in a wooden hut with planks raised just six inches from the floor and the various "fatigue duties" that were an inescapable part of army life.

The third year of the war was characterised by growing casualty rates, exemplified by the Battle of Passchendaele and no ending in sight. Nevertheless, the Schools still received optimistic sounding letters from Old Caleys, serving in the trenches of the Western Front. Charles H. Scott, writing in December 1917, wanted everyone at the Schools to know that "we are doing our best to bring this job to an end and; it is not as exciting as the old Oxford and Cambridge football matches in days gone by, but still everyone is doing their best to put on the finishing touch." F.R. Logan, who left the Schools in 1899, had transferred to the Royal Flying Corps as a photographer. He was now Officer in Charge of the Photography of the Central Flying School and obviously, proud of his achievements in this important field of work. According to Logan, pupil flyers were called "Huns" and it was his job to teach them how to take accurate aerial photographs. An Old Caley serving in the "Salonica Force" in northern Greece showed no such enthusiasm for his work, reflecting the lack of progress by allied forces on the Balkan Front.

It is unsurprising that Old Caleys who were children of serving soldiers or sailors should have volunteered for the forces so readily in 1914. However, a connection with the armed forces had been maintained since 1815. It was part of the ethos and would influence all attending the Schools. This was reinforced by displays of flags and artefacts such as the pipes played by Piper John Smith as part of the "Thin Red Line" of the 93rd Sutherland Highlanders at the Battle of Balaclava on 25 October 1854. The children attending the Schools from 1914 to 1918 were more affected than most by the stresses on families as fathers went to war. There were 49 children on roll whose fathers had been killed in action. The King's Chaplain at the time was the Rev. J.M. Simms, Major General and Moderator of the Church of Ireland. He addressed the Schools' staff and pupils. Noting the significant number of Old Caleys killed and wounded, he explained that this reflected the sense of duty that had characterised the schools since the opening of the Caledonian Asylum in 1828. The spirit of self-sacrifice shown by those who had attended the schools, might best be expressed, in his opinion, by the quotation from the Bible, as set out in 1st Corinthians verses 51 to 57: "Greater love have no man than this, that a man lay down his life for his friends."

Every effort was made to give the children a happy Christmas in 1918. Supporters provided Christmas gifts. These included Christmas cards for each child presented by General Moncrieff, the Schools' president, £10 from Mrs Crawford and Mrs Ritchie, dates from Mr Gray and oranges from Mrs Bernside and Mrs Grant. Fun began on Christmas Eve, with a boy dressed as Father Christmas filling the stockings laid out by every bed. Early on Christmas morning the girls walked around the holly-decorated buildings singing carols.

After prayers and breakfast, the children were at last able to open their presents. These came from parents or otherwise were purchased from school funds. The call for Christmas dinner came from the playing of the pipes. Piping had long been a feature of school life. A subscriber, Mr Cameron had introduced piping in 1826 and before long had established a pipe band. The day ended with a pantomime written by the teachers.

The matron's account books give a very clear picture of domestic items purchased each week. In December 1916 the following items were purchased from the Civil Service Supplies Association: Colman's Mustard at 10 shillings and four pence per pound; Ceylon tea at two shillings per pound; Lyle's Golden Syrup; Knights Yellow Best Soap six shillings and eight pence in 14-pound tins; Emery Paper at one pound

Four old boys of the Royal Caledonian Schools who were killed in action during the Great War. (Royal Caledonian Education Trust)

OUR DEAD HEROES.

THOMAS FINDLAY.

WILLIAM McFALL.

THOMAS McKIM.

HARRY GRAHAM.

one shilling per quire; Hearth Stones at five shillings per dozen; and safety matches at 11 shillings per dozen boxes. The Blind Association provided boot brushes at seven shillings per dozen; black lead brushes at 6d each; scrubbing brushes at nine shillings per dozen.

Rules and routines for girls were considerably more onerous than those for boys. House duties were set out for each day of the week, together with instructions on bedmaking and general tidiness. A feature in the magazine *Living London* gave an insight into life at the Schools. The article notes the tartan uniforms, Scottish dancing and bagpipes. The view is expressed though that the children are "well cared for, well fed and well taught."

News of, albeit temporary, British success at the Battle of Loos in 1915 led to an upbeat atmosphere at the Schools. Thus encouraged, the girls were told to make every effort to look their best and maintain a cheerful demeanour always. This was difficult given the shortage of materials for school clothing. However, they were assured that "old and frayed skirts will only be rendered more modish by being docked an inch of their length." The girls were given responsibility for cultivation of their playground area. They had erected poultry runs and ploughed what space remained for growing potatoes. The boys were cultivating flowers, fruit and potatoes. By 1917, the grounds had the look of a small farm.

Annual prize giving was combined with school sports day. In 1914 this was held on Saturday 27 June, the day before the assassination of Archduke Ferdinand and his wife Sophie in Sarajevo. The chairman was Lieutenant General G.H. Moncrieff VD, vice-president and chairman of directors.

On 25 January 1917, a concert in aid of the Schools was held in London's Queen's Hall. It was arranged by the London Robert Burns Club. Lord Derby, Secretary of State for War, presided while Sir Harry Lauder headed an impressive list of performers, supported by the London Scottish Choir. Many wounded colonial soldiers attended as guests of the Burns Club.

On 21 March 1918, General Ludendorff launched the last great German offensive of the war. He hoped to secure victory before the arrival of American troops in over-whelming numbers. For a while the outcome remained in the balance, until the Battle of Amiens on 8 August resulted in the 100 days' advance that ended in the Armistice of 11 November 1918. The staff and children at the Schools were aware of the critical nature of these events. The headmaster sought to prevent the children's thoughts from dwelling too much on what was happening on the battlefronts. He wanted them to concentrate on what good they might be able to do at home. His message to the assembled children in late March was to the effect that "despite the present upheaval of the world's affairs and of mankind generally, we may rejoice that there are still generous hearts in which benevolence is a spontaneous pleasure." He went on to urge his listeners to find ways they might "relieve distress and do good."

The Armistice caught the Schools by surprise. The "booming of the guns and the sound of hooters" at 11:00 a.m. caused much excitement, as the children realised that something momentous had occurred and soon "there was no room for doubt." By coincidence, the Committee of Directors' monthly meeting was held on that day. They decided to send telegrams of congratulation to King George V, Field Marshal Sir Douglas Haig and Admiral Sir David Beatty. The telegram sent to the King read "The Directors of the Royal Caledonian Schools, in monthly Court assembled, offer Your Majesty their humble and loyal congratulations on the triumph of Right over Might – Andrew Cunningham Chairman."

There were 30 Old Caleys killed in the Great War. A memorial service was held at the Schools on 1 May 1920.

It was conducted by the Rev. Archibald Fleming, Minister at St Columba's Church of Scotland in Chelsea, and Chaplain to the Schools. The opening hymn was *For Men Who Heard their Country's Call* by Terrot Reaveley Glover. This was followed by an address from Rev. Simms, The Memorial to those killed was unveiled by Mrs George W. Paton and this was followed by the singing of William Walsham How's hymn *For All the Saints*. After Rev. Fleming's blessing, Pipe Major Alexander Russell played the lament, *Lochaber No More*. At the end of the service, a bugler of the Scots Guards played the *Last Post* and Mrs Paton placed a brass plate beneath the memorial. This was presented by George W. Paton, a Director of the Schools, in memory of his son Captain G.H. Tatham Paton VC MC of the Grenadier Guards. Captain Paton had been killed in action in France on 1 December 1917.

As the war ended, the Schools might, quite reasonably, have expected to return to normal routines. In the event, the Schools faced a whole set of new challenges. David Lloyd George's Coalition Government had concentrated primarily on winning the war. However, from the summer of 1918 they were giving serious thought to post war re-construction. H.A.L. Fisher, President of the Board of Education looked to improve the country's education system. The "Fisher Act" of 1918 raised the school leaving age to 14 years. Ancillary services were introduced: medical inspections, nursery schools and centres for children having special educational needs. These reforms made it difficult for the Schools to meet the standards set for state-run schools. The subsequent Hadow Reports of 1926, 1931 and 1933 led to the division of primary education into infant and junior phases. The Spens Report of 1938 led to all children between the ages of 12 and 14, in attendance at state schools receiving a secondary school education.

The Schools had nevertheless adjusted to post-war conditions by 1922. The wartime president of the Schools was Lieutenant General G.H. Moncrieff. A fine portrait of Moncrieff was handed to the Schools in 1918. He had served with distinction in the Crimean War and had retired from the Army in 1900. From then onwards he was heavily involved in the London Scottish charities. He had been involved with the Schools for 45 years until his death on 15 October 1918. This had encompassed serving as chairman of directors, treasurer and vice-president and then as President, presiding at the 99th anniversary Festival Dinner in 1914. Moncrieff was born in 1836 in Fife, and was educated at Lymington College and the Royal Military College Sandhurst, before joining the Scots Guards. He was twice Mentioned in Despatches, served in Canada and was Assistant Military Secretary at the War Office. He commanded the Curragh Camp in Ireland, and served as Colonel of the Royal Scots.

The Annual Report of 1922 listed those who, like Moncrieff, had presided over the Annual Festival Dinners. In the early years, from 1815 onwards the chair had been taken by the royal princes. Between 1816 and 1818 the Duke of Clarence, later King William IV presided and in 1825 Prince Albert of Saxe-Cobourg, later husband of Queen Victoria. Prince George, Duke of Cambridge, grandson of King George III, cousin of Queen Victoria and Commander in Chief of the British Army between 1856 and 1895, chaired the Dinner in 1860. Sir Colin Campbell, Field Marshal Lord Clyde, chaired it in 1857. He commanded the force that relieved Lucknow during the Indian Mutiny. Union Castle's Sir Donald Currie presided in 1894 and Liberal Prime Minister Sir Henry Campbell Bannerman 1897.

The Annual Court of Guardians and the Committee of Directors had two main responsibilities. They had to ensure that the Schools were run efficiently and the premises maintained properly. In addition, they had to raise the necessary funds to do so. This involved sustaining the list of subscribers. The children came from families lacking the means to pay fees, either for boarding or their lessons. However, after the

LIST OF
Guardians, Donors, and Annual Subscribers.

(*Subscriptions and Donations corrected to 31st March, 1914.*)

The Names printed in CAPITALS in the Alphabetical List are Directors for Life, being Subscribers of One Hundred Guineas and upwards.

The Secretary would be obliged by being informed of any inaccuracy in this List.

No. of Votes.	Names and Residences.	Life Govrs. and accumulated Subs. from 1893. £ s.	Annual Subs. £ s.	Dona- tions. £ s.
1 14	HIS MOST GRACIOUS MAJESTY THE KING, Buckingham Palace, S.W.	47 5	10 10	
2 17	HER MOST GRACIOUS MAJESTY QUEEN ALEXANDRA, Marlborough House, S.W.	120 15	5 5	
3 9	Ditto, ditto, from "The Queen's Gift Book Fund"	100 0		
4 5	H.R.H.THE DUKE OF CONNAUGHT, K.G., Clarence House, St. James's, S.W.	57 15		
5 1	H.R.H. THE PRINCESS CHRISTIAN, Cumberland Lodge, Windsor Park	10 10		
6 3	H.R.H. THE PRINCE CHRISTIAN, K.G., Cumberland Lodge, Windsor Park	31 10		
7 1	H.R.H. THE DUCHESS OF ALBANY, Claremont, Esher, Surrey	5 5		
8 2	H.R.H. PRINCE ARTHUR OF CONNAUGHT, K.G.,K.T., G.C.V.O.,&c. Clarence House, St. James's, S.W.	25 0		
9 5	H.R.H. THE PRINCESS ROYAL, 15, Portman Square, W.		5 5	
10 19	Aberconway, Lord, 43, Belgrave Square, S.W.	7 2		20 0
11 2	Abercrombie, Peter, H., M.D., 56, Harley Street, W.	9 9	2 :	
12 11	Abercromby, David James, 14 Collingham Road, Cromwell Road, S.W.	92 8	3 3	
13 1	Abercromby, Lord, 41 Brompton Square, S.W., and Tullibody House, Clackmannanshire, N.B.	10 10		

The king and queen head this list of supporters of the Royal Caledonian Schools in March 1914. (Royal Caledonian Education Trust)

Great War, the Schools could still count on royalty and members of the nobility for support.

King George V, Queen Mary and Queen Alexandra were patronesses; Edward Prince of Wales and Prince Arthur of Connaught were vice-patrons; The Princess Royal, Princess Louise Duchess of Argyll, Princess Beatrice, Lady Grant and Lady Pentland were vice-patronesses.

The Duke of Atholl was president. The Duke of Portland, the Marquis of Aberdeen, the Earl of Shrewsbury, Viscount Finlay, Lord Faringdon, Lord Inchcape of Strathnaver, Lord Inverforth of Southgate, Lord Pentland, Andrew Fisher, and Andrew Cunningham, were vice-presidents; Cunningham was chairman of the committee of directors and Patrick Gardiner deputy chairman.

Between the wars, the Scottish ethos remained the defining feature of the Schools. As *The Scotsman* newspaper put it: "in no other schools in England is Scottish dress always worn and the sound of the pipes the familiar music of every day." Yet the Schools would continue to struggle to meet the changing requirements of the education system in England.

However, the coming of the Second World War prevented Parliament from introducing any significant new legislation on educational matters. That would change as the threat of invasion receded and the Government began to think about the shape of the post war world. The year 1944 saw the "Butler Act", landmark legislation designed to transform state education. This put great pressure on the Royal Caledonian Schools. The Schools offered only an elementary education. The Act, as promoted by R.A. Butler, President of the Board of Education, made education for all from the ages of 11 to 15 a legal requirement. The Schools lacked the capacity and the funds necessary to deliver the expected range of courses at secondary level.

The Schools had moreover suffered serious setbacks during the Second World War. In 1940, accidental fire seriously damaged the Hall of the Clans. Then in 1941 the chapel was destroyed by fire resulting from enemy action. Otherwise, the Schools came through the war unscathed but unprepared for the post war legislative changes. After examination of the possible alternatives the Committee of Directors determined to end all teaching at the Bushey premises after 1947. The Schools would continue to provide a boarding facility and the children educated at local state schools. This placed the viability of the Schools in doubt.

It was far from obvious that the days of the Schools were numbered in 1948.

Most of the children were from armed forces families. Deployment of servicemen and women was still determined by the need to defend British colonies. In addition, with the advent of the cold war, Great Britain's obligations to NATO involved the setting up of military bases in continental Europe, with housing and school provision. Government-funded Service Children's Education (SCE) schools are now established in Germany, Cyprus, Belgium, Brunei, Canada, Falkland Islands, Italy and the Netherlands. Nevertheless, the Schools provided boarding and continuity of education within England, while their parents are posted and re-posted, around different parts of the world. The Committee of Directors sought to modernise and refurbish the residential accommodation and raise funds for further improvements. In doing so, they made full use of their royal patrons. On the initiative of two boys, an appeal was mounted for funds to restore the Hall of the Clans. This was a major exercise and took time. The new Hall was opened finally, by Queen Elizabeth the Queen Mother in 1963.

James Milne Coltart was chairman of the Schools in 1983. The British Empire scarcely existed by the 1980s. Between Indian independence in 1947 and the handing over of Hong Kong to China in 1997, most British colonies had become self-governing nations. Coltart had the foresight to see that this would reduce demand for overseas deployment of British forces and therefore, reduce demand for places at the Schools. He had been manager of the *Scottish Daily Express,* chairman of Scottish Television and deputy chairman of the Thomson International Media Organisation.

Coltart's idea was to take the intake of children beyond age 15 up to 18. To achieve this there would need to be dedicated sixth form provision. Again, following an appeal sufficient funds were raised and the new block was built. Accordingly, the foundation stone was laid by the Mayor of Herstmere on 18 September 1985. The stone was taken from the main hall that had been damaged by fire in 1940. On 15 May 1986, the sixth form block, named the James Coltart House, was opened formally by Her Majesty the Queen.

The final Royal visit occurred in 1989. General Sir Michael Gow, a vice-president of the Schools, conceived of the idea that links might be established between the Schools and individual Scottish regiments. He felt that a Hall of the Regiments might complement the family connections displayed through the Hall of the Clans. The idea was that each regiment might provide a badge with an emblem and a picture showing soldiers wearing the tartan associated with it. This was endorsed by the Committee of Directors and each of the Regiments themselves. The Queen Mother opened the Hall of the Regiments on 7 March 1989. At the start of the proceedings, she was introduced to Jack Haines, the only staff member present who had witnessed her opening the Hall of the Clans in 1963.

It was entirely fitting that the Queen Mother should have been present on that occasion. She had maintained a connection with Schools from her first visit, as Duchess of York, in 1925, spanning 64 years. The connection between the Royal Family and the Schools was impressive and probably decisive in keeping the Schools going for so long. Edward Duke of Kent, the first president, had taken the critical decision that the Caledonian Asylum should be established in London and not Edinburgh. The royal princes, the Dukes of York and Clarence, subsequently Kings George IV and William IV had presided over Anniversary Dinners, as had their brother the Duke of Sussex. Queen Victoria had become Patron in 1852. George V, as Prince of Wales, had chaired the Anniversary Festival Dinner in 1898. He and Queen Mary had visited the Schools. Edward VIII, as Prince of Wales, had visited in 1925. King George VI visited with Queen Elizabeth in 1937. Queen Elizabeth II visited in 1986.

Despite the improvements to the buildings and facilities, numbers fell during the 1980s and 1990s. The fact that the Schools provided accommodation but not education, made it less attractive to parents over this period. At the time of the Queen Mother's visit in 1989, there were 124 children on roll. By 1994, numbers had fallen to 54. In 1995 the Committee of Directors decided to close the Schools. After the departure of the last remaining children in June 1996, the premises were sold to the Purcell School of Music. The capital from the sale was invested and the income from it used to fund individual grant applications.

After 1996, there would be no aspiration to offer education or to accommodate eligible children. From then onwards, the Committee of Directors aimed to meet the objectives set by the Charter of Incorporation. The same criteria applied as for admission to the Schools. An analysis carried out 10 years later showed the bulk of grants being awarded were to the children of Army families. The spread of awards was as follows: 280 grants to Army families, 50 grants to Royal Air Force families, and 20 grants each for Royal Navy and poor Scots in London. The breakdown on costs were: £50,000 on living expenses, £39,000 for school clothing, £22,000 after school activities, £18,000 miscellaneous and £10,000 school fees. Over the period, grants to poor Scots in London fell year on year.

In addition to grants for the benefit of individuals, support was offered to organisations and institutions. One example, was the funding for Colinton primary school in Edinburgh, to erect a "Place to Be" in the school grounds and an adjoining family room. These provided sanctuaries for parents and children affected by the wars in Iraq and Afghanistan. The school served communities around the Dreghorn and Redford Army barracks.

The name, the Royal Caledonian Schools, was misleading as the charity no longer offered educational provision either directly or indirectly. Accordingly, the name was changed in 2012 to the Royal Caledonian Education Trust. The Trust became involved in two main areas of activity, individual grants and the development of an educational programme in Scotland. In the first case, the beneficiaries received direct support to assist them in school or college. The education programme involved working with schools and colleges, universities, military communities, the military itself, armed forces charities, the Scottish Government and local authorities.

The Trust has had to adapt to an altered environment. The Caledonian Asylum was formed to meet the need of destitute and orphaned children in London, most of them from armed forces families. The Asylum did so by providing the rudiments of education necessary to find work. Later the curriculum was broadened up to the standards of elementary education in state schools. In the early part of the 21st century, armed forces children faced the stresses arising from deployment in a war zone and moving between schools or even education systems. The challenge for the Trust was to find new ways of supporting armed forces children effectively.

The aims of the Education Programme are: to promote good practice in mitigating the effects of mobility on children from armed forces families; to improve support for children prior to, during and after deployment of a parent to an operational zone; and to influence policy to meet the educational needs and wellbeing of armed forces children in Scotland.

As war came in 1914, the headmaster and staff at the Schools had no specialist guidance, or experience to draw on. Great Britain had not been involved in a major European war since the Battle of Waterloo in 1815. However, they knew intuitively that the children should be encouraged to talk about the war and understand its consequences for those involved and their families at home. The wounded soldiers brought to Bushey could enjoy the piping, dancing and the break from recuperating in a hospital. The children, through observation and talking to the soldiers gained insights into the effects of war. By being kept active, in this way it was hoped that they would be better able to cope with their fear over what might happen to a parent serving in the trenches.

The equivalent in recent years has been the roadside bomb in Helmand province of Afghanistan. In *This is My Life*, a short film produced and funded by the Royal

Caledonian Education Trust, children talked about their coping strategies and how they might support the parents staying at home and younger siblings. As one child put it:

> I know a friend of mine, he got really, really frustrated. He broke his hand hitting a wall because of what happened. He was just so frustrated at it all. The best thing to do is not to talk to your family as such, rather to talk to your friends, people who understand or others who don't actually understand but can take your mind off it; or perhaps just hit something softer like a pillow.

Aside from the fear, is a sense of pride that the parent serving in Afghanistan is doing their duty, as one child put it: "when he takes his bagpipes somewhere and he plays them for people who are away from Scotland, it reminds them that they are Scottish and where they come from." That is not so very different from feelings expressed by the children attending the schools between 1914 and 1918.

In early 1915, the committee of directors were arranging the centenary festival dinner. This was scheduled to take place exactly 100 years after the institutory dinner presided over by Edward Duke of Kent and Strathearn. King George V and Queen Mary agreed to attend. It was scheduled for a day in March 1915. However, early in the year King George agreed to give up drinking alcohol for the duration of the war. He felt, therefore, that it would be inappropriate to attend a large-scale social function where many present would be drinking wine. The Committee of Directors were left with little choice but to cancel the function.

Fast forward nearly 200 years to 2013 at which point the Committee of Directors started to consider how they would mark the Trust's bicentenary. After considering possible alternatives they decided to hold a formal dinner in London's Caledonian Club in collaboration with the Caledonian Society of London. The Caledonian Club decided to mark the occasion by making the Trust sole beneficiary of their Waterloo Ball. This was based on the Duchess of Richmond's Ball held in Brussels on 17 June 1815, the eve of the battle. The Act of Parliament founding the Caledonian Asylum had passed into law on the 14 June.

The Trust marked the bicentenary by commissioning a theatre production *Forces Kids*. The performance follows the story of "Kevin" whose father is a marine. He is anxious about his father's current deployment and misses him terribly. Kevin also has to take on additional responsibilities at home, while adjusting to life at his new school. School children watching the play follow Kevin on his journey as he learns to cope with fear, loss and bullying.

In November 2014 the Committee of Directors met in Edinburgh to consider the future direction of the Trust. The administrative headquarters was then based in the Soldiers, Sailors, Airmen and Families Association (SSAFA) offices in the City of London. A branch office had been opened at the headquarters of the Church of Scotland, 121 George Street, Edinburgh. However, as most Trust activity now took place in Scotland there were obvious advantages to be had from basing the chief executive and the administration of the Trust in the same place. The decision was taken that the Trust would move its entire operation to Scotland in 2015. New and expanded office space was acquired at 121 George Street. The Trust has long had a close relationship with Scotland's national church. The Very Rev. John Chalmers, retired Principal Clerk to the General Assembly, was a keynote speaker at the Trust's conference in 2015.

"A National Institution of the Scottish Nation" was how Edward Duke of Kent and Strathearn saw the Caledonian Asylum, at its inception in 1815. Today the Royal Caledonian Education Trust is at the centre of support for armed forces children in Scotland. The Trust depends for its effectiveness on the quality and commitment of its staff, and ability to maintain income levels and continuing good relations with its stakeholders. These are education providers, the Scottish and United Kingdom Governments, the Scottish local authorities and the military from all three Services in Scotland. However, the Trust has committed to retain its London connections.

The principle that followed in 1815 involved providing for Scottish children in need but not eligible for any other sources of support in London. Later and certainly when the Royal Caledonian Schools opened the new premises in Bushey, the Schools met the requirements of parents who wanted their children to have a stable education, while they themselves were deployed in the armed forces across the British Empire.

The Great War was the watershed in the history of the Schools. The committee of directors, the headmaster and staff and various supporters sought to ensure that the children under their care, might cope with the exigencies of war. The over-riding need to support the children while being separated from their parents, the majority of whom feared they would lose a parent serving their country on land or sea. This was the clear priority during the war. At the war's end, the Schools faced a different set of challenges. In this, they were in the end unsuccessful. The Schools were unable to adjust to changed circumstances. After the Second World War, efforts were made to update the buildings, including the provision of the new sixth form block. However, the problem lay with the capacity to meet new educational requirements. The response was to arrange for the children to be taught in local state schools. This proved to be an inadequate response, as prospective parents saw little point in placing the children with an educational charity that was unable to offer education beyond the elementary level.

However, at this point the Schools did make necessary changes. Becoming a grant-awarding charity enabled the now renamed Royal Caledonian Education Trust to survive. The Trust's education programme became, and still is, the primary source of advice, support, training, resources for learning and good practice for the education of armed forces children in Scotland. The Trust is well on the way to fulfilling the Duke of Kent's mission, to being fully recognised as a "National Institution of the Scottish Nation."

11

The King's Regulars Based Down South: The Scots Guards

Randall Nicol

Background to the Scots Guards and London in the First World War

The origin of the Scots Guards lies in 1642 on King Charles I commissioning Archibald Campbell, Marquess of Argyll, to raise a regiment of 1,500 men in Scotland. He was their first Colonel, but, politician and administrator, rather than soldier, he delegated military authority to his cousin, Sir Duncan Campbell of Auchinbreck, to command as his Lieutenant Colonel. The connection with London began in 1686, when King James VII of Scotland (in that capacity and not as King James II) ordered a battalion, one half of the Regiment, to travel from Edinburgh to the military camp on Hounslow Heath. They landed at Gravesend and were seen in London for the first time. On Hounslow Heath they encamped with the forerunners of the Regiments now known as the Grenadier and Coldstream Guards. The name "Scots Guards" first appeared subsequent to this, though was not finally adopted until 1877. Ever since 1686 the Scots Guards have had the strongest association with London, most visibly in ceremonial roles, and have been regularly stationed there, though often abroad on operations or garrison duty.

In London during the First World War, in support of the two battalions in the British Expeditionary Force (BEF), were, first, Regimental Headquarters in Buckingham Gate, secondly, the 3rd (Reserve) Battalion, from early October 1914 at Wellington Barracks, and, thirdly, the Regimental Band. All were essential and integral to the life and duties of the Regiment. The Guards Depot was at Caterham, Surrey, where men joining the ranks underwent the very strict process of discipline and basic training which turned them from civilians into Scots Guardsmen, indispensable preparation for what they were to face in France and Belgium. Standing Orders of the Scots Guards 1901 stated that "real discipline implies respect and obedience wherever it is due on the one hand, and on the other a just but energetic use of command and of responsibility." Those well-chosen words set the whole scene very succinctly and entirely for every member of the Regiment of whatever rank and appointment.

Pipe Major David Smith and the Pipes and Drums 3rd Battalion Scots Guards on the steps of the Guards Chapel, c. 1916–1920. (Courtesy of the Regimental Trustees Scots Guards)

After the outbreak of war, the 1st Battalion Scots Guards, then stationed in Aldershot, were in the BEF during the Retreat from Mons and the Battle of the Aisne before going north to Ypres later in October 1914. The 2nd Battalion, at the Tower of London previously, landed at Zeebrugge on 7 October and became directly involved in the First Battle of Ypres slightly earlier than the 1st Battalion. Both were on the Western Front till the Armistice and afterwards in Cologne. On 22 November 1918 King George V, Colonel-in-Chief of all the Regiments of Foot Guards, ordered that Privates in the Brigade of Guards were to be known as Guardsmen.

Regimental Headquarters

Following on the structure from the earliest days of the Regiment, in 1914 Field Marshal Lord Methuen was Colonel of the Scots Guards, an official, but neither executive nor honorary appointment, with great scope for playing a positive part by way of influence and human interest. However, the officer in command, in the rank of Colonel, but holding the military appointment of Lieutenant Colonel Commanding Scots Guards, had a full-time post. This command he exercised in all respects, excepting training, operations and matters within the jurisdiction of the commanding officers of the battalions. Thus he appointed commanding officers and made all other senior appointments, including non-commissioned ranks, selected new officers, coordinated and directed recruiting, supervised those employed in the Army away from the Regiment and ran the regimental charities. During the war Colonel Henry

Fludyer, who had re-joined the Army from full retirement but had previously been Lieutenant Colonel, took up the post again for two years, replaced in 1916 by Colonel James Smith Neill.

His principal staff officer was the Regimental Adjutant, till 1916 Major The Honourable Archibald Campbell Douglas, then Major Malcolm Romer, then from mid-1917 Captain Arthur Clarke Jervoise. They were supported by a Warrant Officer Class I as Superintending Clerk and a substantial team of clerks, storemen, grooms and others.

The Lieutenant Colonel's other appointment was Officer in Charge of Records Scots Guards. So all details of soldiers were held and maintained at Regimental Headquarters, a massive task as recruiting took off after the declaration of war. It also meant that for soldiers, but not officers, who were dealt with by the War Office, Regimental Headquarters handled the notification of casualties. If a sick or wounded soldier returned from the BEF he was posted onto the strength of the 3rd Battalion, even though he was in hospital. It was essential that Regimental Headquarters knew where he was, what his progress was and what the medical disposal was: discharged if unfit or disabled, or recovered to return to duty, which meant re-joining the 3rd Battalion. This also kept many occupied.

Early on in the war new officers, other than those with regular commissions from the Royal Military College Sandhurst, transferring from other regiments, or passed out from Officers Training Corps, were given their basic training within the 3rd Battalion at Wellington. However, almost all officers would pass through the hands of the Battalion at some stage before going to the Western Front. From the formation of the Household Brigade Officer Cadet Battalion at Bushey, Hertfordshire, in February 1917 new wartime officers were trained there.

The Guards Depot, Caterham, Surrey

At the Guards Depot, known as "Little Sparta," a very rigorous disciplinary environment, recruits received basic training in drill and in using, cleaning and looking after both their uniform and equipment and their barrack rooms. Personal hygiene played an important part and so did physical training. Significantly, they were briefed and tested on regimental history and customs. While intended to develop instinctive obedience, for their own good and for the greater good of the Regiment, there was more to it than that. The building up of comradeship, teamwork and *esprit de corps* were fundamental to the future interrelationship of discipline, self-discipline, respect, self-respect, confidence and self-confidence. The process, intense and harsh, but with purpose, continued through the war. Significantly, in the battalions on the Western Front drill played a major part. Once they came out of the line after a trench tour or a battle and had had time to rest and clean up, drill soon started up next. Everybody was used to it and it had a settling effect done as a team, also being a means by which new arrivals were quickly assimilated.

Douglas Cuddeford had by 1914 been a trader in Nigeria for eight years. The following spring, aged 28, he came home to Glasgow and in July enlisted as 14149 Private Douglas Cuddeford. In *And All For What: Some Wartime Experiences,* published in 1933, he wrote of his time as a Scots Guardsman and later. When he went into the recruiting office in Bath Street he was put through a very stiff medical examination "rather an ordeal for one of my modest nature. One might have thought I was aspiring to membership of a Russian ballet, the way they put me through it in a state of nature in that chilly room." Basic training was limited to 14 weeks at Caterham. His initial reaction to the barrack rooms with their bed spaces for 40 was of their airiness and spotless cleanliness, only very quickly to find that the explanation was entirely down to the work that the recruits themselves put into maintaining it, including buying the soap out of their pay of one shilling and a penny per day. At that stage the recruits were volunteers, motivated to complete their training quickly and proficiently in order to go abroad. So "a constant threat held over our heads was that if we didn't smarten up we wouldn't "get going to the front." He understood at once that the discipline at Caterham was "iron" and wondered whether he was going to cope with this rigorous training.

> At first I found it very hard work indeed; harder than I ever supposed any work could be, and the discipline was, to say the least, irksome at the beginning. After a week or two, however, I was surprised to find that I could go through the heaviest day without being unduly distressed. At the same time I think I must have shed pounds and pounds of flesh in the form of sweat on that accursed parade ground.

Many NCOs there had re-enlisted to serve abroad with the battalions only to find themselves instructors at the Depot where the need for them was greater. Those who had not been abroad probably resented not having been at the Front. Once his recruit squad assembled their first squad instructor was characteristic of "a typical pre-war guardsman of the old school: foul-mouthed and coarse, fairly honest, but a good-hearted and decent fellow for all that." However, he was only with them briefly and they heard he had been locked up for getting drunk, which may have led to his being reduced to the ranks. His replacement was Corporal William Twohig "and we couldn't have had a more efficient instructor." A few of the instructors were "downright pigs" but the majority were "quite decent fellows when you got to know them." 7232 Corporal Twohig, born in Bermondsey, London, had been in the Army since October 1908 after enlisting in Liverpool. He was a Depot instructor from before the war and did not go abroad until June 1918. Then he became a Sergeant and was wounded in the knee during the attack on 27 September 1918 across the Canal du Nord which led to the capture of the Hindenburg Support Line west of Cambrai.

Cleanliness of person and tidiness of barracks went hand in hand and once a week there was a "General Barrack Fatigue," often involving something beyond the more obvious tasks. Once they had to use their issue food knives to scrape old whitewash off

Sports Day for the 3rd Battalion Scots Guards – fighting on horseback with mops, c. 1915–1918, probably at Burton's Court. (Courtesy of the Regimental Trustees Scots Guards)

the staircase before putting on a new coating. From time to time teams of men scoured the grounds of the barracks looking for odd matches and cigarette ends, collected in dustbin lids. Quickly wise to this, in order to get time off they slyly struck a full box of matches in order to show evidence of their diligence. Private Cuddeford was once detailed with another recruit to take a dirty and obstinate prisoner from the Guardroom to the Bathhouse and clean him thoroughly with scrubbing brushes.

Breakfast at Caterham was limited to a small bit of bacon and a piece of bread rubbed in "gyppo," as all fat and dripping was known. Dinner at midday was the main meal and this, though plain, was of good quality and well cooked "and there was certainly plenty of it." Private Cuddeford's concern was more that "the manner of serving it up rather handicapped the man with a fastidious stomach." All the same by late afternoon, after more hard work, they were likely to be very hungry. At teatime there was only tea with bread and margarine. So any supper they had to pay for themselves. A few pence would provide a filling meal in the barracks coffee bar. Just outside the gate was

> a little "sausage and mashed" shop near the barracks which did a roaring trade with us. One sausage with some mashed potatoes cost threepence; ditto with two sausages sixpence. In this local Restaurant de Luxe, clients were not provided with knives, and the forks were chained to the table! The young ladies who waited on patrons were under strict instructions not to walk out with soldiers!

On regimental spirit he wrote:

> In the Brigade of Guards *esprit-de-corps* is very strong. Every guardsman, whatever his regiment, is proud of being a guardsman, and there is no regiment to compare with his own. This spirit in recruits is encouraged right from the beginning, and is in fact made part of the training.

While he was there he thought the instruction on regimental history a waste of time, but subsequently he recognised its value and appreciated that the way he had first been trained as a soldier was the right one.

> Later on I served in a regiment in France in which the *esprit-de-corps* was weak, and I saw the difference. Still later, when I was with the 2nd King's African Rifles, a regiment recruited in the wilds of Nyasaland, I saw *esprit de corps* as strong as ever it was in the Guards, and we fostered it with good results.

Before he left the Depot Private Cuddeford was selected for promotion, though much had to be gone through before that was confirmed, including prospective NCOs going daily for 10 days to Hoxton's Field at Caterham "where we did nothing but drill one another and bawl commands at distances of up to three hundred yards." The immediate consequence was being completely hoarse, but they found that their voices gained strength with repeated practice.

No one can have enjoyed being a recruit at the Guards Depot, but he was a volunteer and keen to get on with it. The other Scots Guardsman to write a published account of his experiences, *A Private In The Guards,* which came out in 1919, was 17021 Private Stephen Graham, born in Edinburgh and called up in September 1917 as a conscript in London, who approached it from a very different standpoint. He was a well-known writer and author, in particular on Russia, where he had lived and travelled. Temperamentally inclined towards a display of unconventional style and manner, he wrote "When I came to Little Sparta the whole army seemed to glare at me, as uniformity stares at diversity and discipline at freedom." He took, as far as possible, a detached view, did what he had to do and got through it, while regarding what was to him the uneducated and unenlightened military methodology with disdain. As his squad was forming an older man who had broken down in training and was retained at Caterham as a tailor warned some of them not to take what was said to them to heart. "The great process of bullying and intimidation has set in," he said. "They try and break you at the beginning and take all your pride out of you. But it'll be better later on. Never answer any of them back or get angry. It's not worth it." Another man also gave us excellent advice. "Never catch the sergeant's eye," he said. "The sergeants hate being looked at."

3218 Sergeant Major Joseph Barwick, Scots Guards, became Sergeant Major (Regimental Sergeant Major) of the Depot in 1916. From Burley, Yorkshire, he enlisted in Leeds in January 1900 and in 1914 was a Company Sergeant Major in the 1st Battalion until wounded during First Ypres. Private Graham very much approved of him. "A very great personage to us was the brigade sergeant major, with the royal arms embroidered on his sleeve. He was kind to the recruits but a terror to the non-commissioned officers." He had a particularly sharp eye for any physical abuse of recruits by instructors, but less impact on their deployment of verbal abuse. "Even when he was quite near them, the latter had a way of standing quite close to you and delivering a whispered imprecatory address on adultery, the birth of Jesus, the sins of Sodom, and what not."

Because of the tensions of the daytime routines and the endless effort not to attract attention, it was in the barrack room in the evenings that everyone became most relaxed, singing, swearing and shouting as they tended their equipment, oiled their rifles and pressed their trousers until lights out. This was outside Private Graham's natural territory and he remained quiet "but I cannot help smiling at a lusty coster nearby who all the while he is cleaning his buttons keeps bawling in a staccato barrow voice: 'Tuppence a pound plums. Syme pryce figs.' He had sold them in civilian life."

Once he had a visit from a long-haired Eastern European friend who happened to arrive just as the first parade of the whole Depot was forming up on the square at half past eight in the morning and watched and listened in astonishment at the sound of the stamping, rushing, yelling tumult. His visitor said when they met up later, "'Twas like hobgoblins striving against one another in hell."

Very different from when Private Cuddeford enlisted was the physical standard of many recruits. In the early stages of the war, not only were unfit volunteers rejected at recruiting offices, but many others failed to make it through basic training. By late 1917, as Private Graham described, several of his fellow conscripts were well below that earlier standard, with one even wearing a truss. In the event almost all passed out and almost all went on to serve effectively in France.

While resenting the uncouth methods of instilling absolute obedience and the sheer vulgar coarseness, Private Graham responded positively at once to the building up of *esprit de corps*, both by way of regimental history, customs and insignia and by cleanliness and turnout. So, he and his fellows prided themselves on the best polished cap stars, buttons and boots, best oiled rifles and best cleaned equipment. So, they stepped taller and looked smarter to themselves whenever marching on the Square, as they did on Wednesdays and Saturdays to a band, even one playing American popular tunes. So, as he recognised, they learned how to die and some of those he knew at Caterham did die before the Armistice.

3rd (Reserve) Battalion Scots Guards

The main role of the 3rd Battalion was to provide drafts of officers and men for the two battalions on the Western Front, while also carrying out both normal and wartime duties in London. Those who had recovered from wounds or sickness were there, though several were on light duties and not yet nor ever fit again to go on active service, but the main component was men who had passed out of the Depot.

Recruits did not do field training at the Depot so, for example, the first time that a new private soldier fired his rifle would be after he arrived in a battalion. Normally this did not matter in peacetime. In the early stages of the First World War, however, the lack of time to train and prepare reinforcements in England before they were needed in France, notably in the aftermath of First Ypres, meant that new arrivals in the battalions abroad then had to learn there most of what they needed. It was some time before the levels of training met the requirements of real life in the BEF. One example was the correct use of construction with sandbags. On 30 May 1915 Lieutenant Colonel The Honourable Walter Hore Ruthven, Commanding the 1st Battalion, by then near Loos, where trenches were dug in the chalk, wrote to Lieutenant Colonel Sherard Godman, Commanding the 3rd Battalion, complaining that men coming out in drafts did not know how to build breastworks or traverses or generally to use sandbags. He pointed out that they needed to be able to do this not only in daylight, but very much more so in the dark, and suggested that a corner of the barrack square at Wellington Barracks should be set aside for instruction.

Later on, training for all ranks became much more intensive and sophisticated, so that those going overseas would be as fully familiar as possible with what they were going to find. Selected men were trained as signallers and as machine gunners on Lewis and Vickers Guns. Field training for all took place principally either at Tadworth, Surrey, or at Corsham, Wiltshire, the home of Field Marshal Lord Methuen. Everyone was shown the correct use and maintenance of gas masks and everyone was trained in the throwing of grenades. The rifle ranges were in Essex at Purfleet and Rainham and there was field firing on the Ash Ranges at Aldershot.

When Private Cuddeford arrived at Wellington Barracks his first 20 days were spent in musketry training, the working, aiming and firing of a rifle. Ten days of instruction were entirely in barracks, without ammunition. For the next 10 they went off every day, travelling "by the Tube and District Railway" to the ranges at Rainham. They left very early in the morning and were usually back in barracks by one o'clock, subsequently had a parade to show their rifles cleaned and then had the rest of the day off. The standard of shooting was variable, but everyone seemed to pass the tests, though one misty morning, when the shooting was particularly bad, an exasperated company sergeant major "shouted out 'For God's sake fix bayonets and charge the bloody targets; it's your only hope!'"

By comparison with the Depot the regime at Wellington was much more relaxed, all of them being trained soldiers, with NCOs not collectively of the same standard as those at the Depot. While discipline on duty or on parade was as strict as Caterham, otherwise they were left mostly to themselves. So, for example, there were no formal bathing parades, taking baths being voluntary in the well-equipped bathrooms, with ample hot water between 11 in the morning and 5 in the afternoon. One thing many had learned at the Depot for the first time was brushing their teeth.

After breakfast the whole battalion paraded at 9. Usually they then all went on a three-hour route march round London, which had many attractions, there being much to look at. They carried full kit, including packs weighing about 50 pounds. Their other activities were training in bayonet fighting, for which they marched to Kensington Gardens and back, or company drill in Hyde Park. Route marching was partly exercise, but also for training. Though later in the war much more movement was by train and motor vehicle, marching was an unavoidable part of the infantry-man's life in the BEF.

At Wellington Private Cuddeford's company commander was Captain The Honourable John Yarde-Buller, who was commissioned in 1896 and served in the Boer War, left the Army in 1907 and returned in 1914, but did not go abroad. They liked him very much. After leaving Wellington under his command they would go past Buckingham Palace, marching correctly at attention, but as soon as they were comfortably round the corner up Constitution Hill he would order them to "march easy" and smoke "If you have got any fags!" At this point he would move across to the footpath, light up a favourite old pipe and amble along beside the company. "He was a very unmilitary sort of person altogether."

Guard duties, in service dress, went on at a number of places, from the obvious and generally more interesting, such as Buckingham Palace, to the unexpected, such as the very large underground powder magazine in Kensington Gardens, incon-spicuous above ground as "a very ordinary-looking squat concrete building." All guards were for 24 hours with a complete 24 hours off afterwards. The Regimental Band, still at this period in scarlet tunics, would lead the New Guard out to relieve the Old Guard at Buckingham Palace, the Scots Guards also having Pipes and Drums and Corps of Drums, drums and fifes. At night, when most of the interest had disappeared and nothing was going on, the sentries, cold and bored, resented seeing carloads of revellers driving past "enjoying themselves so utterly regardless of the war." It was at St James's Palace that there was diversion as "the servant girls would sometimes bring us hot coffee during the night, and maybe keep us company for a while. Very irregular, no doubt, but it helped to pass the time." He also mentioned that lots of women used to hang around the barrack gates, some of whom even "paid soldiers to take them out!" Female munitions workers were paid more than infantry soldiers.

Although those with homes nearby could get overnight passes the men normally had to be back in barracks by midnight, but that left plenty of time for relaxation when off duty. One of Private Cuddeford's particular cronies was from the East End and with him

> I often attended the big shows at Wonderland and other centres of the boxing fancy. It was he who first took me to the weekly "ball" held in a dancing hall in a street off the Commercial Road. The entrance fee for gentlemen was 1s (increased price owing to the war!) but ladies were free if accompanied by a gentleman; if not, they weren't allowed in at all. The proceedings at those "balls" were remarkably free from ceremony, and as a rule introductions were looked on as quite superfluous.

Private Cuddeford noted "the intense rivalry, amounting almost to animosity, between the different regiments." As far as the Scots Guards were concerned at Wellington, because the other reserve battalions were all outside London, there was only one set of rivals, the Grenadier Guards at Chelsea Barracks. "The boundary between our respective areas, the 'no man's land' as it were, was the region of Victoria Station, and many a disturbance arose in the pubs of that neighbourhood for no other cause than that we belonged to different regiments." In spite of the large numbers of Cockneys in both, their tribal allegiance was either Grenadier or Scots, many of the latter having adopted Scots accents and all addressing each other as "Jock." In the ranks the Scots Guards were known among themselves and to the other Foot Guards as "The Jocks."

Then he was promoted, to find that being an unpaid lance corporal simply meant a lot more work and responsibility. On Christmas Eve he was Corporal of the Barrack Guard at Wellington. Consequent on the festivities there were several latecomers, but as these were often equipped with the liquid means to bribe their way in without penalty, and in the general interests of goodwill, the Guard let them pass. However, the Sergeant of the Guard enjoyed the free drinks so much that he "staggered out into the middle of Birdcage Walk and challenged anybody in the world to a fight!" They had to put him to bed and Lance Corporal Cuddeford had to deal with everything himself. Just as he was standing outside for fresh air in the early morning, before cleaning up the Guardroom ahead of the daytime relief, news was brought to him by the regimental tailor that he was being commissioned into The Highland Light Infantry. It was his last day as a Scots Guardsman.

Soldiers of the American Expeditionary Force at Wellington Barracks after the United States entered the war in April 1917. (Courtesy of the Regimental Trustees Scots Guards)

He went to France in August 1916, fought in the later stages of the Somme, endured the following winter, was in the Battle of Arras and then in July 1917, just before the beginning of the Third Battle of Ypres, posted to the 2nd Battalion The King's African Rifles. So he sailed to Africa, where he was for the rest of the war.

After the disappointments of Third Ypres, the mixed results of Cambrai, and the crushing German and Austro-Hungarian defeat of the Italian Army at Caporetto there was growing awareness by late 1917 that, while the Americans were on their way, the collapse of Russia was going to enable the Germans to strike first in the west if they chose. Private Graham was in the 3rd Battalion then and into 1918, where his experiences were very similar to Lance Corporal Cuddeford's, but it was two years further on and there was a sense of war weariness, guard mounting being the main diversion.

So he remarked that as the time for the Changing of the Guard approached:

> A crowd of accidental passers-by collects. The old guard at the Palace marches into position to be relieved, the new guard, preceded by the band and the colours of the regiment, marches out of barracks. Off we go to a jingling music-hall air, and a sense of mortification steals into the heart that the pipes have not preceded us. For the pipes are always national, or at least in good taste, whereas these wretched ragtime songs of the brass band put us on the level of some sort of South American Republic or less. If the music be wrong the whole ritual is wrong, and the other impressiveness counts for nought.

He occupied his mind on sentry go with poetry. "It is very pleasant to say poetry to oneself whilst marching to and fro. Two lines of Gray's *Elegy* will take the sentry up and the other two lines of the verse will bring him back again. One verse of Omar will take him up, another will take him down."

One night there was an air raid. "Stand to!" We all get up and stand ready with our rifles for any emergency. Every one grumbles. But the guard-room fire blazes merrily, and the guns keep up a joyful hubbub." After a while and just before the bugles sounded the All Clear, Private Graham marched out on time with his relief of the sentry posts. While there:

> In a moment of ennui I notice some words vaguely scratched on a pillar, done by a sentry with his bayonet on some past night in the dark and empty hours when there is no one to see what is done. And these were the words:

> Roll on the Duration.
> Roll on Peace.
> Roll on the Revolution.

And in those lines I felt expressed how exasperating and boring the Great War had become.

Ever and always there were the summons to go to France. At this period the Guards Division, having fought at Cambrai, first rested for nearly a month southwest of Arras and then went into the line east of there. It was generally a quiet period but there were a few casualties in the trenches, men had to be sent down sick and there was always a degree of coming and going for military reasons. So there were drafts and so there would be notices put up at Wellington Barracks reading "The following are warned to be in readiness to proceed overseas." Not all those listed would ultimately go with a particular draft, because more were listed than needed, but all were to be ready to fill any gap in the ranks when the draft formed up for departure.

> Ah, the very rumour of that notice raises a tremulous breeze in the whole barracks, a breeze that plays on the wind-harps of men's affections. It causes a consternation among us as if at some bygone period we had sold ourselves to the Devil for seven years' happiness, and now suddenly we saw this sinister figure appear claiming the execution of his bargain.

In routine wearing of uniform at home the regimental identity of a Scots Guards soldier was indicated by a metal thistle with the letters S G in brass fixed below it on the shoulder strap of his khaki tunic. In the BEF these were awkward with equipment. So instead:

> Immediately the warning is given blood-red tabs with the name of the regiment are sewn on the shoulders of our tunics. We are marked, as it were, with blood, and are like trees with the gash of the hatchet designing them to be felled, or like rams marked for sacrifice to the idol. "I see you've *got them up*," says one to the other with the curious hush of awe.

Private Graham noticed that it was those who had been wounded before who were calmest and more philosophical about it. One or two of those detailed would try various methods of avoiding the draft, absconding being the only certain way immediately and the surest way of ensuring going out next time. "The call brings out the courage in most and the selfishness in some. For it is selfish to escape: if one man's name is crossed off the list for any reason another's must be put on."

Otherwise training continued in a relaxed and unhurried way and Private Graham and others were about to go away for a month's field training, when everything changed. That there was going to be a major German offensive was self-evident in the BEF, where and when not so clear. On 21 March 1918 it started with immediate and dramatic tactical success, notably against the British Fifth Army westwards down the valley of the Somme. The Guards Division, very recently relieved in the line east of Arras and resting in and around the town, were ordered to take up defensive positions just to the south. A subsequent German move against the British near Arras was held, other later attacks elsewhere against the British and French having varying degrees of success, but all ultimately being contained. Nevertheless it was a severe fright.

At home it led to a major change, in particular to Government authorisation of the deployment to the BEF of large numbers of trained men held back since the end of Third Ypres. Private Graham wrote of the instantaneous increase in tempo. "The tragic nature of the moment dispelled the selfish and sickly ways of looking on the fight, and it was marvellous what a good, quiet, patriotic fervour developed in a few days then." For those who had been in the Army in the early days of the war it struck a chord of recollection. Private Graham overheard an officer saying "August 1914 is going to repeat itself." There was a climax at hand.

At very short notice all those many now listed for a large Scots Guards draft were got ready. After being quickly passed by the doctor "We received new metal helmets, waterproof capes, and draft-kit, field-dressings, identification discs, pay-books. Our wills were filed at the orderly room." All the preparations went on amid rumours and counter rumours about the draft as a group and about its individuals, whether going sooner or later or not at all.

> We went on Good Friday, and it was at noon … that we stood finally in the barrack-square in full field-service marching order, weighed down by what we carried. We were all very tense with emotion, and our hands shook comrades' hands in Good-bye with a regularity and continuity that only a practised demagogue leaving the platform could do well. Tears stood in many eyes. We knew, however, that it was an ordeal for the nerves of the affections, and steeled ourselves to think of other things, as we stood there, and be hard.

After a final Inspection by the Commanding Officer, Lieutenant Colonel The Earl of Stair, there followed the order to step off.

Then the regimental band in all its brazenness blared out its melodies:

> If the Sergeant drinks your rum,
> Never mind!

And the rest. And the civilian population, with the women we knew, flung itself upon us, scattering flowers and kisses, shouting and halloing, or gently sobbing and hurrying to keep step with us. Beads of perspiration rolled down our brows and cheeks, our close hair on our heads rose with excitement. Men wreathed their Service hats with primroses. Girls and wives were inside the ranks walking arm-in-arm with their soldier-boys. A mother held out her baby at arm's length for the soldier-father to kiss, and all the while the band ahead of us blasted away in quick-time – and then the band gave way more happily to the pipes, as all our pipers in glorious array took up the slogan and played us to the train. The populace was rolled back by the police, our ranks restored in all their brightness and sparkle, and every man's rifle seemed to be at the same angle across his left shoulder. So in a fine strapping style, all together and with one step, we entered the stern confines of the terminus where the troop-train was waiting, marched past a large draft of silent Gordon Highlanders with aprons over their kilts, and past a draft of Dorsets to the far end of the platform.

We were soon in the train, and then the civilians were allowed to us once more, and then the last tender farewells and embraces. Then the official farewell of the C.O. "Good-b'ye and spare none!" And then the cry, "All aboard!" and then, "We're off, boys!"

And the train rolls slowly out.

Private Graham joined the 2nd Battalion soon afterwards, quickly becoming orderly to his pre-war friend, Captain Wilfrid Ewart. He wrote much about the last months of the war, taking the story to Cologne, where they were for several weeks as part of the Army of Occupation. He was discharged in February 1919.

Coming Home: on return from the Army of Occupation in Cologne the 1st Battalion Scots Guards, led by the Regimental Band, march from St Pancras Station on 3 March 1919. (Courtesy of the Regimental Trustees Scots Guards)

The London Scottish

Towards the end of First Ypres the 1st London Scottish were posted to the 1st (Guards) Brigade, by then down to a fighting strength of five officers and just over 300 men, the weakest of the three surviving battalions being the 1st Scots Guards. They would serve alongside each other till August 1915 when the 1st Scots Guards left to join the newly forming Guards Division. The only other time that they were at close quarters was in August 1916 when they were either side of a divisional boundary in the front line at Hébuterne on the west of the Somme battlefield.

Early in March 1915 Brigadier General Cecil Lowther, the Brigade Commander, lost the filling from one of his front teeth. He recorded in his diary that this was quickly fixed by 3189 Corporal William Meeke of the London Scottish, a dentist with a practice in Harley Street. A little later he heard that Corporal Meeke was told one day that an officer in a car was outside the billets looking for him. On running out and saluting he found that the officer was his chauffeur, commissioned into the Army Service Corps. Soon afterwards Corporal Meeke was commissioned into the Royal Army Medical Corps.

Private Alexander Hepburne Scott, an Oxford undergraduate, from Humbie, East Lothian, enlisted soon after the outbreak of war, went to France with the 1st London Scottish on 14 September 1914 and was at the actions at Messines and Zillebeke, both during First Ypres, and at Givenchy before having to go sick with catarrhal jaundice in January 1915 and being sent back to England. There he recovered quickly and was commissioned into the Scots Guards on 10 March. He returned to France on 15 April, joined the 2nd Scots Guards and was killed at Festubert on 16 May.

Private Guy Dawkins also went to France with the 1st London Scottish at the start and in addition to the battles in which Private Hepburne Scott took part was present at Cuinchy, Neuve Chapelle, Aubers and Festubert, by which time he was a Corporal. He was commissioned directly into the 1st Scots Guards in August 1915. Badly wounded at Loos with a broken left thigh bone, he returned the following spring, this time to the 2nd Scots Guards, and was mortally wounded in the attack on 15 September 1916 near Ginchy, on the Somme. Earlier that summer in the Ypres Salient he had come to the attention of the Rev. Tubby Clayton, who wrote very affectionately of him as an enthusiastic supporter of Talbot House, the soldiers' refuge he set up behind the lines at Poperinghe and forever known as Toc H.

13697 Private Andrew Buchanan was another Scots Guardsman who had been in The London Scottish. He came from Largs but was working as a National Insurance civil servant until he enlisted in March 1915. He went out to France on 3 October 1915 in the large draft sent after the heavy casualties early on at Loos and four days later went straight into the line to join the 1st Scots Guards in the trenches facing the Hohenzollern Redoubt. He was killed in the same attack on 15 September 1916 when Lieutenant Dawkins was mortally wounded.

In March 1918 a working party of prisoners left the main camp at Heuberg in the Black Forest to go to live and work on a farm. Among them were 5620 Private Henry

Butler of the 2nd Scots Guards, a Reservist, originally from Faversham, captured on 23 October 1914 during First Ypres, probably near Reutel, east of Polygon Wood, 84 Lance Corporal George Carlé of the 1st London Rifle Brigade and 5764 Private Richard Thompson of the 1st London Scottish. Both of them were captured on 1 July 1916 near Hébuterne in the failed attack on Gommecourt on the opening day of the Battle of the Somme. Lance Corporal Carlé had already made three unsuccessful escapes and Private Thompson two, in the second of which he very nearly reached Switzerland, being caught at the last moment. On 12 March they all walked out of the farm with as much food as they could carry, travelled, they estimated, 60 miles in two nights, hiding up by day, and crossed the Swiss frontier, where they were warmly welcomed and entertained by the landlady of the Gasthaus zum Post at Schleitheim.

The Caledonian Club

On the Roll of Honour of The Caledonian Club are the names of four Scots Guards officers. Three died during First Ypres and the fourth only a month before the Armistice.

Captain The Honourable Douglas Kinnaird, The Master of Kinnaird, and heir to the 11th Lord from Rossie Priory, Perthshire, was a serving officer in the 2nd Scots Guards and landed with them at Zeebrugge on 7 October when there was still some idea of rescuing Antwerp or facilitating the withdrawal from there, all rapidly overtaken by events. Ypres became their next definite destination and, as the Germans closed in there, he was killed during a counterattack towards the east side of Polygon Wood on 23 October, most of his Company having been killed or captured shortly before, including Private Butler, the escaper.

Captain Colin Campbell, also a serving soldier, whose father was a retired Scots Guards Major General, went out at the start with the 1st Scots Guards on 13 August. He had been in the Retreat from Mons and the Battle of the Aisne, as well as the battalion's first contact during First Ypres with the Germans near Langemarck. From 26 October onwards they were to the north of the Menin Road near Gheluvelt, and he died in the massive German attack on 29 October, which was just and only just held.

Lieutenant The Honourable Godfrey Macdonald, from Ostaig, Skye, served in the Boer War and then retired, later becoming a Special Reserve officer. He left England on 12 October 1914 and so first joined the 1st Scots Guards after the Aisne, arriving just before they became drawn into First Ypres. He was mortally wounded on 29 October, according to an eyewitness, himself about to be taken prisoner, who saw him bleeding to death. Both Captain Campbell and Lieutenant Macdonald were in B Company and close by when they died.

Captain William Ferryman was born in Edinburgh. He served in the ranks of the Volunteer Service Company with the 2nd Scottish Rifles in the Boer War. From 1903 he worked in South Africa. In 1916 he came home, was commissioned on 11 June and went to France in mid-August, but probably joined the 2nd Scots Guards only after the Somme battles in September. In February 1917 he was evacuated home with trench foot. Next he was badly gassed north of Ypres towards the end of July, when the battalion lost many men to gas, including for the first time mustard gas. Working parties were very vulnerable when gas shells landed. He returned to them in September.

On 12 October 1918 by when the Final Advance was progressing rapidly, the Germans being reduced to delaying tactics, though very unpleasant for those who had to face them, the 2nd Scots Guards were involved in a sharp fight at St Python, east of Cambrai, for which Lance Sergeant Harry Wood was awarded the Victoria Cross. Captain Tom Ross, the quartermaster of the battalion throughout the war, was on leave, and Captain Ferryman was standing in. He and eight men were in an unventilated cellar at St Hilaire, nearer Cambrai, when gas shells fell outside, probably Green Cross, of which phosgene was the main constituent. It seeped in while those in the cellar were unaware of their peril. All died, not quickly, from asphyxiation, Captain Ferryman at a nearby Field Ambulance.

St Columba's Pont Street Roll of Honour

The Roll of Honour at St Columba's has the names of five Scots Guardsmen who were members of the congregation and served in the Great War. Two lost their lives.

Lieutenant John Callender-Brodie was commissioned from Sandhurst in January 1915. He went out in mid-September to France before the Battle of Loos to join the 1st Scots Guards, but was rapidly attached instead to the 2nd Guards Brigade Machine Gun Company and with them until evacuated home on in February 1916 with shell shock. Thereafter he was ADC to the Governor of Western Australia for most of the rest of the war, never fit to return to the Western Front. His home was near Forfar.

5632 Private Alexander Garroway, born at Covington, Lanarkshire, who first enlisted in October 1904, was mobilized from the Reserve in August 1914 and went out at the start with the 1st Scots Guards. He was evacuated during the Retreat from Mons with "Sore Feet," not uncommon for reservists issued with new boots, and sent home to recover. In February he went to France again and was promoted in March. The battalion's casualties at the Battle of Aubers on 9 May 1915 were almost all from shelling and Sergeant Garroway was killed.

11382 Piper Donald McArthur from Stornoway was a wartime volunteer in September 1914. He joined the 1st Scots Guards in France and was posted missing as at 27 September 1915 during Loos, after the failed attack on the pit buildings, Puits 14 Bis, downhill to the north of Hill 70.

4999 Private Robert Moffatt, recorded as born at Galford, County Down, (probably Gilford), enlisted in Glasgow in 1903 and served for eight years. He married Margaret Pirie spinster on 4 September 1912, at St Columba's. Mobilised in 1914, he went abroad with the 1st Scots Guards on 13 August, his daughter Roberta having been born the day before. He was captured on 11 November during First Ypres, the battle in which the overwhelming majority of Scots Guardsmen who were POWs were taken prisoner. He was discharged in April 1919.

Viscount Dalrymple was commissioned in 1898 and served in the Boer War, leaving the Army a few years later. In 1914 he was MP for Wigtownshire, re-joined at once and went out with the 2nd Scots Guards to Zeebrugge. During First Ypres he was taken prisoner at Kruiseecke on 26 October 1914. From the spring of 1916 an agreement between the combatants on the Western Front came into effect, provided that the Swiss authorities were satisfied in each case, that those too badly injured or sick for future operational service might be interned in Switzerland. Initially British military internees were at Mürren, Château D'Oex or Leysin. For order and welfare purposes, though the internees were subject to Swiss military discipline, a number of more senior officer prisoners were permitted to go there too and Major The Earl of Stair, as he had become on his father's death in December 1914, was one. He was fortunate to be repatriated on 13 September 1917.

Crown Court, Covent Garden

At Crown Court the Roll of Honour has the names of five Scots Guardsmen and one Chaplain who served with the 2nd Scots Guards on the Western Front.

Lieutenant The Honourable Arthur Kinnaird was the third of the four Kinnaird brothers (not counting two that died in infancy). On the outbreak of war he enlisted in the Royal Fusiliers, was commissioned in April 1915 and from November became an ADC. He transferred in December 1916 and joined the 1st Scots Guards. While commanding C Company in the disastrous attack on Fontaine-Notre-Dame on 27 November 1917 during the Battle of Cambrai he was mortally wounded. Both the

Lieutenant The Honourable Arthur Kinnaird MC was a member of the 1st Battalion Scots Guards and the congregation of Crown Court as well as being a young governor of the Royal Scottish Corporation; he was mortally wounded on 27 November 1917, his elder brother, Douglas, having been killed three years earlier. (Courtesy of the Regimental Trustees Scots Guards)

other officers who went into action were hit, it being the practice since the Somme not to have more than three company officers in a major attack. Sergeant Jock McAulay took command, steadied a very dangerous situation, beat off a counterattack, carried Lieutenant Kinnaird some distance to cover, returned to C Company and held on until relieved. He was awarded the Victoria Cross.

7281 Piper William Grant, born at Abernethy, Inverness-shire, enlisted in 1908 and was with the 2nd Scots Guards when he was hit in the head and eye in the trenches at Rouges Bancs, north of Neuve Chapelle, on 17 November 1914, very soon after they first went into the line there. This was after the battalion had had to be reconstituted after First Ypres. He returned to France the following year but was found to be unfit on arrival and detailed for Permanent Base duties from then on. He was discharged in March 1919.

7263 Sergeant George Gray, from Glasgow, enlisted there in 1908. Little is known of him because his documents followed when he transferred on 31 July 1915 to the 20th Battalion The Middlesex Regiment, then still training in England, but he was wounded, not seriously, in the 2nd Scots Guards sometime in the late autumn of 1914, most likely in the trenches at Rouges Bancs. By February 1919 he was a Regimental Sergeant Major in the RAF.

7743 Pipe Major Andrew McIntosh was born at Killearnan on the Black Isle and enlisted in October 1910. He served as a piper in the 2nd Scots Guards from then on, went out with them to Zeebrugge in October 1914 and was in the battalion continuously. In the spring of 1918 he was sick from what was almost certainly the first onset of Spanish Flu and away for a month. When in Aldershot in 1922 he suffered a hernia, medically attributed as "Caused by excessive blowing of pipes."

The next name, Piper W. McPherson, is uncertain. The most likely person is 15014 Private William McPherson, a clerk at the Seafield Estates Office, Cullen, who enlisted in November 1915 in Aberdeen. He was with the 2nd Scots Guards for two months in the autumn of 1916 and was then sent home sick just before Christmas. This led to his medical discharge on account of phthisis, incurred because of his war service, in February 1917. That a soldier was a piper was not always shown on his documents.

The Rev. Alexander Macrae, Chaplain to the Forces, has an honoured name as

The Rev. Alexander MacRae at a camp near Poperinghe, Belgium, in Spring 1916; Chaplain to the 2nd Battalion Scots Guards, he was also a Corporation honorary chaplain. (Courtesy of the Regimental Trustees Scots Guards)

Minister of Crown Court, as Chaplain to the Royal Scottish Corporation and Royal Caledonian Asylum and from 1915 to 1917 as Padre of the 2nd Scots Guards. He was born and educated in Kingussie and first became a Church of Scotland Minister when licensed by the Presbytery of Lochcarron in 1885.

The Regimental Band

The Regimental Band were at Wellington Barracks, but reported to Regimental Headquarters. Because of the tight field security when the 1st Battalion left Ramillies Barracks, Aldershot, in the early morning of 13 August 1914 there was no fanfare and no music to see them off. Meanwhile the 2nd Battalion, stationed at the Tower of London and serving as a public duties battalion, waited to hear what was to happen next. Before the Retreat from Mons ended it was clear to the government and the War Office that more, many more, troops would be needed across the Channel. So the 7th Division, a new Regular Army division, began to form in the New Forest and the 2nd Scots Guards were ordered to leave London. On 5 September 1914 they marched to Waterloo Station and the Regimental Band played them out of the Tower. Two months later only one in five members of the battalion was still standing.

As they left the Tower Bandmaster Frederick Wood marched beside the Band. He had transferred to the Scots Guards in 1900 and was with them as Bandmaster and later, after he was commissioned in 1919, as Director of Music till 1929.

From soon after the formation of the Guards Division one of the Regimental Bands came out for several weeks at a time to stay with the Division and play for them. The first visit of the Scots Guards Band was from later on in May 1916 to the end of July. During this they went with the representative BEF Detachment to the Bastille Day Parade in Paris. The Detachment was under Lieutenant Colonel Roger Tempest, who commanded the 2nd Scots Guards, and was run by his battalion staff. The Pipes and Drums of both battalions went as well and caused a sensation.

The Regimental Band were again out from early in September 1917 to the end of the year and then finally in Cologne from just before Christmas 1918 till the Guards Division left for home in March 1919.

Separately, the Massed Bands of the Brigade of Guards visited Paris in May 1917 and Rome in February 1918.

Reflections

Captain Wilfrid Ewart served in the 2nd Scots Guards with intervals from early 1915. He was wounded in the leg at Neuve Chapelle, returned, but was then away sick in the summer of 1916, thus just missing the Somme. Finally, late in 1918 he was thrown from his horse and injured. He recorded his experiences in the BEF in *Scots Guard*, first published in 1934, long after his bizarre accidental death in Mexico City on

Captain Wilfrid Ewart served for much of the war in the 2nd Battalion Scots Guards and wrote afterwards that "There was beauty in pain, there was love in death, there was sacrifice in horror, and there seemed very often behind it all a curious, haunting laughter". (Courtesy of the Regimental Trustees Scots Guards)

the night of 31 December 1922. The later part of that book deals with varied ideas, subjects and travel reminiscences. Against the background of Thomas Hardy's poetry, which impressed him deeply, he wrote:

> Popular attitudes were carefully cultivated during the war – if you will, popular fictions. Some of them have been sedulously maintained since the war – adroitly adjusted to suit the necessities of the hour. They had their uses, no doubt – they kept up the fiction of light-heartedness, of sprightliness when, in fact, people's hearts were as heavy as lead. War for the participants was truly defined as: "Months of infinite boredom interspersed with moments of indescribable fear." War was falsely and shamly defined (by the halfpenny press and certain hearty optimists, lookers-on) as young men kicking footballs across no man's land, and as a series of Bairnsfather cartoons of muddy fellows who waxed facetious in the face of death. Others saw only the drab horror and sordid misery of it; others again a sort of spurious heroism based on a Victorian conception of what ought to be, dating from the Peninsular War and the traditions of Inkerman and the Alma, and ascribing to ordinary men the majestic attributes of superhumans. War, in point of fact and upon a more intimate acquaintance, resolved itself into the moral struggle of ordinary mortals against extraordinary forces – of men who grumbled, who were frightened, who got tired and felt ill, who hated

lice and wet feet, who hated cold, mud, tinned food, and discomfort generally, yet were pitted through four-and-a-half years against an Unknown comprising inscrutable powers of Irony and Fate, a perpetual threat, physical degradation and mental torture, and were enmeshed in a web of Destiny from which some lucky star alone could extricate them.

There was beauty in pain, there was love in death, there was sacrifice in horror, and there seemed very often behind it all a curious, haunting laughter. In these years past the only philosophy capable of maintaining a man was the watchword: "What must be must be." Once he lost his grip of this, once let himself think that the future could be eluded or fate cheated, and – himself was lost. The war was ordained for mankind, and mankind had to go through with it for larger and undisclosed purposes, to high and beneficent ends as some say, blindly and fruitlessly according to others.

Bruce Bairnsfather had direct experience of the primitive nature of trench life in the first winter of the war as an officer of the Royal Warwickshire Regiment. To someone who had no direct knowledge of the Western Front who took these drawings at face value Wilfrid Ewart's comment is applicable. To someone who knew and to anybody else with the imagination, these cartoons, wittily and cleverly observed, were very close to the mark, with sufficient hints and tones of the ridiculous to make the awful reality human and the cartoons enjoyable. It is not surprising that "Old Bill," the central character, was such a popular figure with soldiers, because they identified with him.

Humour matters to morale and humour matters to *esprit de corps*. It was those who could see the funny side when there was one, those who could laugh at the preposterous and those who could relax the tensions for others who were themselves most able to cope.

12

Sir Douglas Haig, Religion, and the British Expeditionary Force on the Western Front

Michael Snape

Perhaps the most controversial name associated with St Columba's is that of Sir Douglas Haig (1861–1928). Subsequently Earl Haig of Bemersyde, Haig's relatively brief years as an elder at St Columba's produced some colourful local anecdotes: of the English chauffeur and war veteran, whose faith was lost in the maelstrom of war, only to be found again when he recognised Haig administering the Communion Cup to his Scottish wife. Likewise, the scene of Haig standing next to a humble coachman on the chancel steps, as both were ordained to the Eldership. However touching and picturesque these ecclesiastical vignettes, the fact remains that, while Commander-in Chief of the British Expeditionary Force (or BEF) on the Western Front from late 1915 to the Armistice, Haig presided over the bloodiest battles in the annals of the British Army and, indeed, the British Empire.

A naturally divisive figure (at least outside St. Columba's), Haig has been bitterly condemned and traduced by some (not least, after his death in 1928, by the former wartime Prime Minister David Lloyd George), but firmly and forthrightly defended by others. Given the scale of the slaughter that occurred on the Somme in 1916, around Arras, Ypres and Cambrai in 1917, and on the Western Front during the climactic year of 1918, military historians remain deeply divided over the question of Haig's basic competence as a general, and how well he coped with the scale of the tactical, strategic, and political challenges he faced. Whether billed as a blundering butcher, or as the steady architect of victory, as a callous Olympian warlord or as an enlightened and dogged champion of veterans' rights, few aspects of Haig's character have escaped scrutiny by hostile or sympathetic historians. As the secularisation of British society accelerated in the later decades of the 20th century (and especially from the "long" 1960s, which re-ignited old controversies around the 50th anniversary of the war), the religious aspect of Haig's character and command has been less and less understood, and increasingly side-stepped by wary historians uncomfortable with the nature and character of Haig's religious worldview, deeply influenced as it was by

Biblicism, Calvinism, patriotism, and by the postmillenarian outlook of progressive, late Victorian Protestant theology. While (quite naturally) none of these are easy issues for military historians of an increasingly secular and liberal age to comprehend and appreciate, this essay represents an attempt to place Haig's religious beliefs and convictions in a much wider context, and to dispel the suspicions of dangerous eccentricity that have lingered over the reputation of Haig as a Christian commander.

Haig's Personal Faith

Prior to assuming command of the BEF in December 1915, Haig's religious beliefs and behaviour seem, at first sight, to be somewhat lax. As J. P. Harris has remarked, "until he took supreme

Field-Marshal Sir Douglas Haig, KT GCB GCVO KCIE Commander-in-Chief, France, from 15 December 1915; here painted by Sir William Orpen RA at General Headquarters, 30 May 1917. (© IWM Art.IWM ART 324)

command on the Western Front [Haig's] Christian observance seemed to contemporaries to be of a formal rather than of a particularly personal or passionate kind." However, and though aged 54 when he took command, Haig still bore the religious imprint of his childhood years, and of the influence of his strongly Presbyterian mother, Rachel. Described by his wife Dorothy as "perhaps the most abiding and powerful influence on his whole life," under the tutelage of Rachel he had developed a habit of prayer, a sense of divine oversight, and a marked familiarity with the Bible from an early age; in fact, part of his mother's regime required that he send her written commentaries on designated passages of scripture every week whilst he was away at boarding school. Despite her careful Presbyterian training, Rachel died in 1879, a year before Douglas went up to Oxford, and long before he entered Sandhurst in 1884. Consequently, Haig attended Church of England services for much of his adolescent and adult life, a natural result of the Anglican milieu of his preparatory school, of Clifton College, of his student days at Brasenose, and of the practicalities of army life in England, the Sudan, South Africa and India. As a confident and ambitious undergraduate at Oxford, and with an attitude very different from his later years, Haig had even declared: "It all depends on a man himself how he gets on in any profession. If I went into the Church I'd be a Bishop." Haig's adherence to the English Church was not coldly calculating or merely mercenary. Ever since the Act of Union of 1707, in the British Isles and in the wider Empire, Britain's military and civilian elite had to negotiate the awkward reality of two very different established churches in England and Scotland. Consequently, among army officers it was quite conventional to attend the established Church of the kingdom in which they were stationed— a practice followed, for example, by the Anglican James Wolfe, the future hero of Quebec, when serving in Scotland in the 1740s and '50s. Indeed, Queen Victoria herself provided an illustration of how even the Supreme Governor of the Church of England could be a practising Anglican whilst in England, and a practising Presbyterian whilst in Scotland. Such pragmatism in denominational matters may well have fostered Haig's distinctive, and even enthusiastic, brand of ecumenism. In a telling anecdote, the BEF's senior Jewish chaplain, Michael Adler, remembered being with an Australian brigade, and its two Christian chaplains, when it was unexpectedly visited by Haig in the spring of 1916. As Adler remembered:

> We three Chaplains stood at the end of the line, and Sir Douglas rode up to us and, shaking hands, asked which denominations we represented. "I am glad to see you working so well together," he said, "as you can help us greatly by teaching the men about the noble cause for which we are fighting."

Unconcerned by denominational niceties in early life, Haig's natural wariness of denominationalism appears to have grown under the impact of the First World War. When the Archbishop of York, Cosmo Lang, visited General Headquarters (GHQ) in July 1917, Haig spoke fondly of his vision of "a great Imperial Church to which all honest citizens of the Empire could belong ... Church and State must advance together, and hold together against those forces of revolution which threaten to destroy the State." After the war, and now increasingly fearful of a Russian-style revolution, Haig could envisage no alternative to an even closer integration of church and state, and in April 1919, in a meeting with King George V, even urged upon him the need "to press for the formation of a great-minded Imperial Church to embrace all our Churches except the Roman Catholics." The rationale, he pleaded, was urgent and obvious:

> This would be the means of binding the empire together ... Empires of the past had disappeared because there was no church or religion to bind them together. The British Empire will assuredly share the same fate at no distant date unless an Imperial Church is speedily created to unite us all in the service of God.

Haig pursued this argument in Edinburgh the following month, where he spoke as "an honoured guest" at the General Assembly of the Church of Scotland and addressed a meeting of former army chaplains. Although little more than a pipe dream in practical terms, Haig cherished this vision of the ecclesiastical future of the Empire until his death in 1928. In fact, in 1927 his support for far-reaching church reform caused Haig to cast his vote in the House of Lords in favour of the Church of England's Revised Prayer Book, despite its rather Catholic undertones, being under the firm conviction that "if the Church of England wished to carry out a much-needed reform, it would be in the best interests of both Church and State that it should be left free to do so."

If Haig's pre-war and essentially pragmatic non-denominationalism was by no means eccentric by the standards of his profession and social milieu, this was also true of his pre-war dabbling in Spiritualism, an interest encouraged by his youngest sister, Henrietta Jameson, of whom he was especially fond. In a manner that prefigured his later tendency to harness supernatural power in support of his military career, in one séance at the time of the Haldane reforms Haig dutifully sought advice on the best means of augmenting the newly created Territorial Force. Thus encouraged, the medium assured Haig of the benign interest in his career of "a small man named Napoleon [who] had become changed for the better in the spirit world." More characteristic of Haig's religious outlook, of his Scottish Presbyterian heritage, and of the political tensions of the time (especially around Home Rule and the wartime neutrality of Pope Benedict XV), was his abiding suspicion of the Church of Rome and many (though not all) of its representatives. An enthusiastic returnee to a church whose Church and Nation Committee produced the infamous 1923 report *The Menace of the Irish Race to our Scottish Nationality*, Haig's prejudices (though more circumspect) were quite characteristic of this milieu. In August 1918, and with his ecumenical hackles raised, Haig noted in his personal diary his strong disapproval of the absence of Catholic chaplains from a joint religious service he had sponsored at GHQ. Nor was he impressed by his encounter with Cardinal Francis Bourne in October 1917, of whom he wrote:

> His Eminence Cardinal Bourne from Westminster accompanied by the Rev. B. Rawlinson [the BEF's senior Catholic chaplain] came to dinner. The Cardinal is neither eminent in appearance or in conversation but I expect means well. On the other hand Rawlinson is a most agreeable fellow and seems to have all the qualities of an efficient Jesuit Father! He acts as an assistant to the Rev. Dr Simms who is Principal Chaplain in France.

Haig was wrong on one minor detail: Rawlinson was a Benedictine, not a Jesuit. More significantly, especially in terms of his military reputation, less than a week earlier, and amidst the costly disappointments of the Third Battle of Ypres, Haig had shrugged off accurate if discouraging intelligence reports with the words, "I cannot think why the War Office Intelligence Dept. gives such a wrong picture of the situation except that Gen. Macdonagh … is a Roman Catholic and is (unconsciously) influenced by information which doubtless reaches him from tainted (i.e. Catholic) sources." Similarly, and following the eruption of the German spring offensive on 21 March 1918, Haig voiced some rather crass suspicions as to the reliability of Irish Catholic troops with a harsh assessment of the conduct of the 16th Division, writing in his diary the following day: "Our 16th (Irish) Division … is said not to be so full of fight as the others. In fact, certain Irish units did very badly and gave way immediately the enemy showed." The irony was that, at this stage of the war, recruitment from

Ireland had virtually dried up, and the Division was barely a shadow of its original, Irish and Catholic self.

Although Henrietta continued to encourage her brother with the interest and influence of Napoleon as late as June 1916 (by which time he had been deputed by God to serve Haig in an advisory capacity), Haig's religious outlook had already assumed its earnest and more orthodox wartime form. Haig's new religious seriousness was evident as early as December 1914, when his promotion to command of the BEF's First Army nourished an emerging sense that a "higher power" was overseeing his career. This conviction seemed to deepen over the period of his command. In autumn 1915, and besides praising the work of his chaplains before the Battle of Loos, during that same battle Haig visited the headquarters of Hubert Gough, then one of his corps commanders, and admonished him with the words of Zechariah 4:6 "'Not by might nor by power, but by My Spirit', saith the Lord of hosts." By the time Haig succeeded Sir John French as Commander-in-Chief of the BEF in December 1915, he had arrived at two key conclusions that were to shape his approach to his new command and to what J. P. Harris termed its "truly awesome responsibilities." First, that God had appointed him to this momentous role and, second, that providence would ensure his ultimate success. As Haig confided to his wife, "[A]ll seem to expect success as the result of my arrival, and somehow give me the idea that I am 'meant to win' by some Superior Power." And nor did this conviction diminish in subsequent months and years. According to John Charteris, Haig's Chief Intelligence Officer, a fellow Scot and a son of the manse, by 1918 it seemed perfectly clear that Haig regarded himself "with almost Calvinistic faith as the predestined instrument of Providence for the achievement of victory for the British Armies."

If Haig had acquired a firm belief in divine providence and in his own unique calling by the time he assumed command of the BEF, within a few short weeks at St Omer he had stumbled upon a young and like-minded prophet in the Rev. George S. Duncan, a junior Presbyterian chaplain at GHQ, who became Haig's "faithful chaplain" for the remainder of the war. In fact, as early as May 1916, Archbishop Davidson rather warily noted that "[Haig] has himself a great affection for the Presbyterian Chaplain, Duncan, who is attached to Headquarters, and whose ministry Haig himself, who I suppose is a semi-Presbyterian, often attends." By his own admission, Duncan was an academic whose pastoral experience was practically nil, having spent the years 1902 to 1914 at "various universities" including Edinburgh, Cambridge, St Andrews, and Heidelberg, where he was studying as a postgraduate as late as July 1914. Ordained in 1915 after being offered a temporary commission as a chaplain, Duncan conceded in retrospect that few chaplains were less qualified than him for the work into which he was flung. Nevertheless, Haig plainly perceived a kindred spirit in the young chaplain's preaching and demeanour. Significantly, the two crossed paths on 2 January 1916, the first Sunday of the new year, which the King had designated a national day of prayer. Although the setting was "a small dingy concert-hall" in St Omer, Duncan observed the occasion with "all due solemnity," and his sermon on prayer made an instant and indelible impression on the Commander in Chief. Already wearying of the Church of England, which he thought to be "divided against itself," and whose chaplains he regarded as riven by a "disgraceful" spirit of partisanship "instead of giving us a noble example of unity and good fellowship," Haig was galvanised by Duncan's earnest and forthright manner, which he revealingly admired as "most earnest and impressive:-quite after the old Covenanting style." According to Duncan, in 1917 Haig made a rather provocative claim to the visiting Archbishop of York, a Presbyterian who had become an Anglican:

> I told him … that before I was made Com. in Chief I used always to go round [i.e. to the Church of England]: and that for 3 Sundays or so afterwards I did so out here: [and] one fellow told me what to do with our spare money, but it was only Duncan who told us straight what we ought to do and to be regarding the big things of the present.

It was not, however, a rancorous meeting, for Duncan later recalled that Haig had been "much drawn" to the Archbishop, whom he remembered from his Oxford days, and who seemed "open-minded and sympathetic" to the idea of post-war church reform. He had also "spoken very frankly to the Archbishop about the reasons why he now always attended the Church of Scotland service." As Haig had put it: "I told him how disappointed I had been with some C of E services I had attended. Chaplains ought to deal seriously with the great issues confronting us, and do so in a way that people understand."

If Duncan's emphasis on providence and prayer struck exactly the right chord with Haig, Duncan's example certainly contributed to Haig's emerging vision of the role of the British Army chaplain, which he was to act upon in the coming months. As Haig recalled of their first encounter:

> [Duncan] told us that in our prayers we should be as natural as possible, and tell the Almighty exactly what we feel we want. The Nation is now learning to pray! And that nothing can withstand the prayers of a great united people … The congregation was greatly impressed, and one could have heard a pin fall during his prayers and sermon. So different to the coughing and restlessness which goes on in church in peace time.

Over time, Haig was to grow increasingly reliant on Duncan's sermons, and on their "fine manly Christianity," for both solace and inspiration. As Duncan recalled of this early phase of their developing relationship:

> [Haig] continued to come, not just occasionally, but Sunday by Sunday; and if on any Sunday he was not in his place, it was because he was absent from GHQ. At the end of March 1916 he transferred his headquarters from St Omer to Montreuil; and I found to my surprise that I was to be one of those who were to go there.

With the clear collusion of Dr Simms, the senior Presbyterian minister on the Western Front, Duncan became "generally accepted (unofficially) as the Commander-in-Chief's chaplain." At the beginning of the Third Battle of Ypres in 1917, and alarmed by Duncan's request that he be relieved and moved closer to the front line, Simms wrote in highly revealing terms: "I beg of you to steady your brain. I look on you as a gift of God to our great Chief. Do you not think that that is duty grand enough for any chaplain, to stay & strengthen & uphold his hands in this titanic struggle?" As Simms implied, by this point (August 1917) it appeared that Duncan's support for Haig was analogous to Aaron's support for Moses in Israel's battle against the Amalekites (Exodus 17). As Simms put it in a subsequent letter to Duncan:

> I feel very sure that Aaron had no greatness of conscience as to the propriety of his actions when he st[oo]d on the mountain top upholding his great leader's arms while the battle raged below. Stay & strengthen your soul with that old world story. No one in this Campaign has the sacred claim to our very best as [does] our Chief, for he bears a well nigh crushing burden, & I bless God day and night that he has found a chaplain who he is not afraid to say does help him to bear up under this load. And how mortal man can desire a better, nobler, greater task for his war work I cannot imagine. That the man he delights to honour is a Presbyterian is to me a double cause of thanksgiving for I look upon it as the noblest, strongest form of religious influence that I know on this earth.

By this point, Haig saw in Duncan the epitome of what he wished British Army chaplains to be. In fact, he had a knack of describing Duncan as somebody who "could make anyone fight," and it was with these pointed words that he introduced Duncan to US General John J. Pershing in July 1917. Indeed, it was probably with this thought in mind that, from time to time, Haig released Duncan for temporary service closer to the front line, notably during the 1917 Battles of Arras, Messines and Third Ypres. However, this was not at the cost of losing Duncan's services indefinitely and, for the Somme and the Arras offensives, Duncan was duly posted to Haig's advanced headquarters at Beauquesnes and Bavincourt respectively. In 1917, and as Haig's capacity for command was thrown into question by a succession of stalled offensives and by the evident mistrust of Prime Minister Lloyd George, his relationship to Duncan grew closer still. As Duncan remembered, "During those anxious and arduous months in 1917 my relations with Haig, always pleasant, became much more intimate and personal." By the end of that troubled year, Haig was allowing Duncan to peruse portions of his diary, in which Haig was liable to record his religious reflections on the current situation. Following the Armistice, and in a very personal gesture of gratitude, Haig presented Duncan with a large personal portrait, which soon found its way onto the wall of the vestry of the Scottish Churches Hut at Montreuil, where Haig had worshipped Sunday by Sunday since 1916. The inscription read: "To the Rev. G. S. Duncan, my chaplain 1916 to the end, in all gratitude. D. Haig, F-M. Christmas 1918."

Although Duncan observed that Haig was deeply reluctant to partake in Holy Communion, possibly because his intensely private temperament may have baulked at the public declaration of faith the Church of Scotland required of its communicants, the Bible featured heavily in sustaining Haig's deeply personal, theologically unsophisticated and supremely practical religious faith. Although Haig had been steeped in the Bible as a child, his familiarity with scripture was by no means unusual, for a respectable knowledge of the Bible was, as Duncan rightly stressed, simply part of "an intelligent person's education" rather than the mark of a fanatic. Indeed, it was not unheard of for military figures to be amateur biblical scholars in their own right, an example being the originator of Britain's dreadnought fleet, Admiral Sir John Fisher, whose knowledge of the Bible was held to be "prodigious." However, it was the teachings rather than the text of the Bible that made the impression on Haig. According to Duncan:

> [The Bible] influenced, perhaps unconsciously, both his ways of speech and his general outlook, without necessarily implying that he knew much about its origins or its theology. I have no reason to think that Haig's knowledge of the Bible was either profound or extensive. He certainly gained from it a sense of the divine Presence and Power; and this assurance meant much to him. In a broad general sense he valued it especially for the deep seriousness that characterised its message from the beginning to the end, and for the light which it shed for him on the whole duty of man.

If Duncan may not have considered Haig's knowledge of scripture to have been particularly extensive, we must of course recognise that Duncan's judgment was informed by the Olympian standards of a Scottish Presbyterian minister and biblical scholar. Indeed, it is hard not to discern in Deuteronomy 20:1–4 the scriptural grounds of Haig's 1916 re-conception of British Army chaplaincy:

> When thou goest out to battle against thine enemies, and seest horses, and chariots, and a people more than thou, be not afraid of them: for the LORD thy God is with thee, which brought thee up out of the land of Egypt. And it shall be, when ye are come nigh unto the battle, that the priest shall approach and speak unto the people, And shall say unto them, Hear O Israel, ye approach this day unto battle against your enemies: let not your hearts faint, fear not, and do not tremble, neither be ye terrified because of them; for the LORD your God is he that goeth with you, to fight for you against your enemies, to save you.

While it probably influenced his policy on padres, the Bible also served as a great source of personal consolation to Haig while Commander-in-Chief, and he frequently reflected on its contents, both in his diary and to a select body of confidants. For example, at the height of the Third Battle of Ypres in the autumn of 1917, and in light of Duncan's sermon on Luke 22:41–43 ("And he was withdrawn from them about a stone's cast, and kneeled down, and prayed, Saying, Father, if thou be willing, remove this cup from me: nevertheless not my will, but thine, be done. And there appeared an angel unto him from heaven, strengthening him") Haig insisted that "When things are difficult, there is no reason to be downhearted. We must do our best, and *for a certainty* a ministering angel will help." A further, more obscure, text proved a handy spiritual crutch during the massive German offensives of the following year. Spoken to King Jehoshaphat of Judah when faced by a coalition of Moabites and Ammonites, the words of 2 Chronicles 20.15 seemed especially pertinent to the beleaguered position of the BEF: "Thus saith the LORD unto you, Be not afraid nor dismayed by reason of this great multitude; for the battle is not yours, but God's." Significantly, Haig invoked these words both before and during this crisis, alluding to them in a letter to his wife in February of that year, and admonishing Duncan with them on the bleak morning of Sunday 24 March, when much of the BEF was in headlong retreat. Seven months later, and in the more favourable circumstances of impending Allied victory, Haig was tempted to draw a further comparison, this time between the fate of Imperial Germany and the humbling of Assyria, writing in his diary on 20 October: "Colonel Wigram … states that a telegram just rec'd states that cholera in a bad form has broken out in Berlin. It looks as if the prophecy of II Kings is to be fulfilled re the Assyrians being slain in battle and many thousands by the Lord in pestilence!"

Fed by Duncan, by Holy Writ, and by his own sense of divine calling, Haig's piety also set the tone for his senior staff officers, and for the sober and Spartan mood of GHQ. Described by Duncan as "monastic" in temper, not least because of Haig's immediate ban on female visitors, the prevailing mood was nonetheless more of the kirk than the cloister. For example, in April 1917 Charteris tellingly described one Sabbath day as "a regular Scottish Sunday," in which he and Haig discussed the day's sermon "as one used to do as a boy in Scotland." Given that Haig lived the lifestyle of a respectable Lowland laird, it is hardly surprising that at least one senior staff officer, the artilleryman J.F. Birch, opted to abandon the Church of England for the Church of Scotland for the duration. Even amidst the turmoil of the German spring offensive of 1918, Haig diligently attended church, and Duncan even confessed some surprise at seeing his car appear, "as usual," on the Sunday after the storm had finally broken. Furthermore, and with his great counter-offensive at hand, Haig sanctioned a special service of thanksgiving at GHQ on Sunday 4 August, one that would correspond with a national day of prayer marking the fourth anniversary of Britain's declaration of war. Conceived by Duncan and his Anglican colleague, J.N. Bateman Champain, "Haig received the proposal with enthusiasm." Not only that, but as Charteris noted:

> [Haig] summoned the appropriate Staff Officers and directed them to make arrangements for a Special Thanksgiving Service to be held at Montreuil on August 4th to give thanks to God for the guidance of Providence which had brought the Empire and the Army through these four years of toil and strain, and to entreat that it might not be withdrawn until final success crowned their efforts.

The theme of this service was, of course, emblematic of Haig's deep sense of divine purpose and of his ultimate reliance on God. Although considered to have been typically uncommunicative on matters of faith, even in private conversation or correspondence, Haig's closest associates were under no illusion as to the influence which his faith had upon him. In 1916, on the eve of the Somme offensive, Haig wrote to his wife:

> I note what you wrote in Tuesday's letter that 'for this coming offensive ask for God's help.' Now you must know that *I feel* that every step in my plan has been taken with the Divine help and I ask daily for aid, not merely in making the plan, but in carrying it out, and this I hope I shall continue to do until the end of all things which concern me on earth. I think it is the Divine help which gives me tranquillity of mind and enables me to carry on without feeling the strain of responsibility to be too excessive ...

Following early successes in the Battle of Arras the following April, he again confided to her:

> As to the Battle of Arras, I know quite well that I am being used as a tool in the hands of the Divine Power, so I am not at all conceited, and you may rest assured that I am not likely to forget to whom belongs the honour and glory for all our good work and success.

Nor was Duncan disposed to question this certainty. On the contrary, in April 1918, he sent Haig a timely message reminding him that "There is no man under heaven for whom these days a greater volume of prayer ascends to heaven than for you. May the knowledge of that strengthen you." Haig's reply was characteristic: "I am very grateful for your thinking of me at this time, and *I know* I am sustained in my efforts by that Great Unseen Power, otherwise I could not be standing the strain as I am doing."

Inevitably, his profound and unshakeable conviction that he was simply an instrument of divine providence has become a matter of controversy between Haig's many critics and admirers. Even his friends could be unsettled by its persistence and implications. Charteris, for example, was wary of its "fatalistic" undertones and remarked that, because the outcome of the war was unclear, the same providential discourse which Haig found so inspiring could just as easily have fortified Hindenburg. Furthermore, the historian Gerard DeGroot has rightly drawn attention to the emphasis on the sacrificial, purgative and regenerative aspects of war which featured in Duncan's preaching. Although the precise texts of Duncan's sermons have not survived, such themes were commonly expounded by British Army chaplains of the day. Furthermore, it is quite possible that Haig derived from these sermons (whose thrust he routinely summarised in his diary) the problematic understanding that human suffering was fundamentally purposive, and tended towards higher ends. For example, on 21 October 1917, Haig wrote in his diary:

At 9.30 am I attended Church of Scotland. The Rev. Capt. Duncan officiated. He preached on a passage in the Psalms [Psalm 78] which speaks of the "God of our Fathers" and urges the children of Israel to "teach this" (the story of how God had delivered them) "to your children" … We too must, he said. Place on record how God is now delivering us, just as he did our forefathers in the days of Napoleon. He truly is a *living* God.

A month later, Haig recorded in the aftermath of Third Ypres:

I attended Church of Scotland at 0930 am. The Rev Duncan officiated: he took as his text a chapter of the Acts. Christ never spoke to his disciples of dying but He said "When I leave you I will send my Comforter to you, and he will go with thee wheresoever thou goest." This is the spirit of the Lord Jesus …

In light of such evidence, DeGroot has criticised Haig for being too inclined to rely on blind faith rather than hard evidence in his overall vision of the war. As DeGroot put it,

Haig's religious faith did occasionally obscure the real war. If intelligence from the front conflicted with his vision of the war, he often either ignored or subconsciously misinterpreted it … With the end predetermined, events along the way diminished in importance. If data was occasionally ignored, it was because Haig believed that the goodness of God was the most reliable indicator of the way the war would be resolved.

Nevertheless, even DeGroot ultimately conceded the "sad fact," as he termed it, that "in order to win, Britain needed Haig and Haig needed religion." Seen from this perspective, Haig's religious faith was an asset to the British war effort, a personal gift that enabled him to rise above all military and political adversity until final victory was attained in November 1918.

Still, more hostile critics have seen things differently, arguing that the depth and nature of Haig's personal faith necessarily weakened the competence of his command. According to Basil Liddell Hart, who did much to shape posterity's impressions of British generalship in the First World War, Haig's faith served to preclude a sober and objective handling of the BEF on the Western Front. Furthermore, for Denis Winter, one of the shrillest of Haig's critics, the maturation of Haig's religious views during the war represented "an unhealthy development in a man already tending towards delusions of infallibility." Nevertheless, from Duncan's unique vantage point, and even after the passage of half a century, Haig's case did not amount to a particularly crass and dangerous example of spiritual presumption. According to Duncan, Haig's understanding of his own situation in the providential ordering of human affairs was held "in all humility, not out of egotism or wishful thinking, but with a sober grasp of the situation as he saw it." In fact, Duncan flatly confronted and rejected the suggestion that a colossal spiritual conceit had closed Haig's mind and warped his military judgement. As Duncan saw it, Haig's convictions had scriptural and historic precedents on their side:

> With some men, no doubt, belief in a divine "call" leads easily to fanaticism. But Haig was no fanatic. There was about him a mental balance which was associated not a little with his stern sense of duty; and like other devout men down the ages he heard in the call of duty the voice of God. He takes his place with those heroic figures (like Moses and Joshua in the Scripture records, or like Cromwell and Lincoln in the story of the nations) who in some critical hour of history begin by recognising the need for action in the situation which confronts them, and then, in a spirit of obedience and faith in God, find themselves braced to meet it with courage and resolution, and in so doing draw strength from unseen sources.

In justice to Haig, it must be stressed that he was by no means unique in being sustained by a providential conception of his role in the war. In a remarkable entry in his personal diary, Bishop Llewellyn Henry Gwynne, the senior Anglican chaplain on the Western Front, wrote of a telling encounter with Sir Julian Byng in September 1917. Appointed to the command of Third Army only three months earlier, Byng's promotion clearly struck a religious chord, and he was confirmed as an Anglican early in 1918. Of their meeting the previous autumn, Gwynne noted that:

> It was quite a short interview but that gave me an insight into what some of our best believe. He began by asking whether I thought that the clergy were seeing the great vision of what was in front of them – the great difficulties and at the same time the grand prospects. He also went on to say that even this great material force was an expression of the spiritual power behind the material and thought that all the big men here were called out by God for this work; that God gave him his present job and though he did not feel big enough or good enough for it, he felt he had a claim on God for equipment for the work given to him. I came away feeling that if this is the spirit of our leaders then we need have no fear about the ultimate victory.

If Byng testified to the presence of similar sentiments among senior commanders of the British Army, a much more public example was that of US President Woodrow Wilson. The most influential Presbyterian layman of his day, Wilson's worldview, like Haig's, was founded on a supreme confidence in the justice and righteousness of God and a profound belief in the moral ordering of the universe. Despite his background as president of Princeton University, a historic bastion of American Presbyterianism, Wilson had no interest in abstruse theological speculation, had no inclination to share his religious experiences, and was quite happy to worship on alternate Sundays with his Episcopalian second wife, Edith Bolling Galt. Like Haig's, Wilson's faith was also expressed in simple terms. As one biographer has put it, "in matters of basic Christian faith, Wilson was like a little child, never doubting, always believing, and drawing spiritual sustenance from Bible reading, church attendance, and prayer." Nevertheless, Wilson's supposedly childlike personal faith was of enormous national and international significance, driving his political and presidential career, mandating his push for war in 1917, and underpinning his (ultimately fruitless) attempt to shape a new world order through the Treaty of Versailles and the League of Nations. Nor, it must be said, was Haig's intimate relationship with Duncan necessarily exceptional. Byng's conversation with Gwynne is symptomatic of the way in which a number of Allied generals were prepared to unburden themselves to trusted chaplains. As Alistair Horne pointed out in his 1962 classic *The Price of Glory*, France's "fighting friar," General Noël Marie Joseph Edouard, Vicomte de Currières de Castelnau, who took the fateful decision to defend Verdun, always had a "private chaplain" in his entourage, in his case a Jesuit priest who was also his nephew. Furthermore, Bishop Charles Henry Brent played an identical role for General John J. Pershing, Commander-in-Chief of the American Expeditionary Force in France. Not only did Pershing regard Brent as his "spiritual adviser," but Brent was perfectly prepared to admonish Pershing over his approach to command: "I told the C. in C. that in times of anxiety he had the right and the duty if we considered this to be a righteous war to throw himself on God. He said he did so."

Haig and His Chaplains

Evidently, Haig's faith influenced his conduct of the war at several levels, from the way in which he ordered his headquarters, to the providential context in which he understood the course of the war. However, its most lasting institutional legacy was the way in which it helped to redefine the role of the British Army chaplain. Throughout the tenure of Sir John French, Haig's predecessor as Commander-in-Chief of the BEF, the role of the growing number of clergymen serving as army chaplains in France and Belgium had been fraught with controversy. Besides the customary in-fighting among Anglican chaplains of different church parties and their civilian sponsors, and tensions between the Church of England and the Church of Scotland over perceptions of Anglican privilege, chaplains of every stripe had been subject to a notional ban on ministering in the front line. Curiously, the exact origin of this prohibition remained (and remains) elusive, although enquiries undertaken by the Archbishop of Canterbury, Randall Davidson, seemed to point in the direction of the forceful and opinionated Lord Kitchener, then Secretary of State for War. However, and in Kitchener's defence, for 50 years chaplains had been classified as ambulance personnel under the Geneva Convention, their unrestricted presence as non-combatants in the front-line trenches posed an additional strain on logistics, and the prospect of dead clergymen littering the battlefield was naturally anticipated as bad for morale. Although this prohibition was widely resented, and often violated by individuals, it was Haig's arrival as Commander-in-Chief which gave chaplaincy in the BEF a new mission, new freedom of action, and a new sense of purpose.

Closely reflecting Haig's developing relationship with Duncan, and coterminous with the introduction of conscription in mainland Britain, from the early weeks of 1916 Haig placed an increasing and explicit emphasis on the role of the chaplain as a morale-builder for the British Army's citizen soldiers. Shortly after assuming command of the BEF, Haig invited Bishop Gwynne to dine at GHQ and, once there, assured him that "A good chaplain is as valuable as a good general." He also marked his approval of Gwynne's efforts to date by having his Christmas sermon printed and distributed among the troops. Moreover, Haig declared to his guest that "no one could do more than a chaplain to sustain morale and explain what our Empire is fighting for," and he urged Gwynne to dismiss chaplains whom he thought were lacking in "spiritual force." Haig himself noted of their conversation: "I spoke to him regarding the importance of sending a message to all the clergy to preach of the great object of the war viz. the freedom of mankind from German tyranny." The chaplains, so Haig thought, "were too narrow in their views. They must be enthusiasts to do good." Haig made his views known to a wider audience during a conference of army commanders at Cassel on 15 January 1916. According to Haig, here it was agreed that:

> Every effort must be made to raise the "moral" [sic] of the troops. Amusements, games, etc. etc. must be organised. I also called attention to the large number of clergymen who are now being sent to join the army. Army commanders must look to the efficiency of these men as well as to any other part of their commands. We must have large minded, sympathetic men as Parsons, who realise the *Great Cause* for which we are fighting, and can imbue their hearers with enthusiasm.
> Any clergyman who is not fit for this work must be sent home.

Undoubtedly, this marked a major development in the British Army's policy towards its chaplains. Hitherto, they had only been obliged to discharge their official functions (as prescribed in King's Regulations) of leading religious services and burying the dead. In addition, since the previous winter on the Western Front, they had been widely expected to provide entertainment and to ensure the well-being of troops when out of the line. The role of the chaplain as elaborated by Haig at Cassel was essentially open-ended, with no clear limit being placed on their potential usefulness.

The effects of this new dispensation became apparent in succeeding months, and especially in the protracted preparations for the Battle of the Somme. Of his visit to Haig's GHQ at Montreuil in May 1916, Archbishop Davidson wrote:

> I found Haig rather shy and difficult to talk to at first, but when he thawed he was delightful in his quiet, earnest frankness of conversation. I pressed him for criticism about the work of the chaplains, but I could not elicit anything except laudation. He was strong on the great value of the changed administrative order which now encourages the chaplains to go forward into the trenches, if they will do so, instead of being, as formerly, kept behind at the casualty clearing stations,

Earl Haig features in the centre of this 1923 caricature of members of the Caledonian Club during the war; St Columba's minister Archibald Fleming, chaplain to both the Corporation and the London Scottish Regiment, is depicted on the left. Haig was in later years an elder at St Columba's and would lie in state there. (*The Sketch*, 21 November 1923)

or even further back. Haig was enthusiastic about the fine type of young Padre now at work in all parts of the line. There was hardly one whom he knew he would wish changed … Both Haig and Fowke [Adjutant-General of the BEF] spoke in terms of real affection about Bishop Gwynne, and the tact and vigour of his administrative work. It is remarkable how Gwynne's simple goodness has evidently been his passport to the affection of these people, while his efficiency wins their respect.

As for Haig, he wrote of their meeting:

> We had quite a large party of clerics at lunch … The Archbishop was very pleased with all he had seen and the work the various chaplains are doing. The latter told him how much they have been helped in their work of late by *all* Commanders, "so different to the old days" whatever that may mean.
>
> I told the Archbishop that I had only two wishes to express and I had already explained them to Bishop Gwynne, and these are:
>
> *First* that the chaplains should preach to us about the objects of Great Britain in carrying on this war. We have no selfish motive, but are fighting for the good of humanity.
>
> *Secondly.* The chaplains of the Church of England must cease quarrelling amongst themselves. In the field we cannot tolerate any narrow sectarian ideas. We must all be united.
>
> The Archbishop thought his people were very united now, but possibly six months ago some were troublesome!

As Haig naturally envisaged, the chaplains' duty as morale-builders could be most effectively and vividly fulfilled through their preaching. Given that King's Regulations technically required that all soldiers attend a parade service once a week whenever practicable, on such occasions their sermons offered a clear and direct means of imbuing their listeners with the desired spirit of determination and aggression— or "enthusiasm," as Haig had put it to his army commanders at Cassel in January 1916. And apparently, in the spring and early summer of 1916, the chaplains of the BEF did not disappoint. In a private letter to King George V dated 28 June 1916 (only three days before the attacking divisions went over the top on the Somme) Haig wrote:

> Everywhere I found the troops in great spirits and full of confidence of their ability to smash the enemy when the moment for action arrives. Several officers have said to me that they never have known troops in such enthusiastic spirits … We must, I think, in fairness give a good deal of credit [for] this to the parsons. I have insisted on them preaching about the cause for which we are all fighting and encouraging the men to play their part. Some parsons too that were no use have been sent home. But, taken as a whole, they have done well and have been a very great help to us commanders.

In a further letter written upon the second anniversary of the outbreak of war, and with the Somme offensive in full swing, Haig wrote to Gwynne:

> My Dear Bishop,
> Very many thanks for your most friendly letter. I appreciate most truly your kindly appreciation of my efforts to help you in your great work. That the troops are in such splendid heart and moral [sic], and fight "without counting the cost" is largely attributable to our chaplains who have so successfully made our men realise what we are fighting for and the justice of our cause.
> Please accept my dear Bishop my heartfelt thanks for your share in this great work and believe me
> Yours very truly
> (Sgd.) D. Haig.

With the pattern set in 1916, Haig remained a staunch patron and promoter of chaplaincy in the BEF for the remainder of the war. Although, among so many different factors, their contribution to the morale of its soldiers defies isolation and quantification, Haig clearly believed that their contribution was crucial to his soldiers' performance— a not unreasonable assumption given the religious temper of contemporary Britain, the paucity of self-identifying atheists in the British Army, and the ubiquitous presence of the churches in civilian society. In an official despatch to the War Office concerning the campaigns of 1917, Haig described the value of the chaplains' work as "incalculable," and he maintained this verdict until the end of the war. Indeed, on the Sunday following the Armistice, Haig wrote an effusive message to Dr Simms, expressing his profound appreciation for the work of the army's chaplains on the Western Front:

> Strengthened as I know I and the whole Army have been by the Divine Power, I cannot adequately express the gratitude which I owe to you and all our chaplains for the grand work which they have rendered to our Cause. –And to you in particular, my dear Dr. Simms, I thank you with all my heart.

Haig's gratitude was again demonstrated on 27 June 1919, the eve of the signing of the Treaty of Versailles, when he attended a memorial service in Westminster Abbey for those Anglican clergy who had served and died as chaplains. On being thanked in the vestry for his attendance by Bishop Ryle, the Dean of Westminster, Haig simply answered "I could not do less." However, such feelings of esteem were not always mutual, and not on the grounds that some of his chaplains were beginning to perceive Haig as a callous butcher. On the contrary, and for one of them at least, peace had not been won with the single-minded vigour they had been instilling for nearly three years. Wounded towards the end of the war on the Western Front, Henry Day, a Jesuit priest serving with the 1st Division, was lying in a London hospital when news of the Armistice broke. Significantly, he felt a strong sense of "disappointment," because he believed that "the peace was premature," an opinion he voiced in a widely-reported speech in Manchester some weeks later. Subsequently, and at a civic reception to mark Haig's investiture with the freedom of the city in March 1919, Day was snubbed by Haig after being introduced to him as "the padre who denounced the Armistice."

Day's case notwithstanding, Haig's appreciation for his loyal chaplains helped ensure a slew of post-war honours, to say nothing of hundreds of wartime decorations including two Victoria Crosses. Duncan was made an Officer of the Order of the British Empire in 1919 and, as Simms recognised, his own CB reflected his standing with Haig and served as "an expression of our great chief's approval of the work of our Chaplains in the Field." There were further honours of a different kind for George S. Duncan, who hankered for a return to academic life. The Chair of Biblical Criticism having fallen vacant at St Andrews in 1916, Duncan was appointed to the post in the summer of 1919. By this time, Haig was Rector of the university, but he was keen to disclaim any personal influence in Duncan's appointment, insisting that "It was your own worth, and hard work which got you the place. And I well know that no better man could have been found if one searched the whole world through, than yourself for the job." While it is hard to conceive that Duncan's appointment owed nothing to his well-known connections with Haig, it is clear that Haig still saw himself in Duncan's debt, writing to him in 1921: "I can truly say you were a great help to me, when I was C. in C., in putting things into proper perspective on the Sundays. But I had a hard trial before I came across you at St Omer."

Haig and the YMCA

If Haig revolutionised the role of the British Army chaplain from 1916 onwards, his support for the expansive, wartime army work of the pan-Protestant YMCA (Young Men's Christian Association) was more in keeping with established precedent. From the 1860s, in the aftermath of the Crimean War and the Indian Mutiny, the British Army had become a major mission field for the British churches, and in consequence a host of "soldiers' homes" had been established in garrison towns across the Empire in the 50 years before the outbreak of war. Often enjoying the high-profile sponsorship of key military figures (Garnet Wolseley, for example, had been a key supporter of Wesleyan soldiers' homes in Ireland), these homes typically offered not only salvation but also wholesome recreation, non-alcoholic refreshments, and (above all) a proper steer for the morally vulnerable young men who made up the greater part of the Army's rank and file. Closely involved in this army work was an auxiliary body of the YMCA, namely the Soldiers' Christian Association, whose representatives took the work of the soldiers' homes into the field (or, more properly, onto the veldt) during the South African War of 1899–1902. Furthermore, in the form of Talbot House, which was opened in Poperinghe, at the base of the Ypres Salient, in the winter of 1915–16, these soldiers' homes found a new iteration on the Western Front. Not coincidentally, the

Anglican chaplain and eponymous founder of Talbot House, Neville Talbot, a son of the Bishop of Winchester, had served as an infantry officer before taking holy orders.

However, more than a year before Talbot House opened for business, the YMCA had begun its work in the French bases of the BEF, an enterprise which extended its work in the burgeoning home camps of the British Army. Increasingly conceived as a Christian, civilising and philanthropic service to the nation-in-arms, rather than as an explicitly evangelistic effort to win lost souls, the varied hut and marquee work of the YMCA no doubt appealed to Haig's sense of piety, practicality, ecumenism and paternalism. Significantly, and as commander of First Army, Haig was the first senior commander to sanction the extension of YMCA (or "Red Triangle") work into the forward areas of the BEF. The timing of this development, namely July 1915, was revealing in itself. The regular and Territorial divisions of the First Army had recently participated in three major – if unsuccessful – offensives at Neuve Chapelle (10–13 March); Aubers Ridge (9 May), and Festubert (15–25 May). Duly reinforced by several divisions of volunteers from Lord Kitchener's New Army, which began to arrive that May, the First Army was earmarked to undertake a fourth and much larger offensive at Loos in September. Significantly, these new arrivals, the archetypal citizen soldiers of the First World War, would play a major role in the fighting at Loos and it seems quite probable that the opening of Red Triangle centres in the First Army area was partly intended to ease their transition to front-line conditions by maintaining the amenities to which they had already become accustomed. The YMCA's First Army work began in a deserted convent at Aire, then home to army headquarters, in July 1915. As J.H. Hunt, the YMCA secretary responsible, reported to Oliver McCowen, the YMCA's senior official on the Western Front:

> You will be pleased to know that the work here is still being maintained success-fully – there are no signs of a re-action. The rooms are packed every night … After the Church Parade on Sunday Sir Douglas Haig, Gen. [Percy] Hobbs [the Deputy-Adjutant and Quartermaster-General] and the Staff came in. Sir Douglas was intensely pleased and with a hearty handshake wished us all success.

As Commander-in-Chief, Haig continued to evince his wholehearted support for the YMCA, sympathy that may have been strengthened by the fact that Lady Haig had become a steadfast worker at a YMCA officers' hostel in London. In April 1917, at the height of the Battle of Arras, Haig endorsed the expanding work of the YMCA by visiting some of its centres near the front line. As the YMCA's *Red Triangle* journal reported:

> A most encouraging incident to our workers was the unexpected visit to two of our centres during this period of the Commander-in-Chief himself. Sir Douglas Haig found time to chat with our men for several minutes, complimented them very warmly on the work they were doing, and expressed the hope that it might be continued.

In a meeting with Oliver McCowen that October, Haig pledged his continued support for the YMCA, McCowen noting how "He was extremely busy, but spoke most sympathetically and gratefully about our work [and] promised to help us in any way he can." Finally, in April 1919, and on his return to England, Haig paid a warm tribute to the Association's war work, which at that time represented the greatest philanthropic effort mounted by British civilian society:

> The conclusion of my period of command in France provides a fitting occasion on which to renew the warm expression of my gratitude to the Y.M.C.A. for the splendid work carried out by their organization during more than four years among the troops serving under me. No difficulties or dangers have been too great for the Y.M.C.A. to overcome in their efforts to provide for the comfort, entertainment and recreation of the men. The value of their work has been inestimable, and I feel confident that it has been deeply appreciated by all ranks.

However, and as with the case of the chaplains of the BEF, this support was by no means simply one way. A key strand of the evolving educational work of the YMCA was the despatch of a host of visiting civilian lecturers to France and Belgium, many of whom possessed real force and charisma. Among the more compelling speakers was Dr John Kelman of the United Free Church, then minister of St George's Church, Edinburgh. In January 1917, McCowen noted that Kelman was having "a magnificent time in the Second Army." That October, and now released by his presbytery for a four-month tour of the Western Front, Kelman worked his magic in Third Army as well. According to another YMCA official, R.G. MacDonald:

> [I]n fourteen days he addressed thirty meetings with an audience averaging from five hundred to six hundred officers and men in each [and] in all he spoke to sixty to eighty Generals, some hundred Staff Officers, one thousand five hundred to two thousand Officers and from anything like twelve thousand to fifteen thousand men. In doing so he aroused the greatest enthusiasm and kindled to a flame the old ideas which were beginning to burn very low for many. Very many officers and men alike said how great an inspiration he had been and how great a tragedy it would be if his mission to the Army in the field were interrupted or ended.

Kelman also made a deep impression on his fellow Scot and Presbyterian, Sir Douglas Haig, and it was by dint of Kelman's efforts that McCowen was able to secure an interview with Haig in October 1917, at the very height of the Third Battle of Ypres.

Appraisals

Haig's obvious but understated faith occasioned some favourable comment at the end of the war. The military correspondent of the influential *Westminster Gazette*, for example, noted that:

> Sir Douglas Haig is a Scotsman, and the Scotsman commonly is brought up in a robust faith ... the influence gives a sense of responsibility; the sense of responsibility makes a man reliable; the reliableness makes him useful ... And the trait leads a man to think and judge for himself, so that he is not buffeted about by every waft of opinion ... On a tough job he has at least double the chance of sticking it out.

As we have seen, subsequent historians have been less sure. A century after the Armistice, the controversy over Sir Douglas Haig's command of British (and British Empire) operations on the Western Front shows little sign of abating. However, whether one ultimately belongs to Haig's persistent band of detractors, or to his growing body of defenders, one thing is clear: Haig's religious faith sustained him as an individual and fundamentally shaped his approach to his military responsibilities.

Setting aside the interminably vexed question of the competence, or otherwise, of his specific judgements as a general, some key observations must be made of the way in which religion affected Haig's exercise of command – an issue that can be readily misunderstood. Firstly, Haig's uncomplicated religious convictions were built on deep personal foundations, and his religiosity as Commander-in-Chief of the BEF was by no means a recent and sudden growth, still less an ignoble manifestation of lifebelt religion. Secondly, such convictions were in no sense an eccentric personal foible. Haig's religious beliefs were quite typical of his generation of British Army officers, and had clear parallels among the senior commanders of other Allied armies – as, indeed, did his close relationship with his *de facto* personal chaplain, George S. Duncan. They were, moreover, comparable to those of President Woodrow Wilson and were evident among British, American, and other Allied commanders during the Second World War – as the examples of Montgomery, Alanbrooke, Marshall, Patton, MacArthur and de Gaulle (among many others) serve to illustrate. Thirdly, the consolation and inspiration that Haig derived from his faith, and from his belief in the hand of providence guiding and guaranteeing the successful outcome of the war, seems to have been operationalised in his dealings with British Army chaplains, whose role he transformed in 1916, and who went on to play a significant part in maintaining the morale of his armies. Fourthly, Haig's rather admirable sympathy with a practical and ecumenical expression of Christianity and Christian service led him to be the principal supporter and facilitator of YMCA work on the Western Front. While the colossal efforts of this organisation on behalf of the bodily, intellectual and spiritual needs of British and Empire soldiers have been unjustly relegated to the footnotes of British military history, in this case Haig's active sympathy made an enormous practical and

The Haig Memorial in St Columba's Church. (St Columba's Church of Scotland)

positive difference to the millions of British and Empire soldiers under his command. Whether Haig as a man, a commander, or as a Christian, appeals to the sensibilities of early 21st century British society, there can be no doubt as to the massive significance of his religious faith for both his contemporaries and subordinates.

Epilogue: The Place Whereon I Stand is Holy Ground

At 0510 hours, in a railway siding in Compiègne, in General Foch's private train, the Armistice was signed – bringing an end to the hostilities of the First World War; agreement that, at the 11th hour of the 11th day of the 11th month, the guns would fall silent; an end to 1,568 days of fighting, the devastation of war and the incomprehensible casualty figures. There was fighting up to the last moments. Lieutenant Colonel Reginald Haine of the Honourable Artillery Company (HAC) remarked: "It wasn't like London, where they all got drunk of course. No, it wasn't like that, it was all very quiet. You were so dazed you just didn't realise that you could stand up straight and not be shot," (quoted in Max Arthur's *Forgotten Voices of the Great War*).

Captain Bob Gorrie, formerly of the Scottish Horse and then the Royal Artillery, recorded in his war diary for Sunday 10 November 1918: "Trotted off to Church of Scotland Church at Sloane Square with Hambo on his crutches – quite good service … " He was more forthcoming about the events of the next day, in a letter to his mother, dated 13 November 1918.

> It wasn't till the morning that we got the great news and it was our splendid luck that we were trundling up Victoria Street on the top of a bus when the rockets and the salvoes went off – and then we were sure. It was a scene that neither of us will forget. Victoria Street was looking more douce and respectably business-like than usual – as if the subduedness of war had come to stay for years – when of a sudden the maroons and guns fired with a reverberating 'boom.' People seemed to stop and think for a moment then a joyous light of devout thankfulness shone on everyone's face, and as if some superman Pied Piper piped into the city, the doors and windows opened and the street filled with hatless and coatless folks.
>
> I've a hazy sort of idea that I found myself standing on the front seat of that long-suffering bus uttering elephantine roars and the whole street seemed to take the cue. From all over the city one could hear an ever-increasing roar as the crowd found its voice and by the time we reached Trafalgar Square the flags were fluttering out at all the windows and the great square was thronged with cheering crowds.

A fellow officer, a subaltern in the Fusiliers:

> spotted an urchin armed with a bugle in the crowd below us, so we hailed him
> up and installed him as a figurehead on our bus-top. He did yeoman service, that
> laddie, and I really thought once that he'd suddenly deflate and become a limp
> corpse – but he didn't, and we carried on trundling around the city – down the
> Strand and Fleet Street and back again to Trafalgar Square with the street filling
> faster and noisier … There was something so spontaneous about the cheering and
> the smiles on that memorable Monday morning, there was such heartfelt relief
> and a sudden lifting of the awful load that it seemed almost worth a four years'
> war to have the joy of finishing it.
>
> *Diaries and Letters of a Frontline Soldier*, R.M. Gorrie

The long years of war had brought a yearning for peace. By June 1917 the description
of a St Columba's church parade for the Cadet Corps commented on the smartness of
their turn-out but also the thoughts of their observers, "no doubt praying that the war
would be over before they reached the military age." In November of the same year a
letter of thanks was placed in the Church Magazine "I sincerely trust your good works
may not be long required. We all wish it an end, and are longing for the day when
we can resume our peaceful occupations." In a "Prayer in Time of War" (*St Columba's
Church Magazine*, June 1918), there is the appeal to the Almighty: "O Father, may this
war be mankind's last appeal to force." The "war to end all wars" would, of course,
prove a vain hope. As early as November 1918 the magazine was quoting the minister:
"We have passed through the major terrors and risks of war; let us beware lest we
succumb to the subtler dangers of imagined peace." A remark followed by the rhetor-
ical question: "The last war? Only if we can say, the 'last wickedness.'"

Though hostilities ended in November 1918 the hospitality offered to troops at St
Columba's continued until October 1919, in recognition of the continuing demands
upon soldiers.

> To help men forget the war is one of our chief aims in St Columba's Hall; polit-
> ical and military problems are kept far away. The love of country, the love of
> music and the love of home gives the atmosphere; and Religion the blessing.
>
> *St Columba's Church Magazine*, February 1918

While the hardships of active duty subsided, the consequences and repercussions of
war, seen and unseen, would continue for years to come. Mrs W.M. MacLeod, one of
the central characters among the Scots in Great War London who had done so much
to galvanise the hospitality of St Columba's during the war years, was lauded on her
death for continuing her care work for years after the war had ended.

> When the War was over, and the zeal of nineteen out of twenty war workers
> throughout the country waxed cold, and whilst ex-Service men hidden away in

chronic disablement became largely forgotten – when the private motor cars that were to be had by the score during the War, and the singers and entertainers innumerable, soon became hard to find – Mrs Macleod gave herself throughout these whole ten years to redoubled efforts on behalf of the wounded and permanently disabled in the Hospitals and elsewhere in and around London.

The consequences and damage of war are both visible and invisible, its wounds both physical and spiritual. Well before the establishment of Armistice Day, its annual Silence, or the services on Remembrance Sunday, the need to come together to honour and mourn loved ones was evident. In June 1918 St Columba's held a commemoration service for "soldiers and sailors of Scottish origin or connection belonging to the British Dominions and the United States of America, who have fallen in the war." It was recorded: "Never, probably in any church, have so many Scots, from so many scattered parts of the globe, joined together in common worship." The congregation that day included Boer soldiers, who worshipped under the window erected to the memory of the London Scots who had fallen in the South African War less than two decades earlier – surely "a dramatic note of reconciliation." In time, the church on Pont Street would play a significant role in the remembering of the fallen of the London Scottish Regiment, the London Scottish Football Club and The Caledonian Club, amongst others.

In those war and early post-war years, one can only imagine the atmosphere of such occasions. At another service of commemoration in October 1918 proposed by the Federated Council of Scottish Associations in London, for members of the Scottish community who had died in the war, the minister Dr Fleming opened his address:

> Never have I felt as I do this afternoon that the place whereon I stand is holy ground. For I know what has brought the majority of you here; and your sacred sorrow would have consecrated this building in which we are met, even had it been a hitherto unconsecrated place.

Such services and subsequent acts of remembrance, appear characterised by considerations of duty, sacrifice, the justice of the cause and service to Crown, to Country and to God. This was not just pulpit talk. By December 1918 a mother whose son had been killed was quoted in the *St Columba's Church Magazine*: "I can only hope to grope my way through the dark by the light of his own beautiful conception of duty and courage."

It may be beyond our reach, to fully comprehend the mind-set and motivations of an earlier generation. Their alignment of Crown, Country and God is not an easy one for contemporaries to grasp. One might hazard that after the words, however fine, stirring, or indeed appropriate, it was the power of music and silence that gave the most profound voice to lament – just as it does today. In April 1918 there appeared the notice: "Our church is open every week day. In its silence there is the opportunity for recollectedness and the medicine of quiet."

The tapestry of faith, duty, service and loyalty to Crown and Country, finds clearest expression in the life and death of Earl Haig. His own faith and the support he received from his personal chaplain, Reverend George Duncan, is well attributed. His post-war years were preoccupied with the care of his former soldiers, via the establishment of the British Legion and the growth of the Poppy Appeal. The Field Marshal

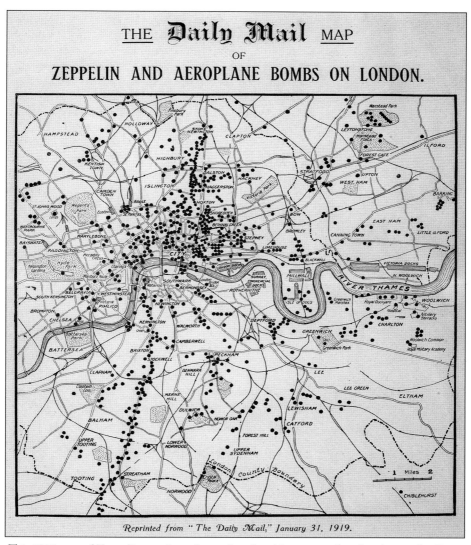

THE **Daily Mail** MAP
OF
ZEPPELIN AND AEROPLANE BOMBS ON LONDON.

Reprinted from " The Daily Mail," January 31, 1919.

This 1919 map of Zeppelin attacks and aeroplane bombings across London during the Great War illustrates how the Home Front could not escape direct experience of the conflict.
(London Metropolitan Archives, City of London)

died in 1928 and the arrangements for his funeral and the crowds that attended make it plain that this was not a "donkey who had led lions," but a saluted leader; there is no hint of the vilification or wretched reputation that would emerge later. This was a grateful nation.

His body lay in St Columba's for three days while mourners processed past. The *London Scottish Regimental Gazette* carried the reflections of one of the sentries who had formed part of the honour guard:

> Whilst on guard in the Church you were truly alone with your own thoughts. With head bowed and standing still for twenty minutes, what were one's impressions? Feet, yes, all one could see were feet – feet – feet, bringing our thoughts back to the times of strife in France. Many of the same feet that trudged the mud of Flanders – under the orders of "Duggie Haig," or the Chief, as he was invariably called – were now shuffling slowly and reverently past the bier of the Chief. There were men, women and children of every walk of life, high and low, rich and poor, in the Church. If a sentry looked out of the corner of his eye – and no

Earl Haig's coffin at St Columba's Church of Scotland in 1928.
(St Columba's Church of Scotland)

one could blame him for doing so – he saw tears and honest grief – yes, individual grief in many eyes.

St Columba's Church Magazine, April 1928

From St Columba's, Haig's coffin was processed to Westminster Abbey; Dr Fleming and the Rev. Duncan part of the escort. Following his state funeral, the body was transported by train to Scotland. A further service was held at St Giles, Edinburgh, before eventual burial in the ruins of Dryburgh Abbey.

In a statement issued by Dr Fleming he referred to his late elder as being known as "the greatest soldier of our time – but we will remember chiefly the dear friend, the humble fellow-worshipper, the honoured office-bearer." Of St Columba's, Fleming recounted what strength Haig found:

in this House of Prayer for his gigantic task; and also, how at Headquarters in France, the faithful ministry, counsel and friendship of his Presbyterian Chaplain, now Professor George Duncan of St Andrews, were an unfailing support and solace to him in many a burdened and anxious hour. If he was less frequently with us in later years, it was largely because he was ceaselessly engaged at the dedication of War Memorials at home, in the Dominions and abroad, and above all in the organisation, through the length and breadth of the country, of means of providing for the necessities of his wounded and impoverished soldiers, and of the dependents of the fallen. Day by day, year by year, the care of his old comrades in arms became his absorbing thought. It might almost be said that latterly he cared for nothing else. And now the British Legion – that vast organisation of compassion, cheer and helpfulness – is left without its chief. It was the greatest piece of staff work that even Lord Haig achieved; it was at the Headquarters of the Legion that he made himself Field-Marshal for the Prince of Peace and Pity. And thus, he won the double title alike of great servant of the King and of the King of Kings.

We mourn him proudly; we shall try to become heirs of his spirit. I know well, from many a conversation, what that spirit was. It was that of the calm, intrepid, industrious pursuit of Duty. It was the resolve to do his best and leave with tranquillity the rest to God. It was to bear despite and frustration with Christian patience and without resentment. It was to love God, his country and his King above all things, and his humblest fellow-soldier as himself. So lived, and so died, the greatest and humblest gentleman I ever knew. He lived without fear and without reproach. He died, coveting no posthumous honours. He has left to the Church, the nation and the Empire the double legacy of his great example, and the care of the soldiers who were his dear solicitude to his latest breath.

A century on from the "war to end all wars," Scottish organisations continue to flourish in London. The congregations of St Columba's and Crown Court uphold the traditions of hospitality to guests through congregational lunches and winter night shelters for the homeless. ScotsCare and the Royal Caledonian Education Trust support those in need. The Caledonian Club, the Caledonian Society and the Burns Club promote Scottish culture and entertainment in the capital. The Scots Guards and London Scottish Regiment (which still has an impressive parade of Pipes and Drums from the regimental HQ ahead of the annual Remembrance Sunday service at St Columba's) continue to add new chapters to their long and proud histories. London Scottish FC remains a club providing rugby for both Scots and others, from the elite end of the game down to five-year-old boys and girls on a Sunday morning.

New threads linking the stories of Scots in Great War London to wider Scottish society are still emerging. Their resonance with 21st century life has been made clear with the centenary commemorations. On 24 November 2017 Lieutenant Harry Graves was remembered by pupils of Perth Academy, his former school. It was exactly 100 years after his death from wounds sustained during the Battle of Cambrai which had been reported in the *St Columba's Church Magazine*. The school had organised an ambitious "Flowers of the Forest" project to commemorate the 168 former pupils who lost their lives in the First World War. Biographical details on each were gathered and the anniversaries of their deaths marked.

At that ceremony was Sheila Macgregor from Dunblane, the great niece of Lieutenant Harry Graves and his sister Phyllis. Mrs Macgregor and her family have done extensive research on them and other relatives. But they did not have much information about their involvement, as noted earlier, in the life of St Columba's in London. Phyllis Graves later married Rev. Robin Scott who became the minister at St Columba's. But Mrs Macgregor was not aware of the reference in the St Columba's magazine in 1917 or the fact noted there that Phyllis lost both her brother and a fiancé in the war. She got in touch after reading a newspaper article on the work for this book. It is a simple illustration of why the life of Scots in London in those wartime years continues to echo.

Good Company and the Weaving of Threads

This commemorative volume, *Scots in Great War London*, began with a summoning of ancestors in a place of presence, memory and prayer – the "good company" of the London Scottish Regimental Chapel, in St Columba's, Pont Street. And via one set of objects and one family story, let us finish where we began.

In the *St Columba's Church Magazine* of March 1915 there is the poignant account of a celebration of communion, or "Lord's Supper," on the Western Front, on the eve of an attack. Its author was Rev. Lauchlan Maclean Watt, a minister of the Church of Scotland and at the time chaplain to the Gordon Highlanders. Maclean Watt was born at Grantown-on-Spey, Morayshire, although his mother was a native of Skye. Educated at Edinburgh University (MA, BD), he was ordained a minister in the Church of Scotland in 1897.

He would serve in various Scottish parishes, including as minister of Glasgow Cathedral (1923–1944) and as Moderator of the General Assembly of the Church of Scotland (1933). He was a prolific author in prose and verse, on folk-lore, history and antiquities, especially Celtic and Gaelic.

In early 1915 he described the following incident:

> Just as I was about to pass on to another place a couple of soldiers of the Black Watch came round the corner. They touched their bonnets and said: "We're going off to the front tonight, sir, and we thought we'd like to have the sacrament before we go. Can you give it to us?" "How many?" I asked. "Oh, maybe sixteen," was the reply. "Well" I answered "at six o'clock in the shed next to this one, be present with your friends." I prepared the place that was for some of them the room of the Last Supper. A tablecloth borrowed from the officers' mess and a little wine from the same source helped our preparations. A notice on the door (ignored!) to keep the room for its temporary designated purpose.

The chaplain recounted that some years previously while minister of St Stephen's, Edinburgh, it was his practice to take communion to the house-bound, be they elderly or sick, "so linking the lonely and setting the solitary in families." In 1912 the Senior Girls' Bible Study Class had presented their minister with a small communion set to aid this part of his ministry. This was the set he would now use with the soldiers, on their way to the Front.

> The men began to gather and sat there reverently as though the dim, little, draughty hut were the chancel of some great cathedral, holy with the deepest memories of Christian generations. "You might wait" said one. "The Camerons and Seaforths may be able to come." So we waited – a hushed and solemn waiting. And at length the others came, stepping softly into the place; and with them comrades who explained that, though they were of a different country and a different church belief, they yet desired to share in the act of worship, preparatory to celebration.
>
> At length about one hundred and twenty were there and we began. They sang the twenty third Psalm – the Lord is my Shepherd – so familiar to many, bringing tears to the eyes of some. It only needed the simplest words to seal that sacrament. And next morning in that grey light, the men who had been touched by the thought of home and the dear ones there … were marching off to grip the very hand of death, in sacrifice, like Christ's, for others.

There is a footnote to all this. In November 2015, the grandson of that wartime padre, gifted his grandfather's immaculately preserved communion set to St Columba's. It bears the original inscription:

Presented to the Revd Lauchlan MacLean Watt BD
By the members of the Senior Girls' Bible Class
Of St Stephen's Parish Church, Edinburgh
In grateful acknowledgement of his
Thought and care for the sick and aged
Easter 1912

The paten (tray for the bread) bears a later addition: "France 1915."

A few days after receiving the communion set, the minister was able to visit a member of the congregation, Mrs Anne Winternitz, then in her 90s. Nine decades earlier, aged three, she had asked Reverend MacLean Watt to marry her! At the time, he was minister to and friend of Anne's parents. Twenty years after that precocious asking, Anne wrote to inform her parents' friend, that she was now actually engaged. Maclean Watt replied with hearty congratulations, but added that he would be contacting his lawyers for breach of promise!

At the end of the visit, Anne and her minister, shared communion. For their bread and wine, they used the same vessels – cup and plate – that had offered comfort to troops a hundred years earlier. It was the completion of one very particular circle. A month later, the same communion set was used in the London Scottish Chapel on Christmas morning. Quite by chance, members of Anne's family were in the congregation that day. Place and people, family and faith; things past, things to come; *Scots in Great War London* and the Scots of London today, continuing to weave their patterns into the fabric of this remarkable city. Long may that continue.

Appendix: Federated Council of Scottish Associations in London, Annual Report 1920

In presenting the Fifth Annual Report I feel sure that you will all agree that it is a fitting time to put on record our profound admiration for all units of His Majesty's fighting forces for their splendid heroism and self-sacrifice which have culminated in such a marked victory for freedom and civilisation. To all arms of HM services we offer our heartfelt thanks, and salute the memory of our Heroic Dead; we owe them all a debt which we can never repay, and their memory must for ever be held in reverence.

It is some satisfaction to us to know that through all the long strain we have been able to ameliorate the condition of the soldiers of our Scottish regiments by supplying much needed comforts. We now know how great the need was, and that it was by the consistent help of enthusiastic contributors that we were never left without the means of supplying requisitions.

The Federated Council was called into being to do what was possible for our Scottish fighting forces, and also to look after the interests of Scottish organisations where these could be directed into channels of service, and we have a right to claim that the combined societies were able to do work which, without co-operation, would have been impossible.

Individual efforts were hopeless as they usually meant that some small units got too many comforts while the larger numbers had to go without, and it was only by a proper system of supervision that overlapping and

John Douglas, honorary secretary of the Caledonian Society and governor of the Corporation was chairman of the Federated Council of Scottish Associations, continuing what had been started "in a small way" at the Corporation at the outbreak of the Great War. (Caledonian Society of London)

waste was prevented. From the start our work was carried on through commanding officers and others equally responsible and so satisfactory was our system that we were the only organisation in London, apart for Regimental Committees, that received official sanction to deal direct with the various Scottish regiments in the field. Only once did we come into adverse contact with the Director-General of Voluntary Organisations, when some bales of comforts destined for Salonika were stooped at Devonport. The delivery was urgent as our men were suffering from extreme cold, and we had to work quickly but it was satisfactory to know that within 24 hours the embargo was removed and the bales were loaded on board the transport for which they were intended.

We refused to join the "Pool" and allow the comforts meant for Scottish regiments to be distributed to all and sundry and, because of this, our regular workers were not allowed to have war-workers badges, but the work went on and in spite of the fact that our workers knew that there would be no badges, and no rewards, their desire to help our Scottish soldiers provided sufficient incentive and, as time went on, the work increased rather than diminished.

The work which we took in hand in October 1914 was in a measure only taking over what had been begun in a small way by the Royal Scottish Corporation, and the policy of getting the various Scottish associations in London to co-operate proved eminently successful. We received help from many organisations in London and the provinces, and also overseas, and it is a proud satisfaction that a large amount of assistance came from English friends who admired the fighting prowess of the Scots. Many church guilds and schools contributed, and we can never forget the magnificent comradeship which we encountered on every hand.

Early in our work we received valuable help from Queen Mary's Needlework Guild, The Queen's Work for Women Fund, The Scottish Society of Edinburgh, the Women's Voluntary Aid, British Red Cross and the Daily Sketch Fund which enabled us to meet requisitions that could not otherwise have been met, and from the start we had contributions of money and goods from many parts of Scotland, England, Wales, Ireland, Canada, United States of America, South Africa, India, Malay States etc. We also had a gratifying contribution of 2000 pairs of socks and a sum of money from the St Andrew Society of the River Plate.

The number of articles, or pairs of articles, which we were able to distribute from start to finish was 75,116, including 37,619 pairs of socks. The general articles included shirts, mufflers, mittens, gloves, hose tops, helmets, coats, towels, bandages, medical comforts, soup squares, pipes, tobacco, cigarettes, soap, games, sets of bagpipes and other musical instruments, books etc. We were also asked in several instances to purchase football accessories and other articles. In some cases we contributed towards the cost of these special lines but, speaking generally, we only acted as buying agents and the officers and men paid for the articles which we procured for them.

Our organisation was recognised as working on good business lines, with a reputation for getting things done, and some Regimental Committees, such as Lady Mansfield's workers for the Black Watch, asked us to undertake the distribution of their comforts to their own battalions.

We were fortunate in having the help of Messrs Pettigrew & Stephens Ltd of Sauchiehall Street, Glasgow as our representatives in Scotland, and we are indebted to them for handling and distributing Scottish consignments free of charge. We also had the advantage of all the main consignments being handled at Douglas Wharf, Putney free of charge. In case of any misapprehension, it may be stated that because we were not connected with the "Pool," carriage had to be paid to the various ports, but none of these charges came against the funds.

We now have 137 pairs of socks in hand, and it is proposed to hand these over to the Royal Scottish Corporation to distribute, and I feel sure you will agree that we can trust Mr Moncrieff to put them out to deserving recipients.

In the early days of the war the Council took a keen interest in the recruiting for the London Scottish, and a memorable meeting of the leading Scots in London, convened by the Federated Council with the Secretary for Scotland in the Chair, took place on 4th November 1915 at the Royal Scottish Corporation to further the interests of the famous regiment. The influence of the Federated Council was considerable, and it was found possible not only to complete the second and form a third battalion, but many of the recruits had to be drafted to other Scottish regiments. It may interest you to know that the records show that over 10,000 passed through the Regiment. Of these, 1380 were killed, 4800 wounded and 115 made prisoners of war. Something like 2000 commissions were granted to men who were serving, and the influence of the London Scottish was thus extended to many other regiments.

On 7th December 1915 we started sending parcels to prisoners of war but when the Central Committee was formed, it relieved us for a time. At the annual meeting held in October 1917, a warning note had to be struck in consequence of the information which had been received at first hand from Scottish prisoners of war who had returned to this country. Each association was asked to support the Regimental Committees by undertaking to provide part of the cost for food for individual prisoners of war and a gratifying response was made to the appeal. The expenditure of the Council in the last year of the war rose to over £150 per month, but so well had the scheme been taken up that at the date of the signing of the Armistice, the rate of expenditure was guaranteed for another six months. We got into direct communication with the senior officers at many of the camps with a view to adopting lonely Scottish soldiers but found that the Regimental Committees had as full information as it was possible to get, and our distribution was done through the various committees.

We arranged with the Bureau de Secours at Berne, Switzerland to supply bread to the prisoners of war adopted by our associations, with the result that the men had the best bread in a fresh condition. Our dealings with the Berne Committee engendered absolute trust on both sides. On one occasion, eight Scottish prisoners' names came to Berne with a request for bread and the Committee at once sent what was required in the name of our Council, knowing we would honour the bill. It is impossible to speak too highly of the Berne organisation – there was nothing to surpass it in real efficiency, and their system of accounting would have been a credit to the best business establishment anywhere. When the Government took over the feeding of our prisoners and sending the food in bulk, your Executive thanked the officials at Berne for the efficient way they had carried out our requisitions, and received the following reply: "we are extremely grateful to you for your generous appreciation of our work and can assure you that it is a matter of great regret to us that we are no longer to co-operate with you under the new scheme."

In connection with this work, we were able to trace men when their anxious relatives failed to find them. One typical case may be given – a mother in Scotland had tried for six months to get some intelligence about her son. She had tried all the usual channels without success and we were appealed to as last resort. Our energetic honorary secretary, Mr Rintoul, took the matter in hand and, in a little over a fortnight the boy was located in a hospital in Germany and put into direct communication with his mother.

In many ways our organisation became known for efficient working, and even the 48th Canadians (Toronto Highlanders) asked us to act as their Regimental Committee in this country, and supervise the supplies for 221 prisoners belonging to the Regiment. It was one of the many compliments which we appreciated but in this case it was decided, after some pleasant interviews, that it was a task for a permanent organisation and not for spare time workers like ourselves.

In May 1917 it was resolved to organise a systematic visitation of wounded Scottish soldiers in London hospitals and we were greatly helped in the work by the English County Folk Visitation Society whose commissioners sent cards giving particulars of all arrivals. We had considerably over 100 visitors and the visiting was carried out over 100 hospitals in the Metropolitan area, Middlesex, Surrey, Kent and Essex. We were greatly indebted to the County Folk Society for the valuable assistance given to us and we know that they, in turn, appreciated the way we tackled each case. From a communication received from the chairman of the Society, I take the following paragraph: "I must say we greatly appreciate the magnificent way you are running Scotland, and I think I can frankly say that we have never had a case of a Scot not being visited." In all, we arranged visitors for 6,037 men.

Many instances could be given of re-unions which were arranged by our visitors where it was made possible for wives and mothers to visit their loved ones, but with such an excellent list of visitors the work was bound to be effectively done. We recall the names of Lady Haddo, Miss Maxwell, Mr and Mrs Benzies and Mr John Wallace as examples of the methodical work which was a credit to any organisation. I would also like to mention the name of Miss Morrish of Douglas Wharf who was responsible for registering full particulars, issuing cards and receiving reports from visitors. She is also entitled to much credit for the admirable way she superintended the receiving, registering and classifying of all parcels of comforts, dealing with requisitions from commanding officers and conducting correspondence with the various transport officers at the different ports.

The Council was approached by the Harry Lauder Fund Committee in Glasgow and asked to look after the interests of the Fund in London but, with so many departments already in hand, it was decided that it would be better to form a separate committee to work this fund. This was agreed to, and the Federated Council was able to form a strong committee which was the means of raising about £7,000 for the benefit of the Fund.

On 18th July 1915, under the able direction of Miss Blackwood of St Columba's Church, a magnificent organisation was started for the entertainment of Scottish soldiers passing through London on leave. It was the habit of the authorities to dump the men at Victoria Station at two o'clock on Sunday mornings and leave them to wander about the streets for 19 hours before their trains left for the north.

Dr Fleming was unfortunately ill and away from London but the moment the state of affairs was realised, an energetic band of workers led by Reverend Douglas Robertson and Mr William Robertson, an esteemed elder of St Columba's, was organised to look after the comforts of the men. The Kirk Session readily granted use of the hall, and one of the finest pieces of work done in London was the result. The men were met at the trains in the bleak early morning and escorted to the hall where a hot cup of cocoa and biscuits were served. After a wash and shave, the men were taken for a stroll in Kensington Gardens, and returned to the hall about 6:30 where the ladies had prepared a hot steaming breakfast. After breakfast, the men went to the baths for a plunge and a change of clothing and again returned to the hall where buses were waiting to take them a three hours trip through London. Members of St Columba's provided dinner; in the afternoon tea was provided in the hall and after supper the men were piped to the stations and given a hearty send off.

It is impossible to speak too highly of the magnificent work which was carried on until last month, and altogether 47,624 men passed through the hall. It was a privilege to be allowed to help in such an undertaking and your Council gave full-hearted support throughout.

The afternoons for wounded soldiers also received support of the Council and some of our individual members. Mr Moncrieff was honorary treasurer and the work was carried out from the Scots Corporation Hall. The men were taken from the various hospitals in buses and cars to the (Royal Caledonian) Schools at Bushey, private gardens in and around London and other places of interest. Entertainments of a suitable kind were provided, and the Committee had the assurance of the Hospital Authorities that the influence on the men was most marked and greatly helped towards their recovery. Altogether 13,611 men were taken out by the Committee.

In reviewing our work, we can look back with pride to the memorable Commemoration Service for sailors and soldiers of the Scottish community in London who died during the war, which was organised by the Federated Council and held at St Columba's Church on Sunday 29th September 1918. Dr Fleming's sermon was powerful and appropriate and will ever be remembered as a fitting tribute to our Glorious Dead.

I have not said much about finances as this is the province of the Honorary Treasurer but it is satisfactory to know that most of the associations contributing towards the support of prisoners of war have paid amounts remaining in their hands to the Council for the purpose of carrying on its ordinary work.

The short review of our work is sufficient to give an index of the whole-hearted support and sympathy which we have received from many organisations and individuals, and to one and all we tender our grateful thanks. Our war work is over but we can look back on it with satisfaction because we were all linked up in a comradeship which was good for ourselves, and meant a large amount of good for others.

Your Executive suggests that a Roll of Honour should be prepared on which names of outstanding individual workers will appear and, if you agree with the suggestion, the preparation of the Roll will be carried out forthwith.

The Federated Council is now respected both at home and abroad and we ought to not only maintain but increase its prestige.

Will you now allow me, as your Chairman for five years, to say how much I appreciate the honour conferred on me by electing me to such a responsible position. We have formed friendships through the Council which have been of a pleasant and lasting kind; it is a privilege which I am proud of and I am grateful to you all for the magnificent support you have given me. Let me say here and now that whoever you elect as your Chairman in future will receive as wholehearted loyalty form me as you have always shown towards myself. Officials may change, but the organisation goes on.

Fifth Annual Report of the
Federated Council of Scottish Associations in London
John Douglas, Chairman
Delivered 25 November 1920

Acknowledgements

Especial thanks must go to our authors – mostly volunteers, but all experts in their fields, and not only for writing and proof reading but for their suggestions on sourcing images and securing permissions. Similarly the editors are grateful to Justine Taylor who, with David Coughtrie, filtered the large number of images submitted and narrowed the selection down to the very best among those available in good reproductive condition; to Sheena Tait for proof-reading the first draft and for editing the bibliography into a manageable list; and to all the colleagues, friends and relations who contributed anecdotes, uncovered photographs, helped with research or proof-read and corrected individual chapters at various kitchen tables.

If only to mention a few of the deserving many, name checks are due to Jan Coughtrie, Andrew Ferguson, David Balden and Alison Davis (Caledonian Club), Sarah McFarland, Hilary Thomas and Richmond-upon-Thames Library and Archives (London Scottish FC), Neil McNair (Caledonian Society), Jen Nash of Panache Communications (Royal Caledonian Education Trust), Susan Pym and Stuart Steele (St Columba's), Shona Fleming and Scott Swinton (ScotsCare). Thanks are also due to the Army Records Society and Pen and Sword Books for permission to quote from the writings of the Rev. George Duncan. We are grateful to Earl Haig and the National Library of Scotland for permission to quote from the diaries of Sir Douglas Haig. We have also relied gratefully on the professional expertise and unfailing support of our friends at Helion, Duncan Rogers, Victoria Powell, Kim McSweeney and Leonni Ward.

Thanks are also due to those who have given permission for the use of the images, especially to Brigadier Harry Nickerson, Chairman of the Regimental Trustees, for permission to use the images in the Scots Guards chapter, Lord de Saumarez for the image of the 2nd Battalion Scots Guards marching out of the Tower of London in October 1914, to the Rennie family for the image of Paton VC MC and to the McCosh family for the image of Edward McCosh; Stefan Kraus and Sung Kwon of Polimekanos for their scans of Royal Scottish Corporation and private collection images; Debbie Mason of the World Rugby Museum for sourcing publishable copies of images, and to Jeremy Smith of the London Metropolitan Archives for his helpful guidance.

And not least, the *Scots in Great War London* team wishes to express its heartfelt thanks to HRH The Princess Royal for her enthusiastic support for the group's 2018 programme of events, and for graciously offering to write the Foreword to this book.

Paul McFarland and Hugh Pym
The Scots in Great War London group

Select Bibliography

Archival Sources:

The Archives of the Royal Caledonian Education Trust can be viewed at the London Metropolitan Archives

The Archives of the Caledonian Society of London can be viewed at the London Metropolitan Archives

The Archives of the Royal Scottish Corporation can be viewed at the Guildhall Library or the London Metropolitan Archives

Imperial War Museum: Copy Diary of Major General Sir Cecil Lowther, IWM/Documents 6388

National Army Museum (NAM): Soldiers' Effects Records, 1901–60, NAM Accession Number: 1991–02–333

National Library of Scotland (NLS): Papers of Field-Marshal Sir Douglas Haig OM, KT, GCB, GCVO, 1st Earl Haig, Acc.3155

National Records of Scotland: CH2/852 Crown Court Church Kirk Session Minutes

National Records of Scotland 1881, 1891, 1901 and 1911 Census returns

Scots Guards Archives: Officers Files for the following: Lieutenant John Callender-Brodie, Captain Colin Campbell, Major Viscount Dalrymple (later Earl of Stair), Lieutenant Guy Dawkins, Captain William Ferryman, Lieutenant Alexander Hepburne-Scott, Lieutenant The Honourable Arthur Kinnaird, Captain The Honourable Douglas Kinnaird, Lieutenant The Honourable Godfrey Macdonald, Captain The Honourable John Yarde-Buller

Scots Guards Archives: Soldiers Personal Records and Enlistment Books for the following: 3218 Sergeant Major Joseph Barwick, 4999 Private Robert Moffatt, 5632 Sergeant Alexander Garroway, 7232 Sergeant William Twohig, 7263 Sergeant George Gray, 7281 Piper William Grant, 7743 Pipe Major Andrew McIntosh, 11382 Piper Donald McArthur, 14149 Private Douglas Cuddeford, 15014 Private William McPherson, 17021 Private Stephen Graham

The National Archives:
  (TNA) ADM 188/451: Admiralty: Royal Navy Registers of Seamen's Services
  (TNA) AIR 76: Air Ministry: Department of the Master-General of Personnel: Officers' Service Records
  (TNA) RG: 1881, 1891, 1901 and 1911 Census returns
  (TNA) WO95: Official War Diaries of various units
  (TNA) WO95/1266/2: 1/14 Battalion London Regiment (London Scottish) War Diary

(TNA) WO95/2422/2: 1 Battalion Cameronians War Diary
(TNA) WO 329: War Office and Air Ministry: Service Medal and Award Rolls, First World War
(TNA) WO 363: War Office: Soldiers' Documents, First World War 'Burnt Documents'
(TNA) WO364: War Office: Soldiers' Documents from Pension Claims, First World War
(TNA) WO 372: War Office: Service Medal and Award Rolls Index, First World War

Newspapers and magazines

Dumfries and Galloway Standard and Advertiser (Dumfries, online via www.findmypast.co.uk or https://www.britishnewspaperarchive.co.uk/)
Edinburgh Evening News (Edinburgh, online via www.findmypast.co.uk or https://www.britishnewspaperarchive.co.uk/)
Local Newspapers online via www.findmypast.co.uk or https://www.britishnewspaperarchive.co.uk
Perthshire Advertiser (Perth, online via www.findmypast.co.uk or https://www.britishnewspaperarchive.co.uk/)
The Graphic (London, online via www.findmypast,co.uk or https://www.britishnewspaperarchive.co.uk/)
The London Gazette (London, online via www.thegazette.co.uk)
The London Scottish Regimental Gazette (London: various, 1914–2017)
The Northern Scot (Elgin, via http://www.northern-scot.co.uk)
The Red Triangle (London: 1917–1924)
Westminster Gazette (London, 1893–1928)
Crown Court Church Magazine (London: 1919–1922)
St. Columba's Church Magazine (London: 1914–1920)

Published Sources

Adams, R.J.Q., *Bonar Law* (London: John Murray, 1999)
Arthur, Max (comp), *Forgotten Voices of the Great War: A New History of World War I by the Men and Women Who Were There* (Guilford, Conn.: Lyons Press, 2004)
Barnes, David & Burns, Peter with Griffiths, John, *Behind the Thistle: Playing Rugby for Scotland* (Edinburgh: Birlinn, 2013)
Buchan, John; *The Thirty-Nine Steps* (Edinburgh: W Blackwood, 1915)
Calder, Jenni, *Scots in Canada* (Edinburgh: Luath Press Limited, 2007)
Cameron, George G., *The Scots Kirk in London* (Oxford: Becket Publications, 1979)
Cameron, George G., *St Columba's (Church of Scotland), Pont Street London* (London: 1980)
Clayton, Rev P.B., *Tales of Talbot House in Poperinghe & Ypres* (London: Chatto & Windus, 1919)
Clutterbuck, Colonel L.A. in association with Dooner, Colonel W.T. and Denison, Commander The Honourable C.A., *Bond Of Sacrifice: Volume I August–December 1914 and*

Volume II January–June 1915: A Biographical Record Of British Officers Who Fell In The Great War (London: Anglo-African Publishing Contractors, 1917)

Committee of the Irish National War Memorial (comp), *Ireland's Memorial Records 1914–1918* (Dublin: Maunsel and Roberts, 1923 online via www.ancestry.co.uk)

Cozzi, Sarah, "When You're a long way from home", *Canadian Military History* (Winter 2011 Volume 20, Issue 1)

Cuddeford, D.W.J., *And All For What?* (London: Heath Cranton Ltd, 1933)

DeGroot, Dr Gerard, "The Reverend George Duncan at GHQ, 1916–1918", *Military Miscellany I* (1996, Volume 12)

Dolden, A. Stuart, *Cannon Fodder: An Infantry Man's Life on the Western Front 1914–18* (London: Blandford Press, 1988)

Duff Cooper, Alfred, *Haig* (London: Faber and Faber, 1936)

Duncan, G.S., *Douglas Haig as I knew him* (London: Allen & Unwin, 1966 and Barnsley: Pen & Sword Books, 2016)

Ewart, Wilfrid, *Scots Guard* (London: Rich & Cowan Ltd, 1934)

Ewart, Wilfrid, Petre, F Loraine & Lowther, Cecil (eds), *The Scots Guards in the Great War 1914–1918* (London: John Murray, 1925)

Fraser, Graham, "World War One: The story of Scotland's rugby stars," *BBC News*, 22 December 2014, (http://www.bbc.co.uk/news/uk-scotland-30519664)

Fraser of Leckelm, Mrs, *Records of the Men of Loch Broom who fell in the European War 1914–1918* (Glasgow: The University Press, 1922, available via http://www.themenoflochbroom.com)

Galt, John, *The Radical: An Autobiography* (London: Dodo Press, 2002 see https://www.amazon.co.uk/Radical-Autobiography-Dodo-Press/dp/140993599X).

Gammie, A.A., *Dr Archibald Fleming of St Columba's* (London: James Clarke & Co, 1932)

Gorrie, Donald (comp), *R. M. Gorrie: Arras 1917–18: Diaries and Letters of a Frontline Soldier* (Edinburgh: Birlinn, 2012)

Graham, Stephen, *A Private in the Guards* (London: Macmillan & Co Ltd, 1919)

Graves, Dianne, *A Crown of Life: the World of John McCrae* (Montreal: Robin Brass Studio, 1997 and 2012)

Griffiths, John, *The Phoenix Book of International Rugby Records* (London: Phoenix House, 1987)

Headlam, Cuthbert, *History of the Guards Division in the Great War 1915–1918*, in two volumes (London: John Murray, 1924)

Hobson, Chris, *Airmen Died in the Great War 1914–1918* (London: Spink & Son Ltd, 1995)

Holmes, Richard, *Tommy: The British Soldier on the Western Front 1914–18* (London: HarperCollins, 2005)

Horn, Lieutenant Colonel Bernd, and Harris, Stephen (eds), *Warrior Chiefs: Perspectives on Canadian Military Leaders* (Toronto and Oxford: Dundurn Press, 2001)

Horne, Alistair, *The Price of Glory: Verdun 1916* (London: Penguin, 1993)

Huntly, Gordon, *The Unreturning Army* (London: Penguin Books, 2013)

Imlah, Mick, *The Lost Leader* (London: Faber and Faber, 2008)

Latham, Edward Bryan, *A Territorial Soldier's War* (Aldershot: Gale and Polden, 1967)

Leslie, Moira, "This is my life" training folder, *Royal Caledonian Education Trust* (London, 2013).

Lindsay, J.H. (ed.), *The London Scottish in the Great War* (London: London Scottish, 1926)

Lownie, Andrew, *John Buchan: The Presbyterian Cavalier* (London: Constable, 1995)

Ludendorff, Erich, *The Great War from the Siege of Liege to the Signing of the Armistice As Viewed From the Grand Headquarters of the German Army August 1914 to November 1918* (New York: Harper Brothers, 1923)

McCrery, Nigel, *Into Touch: Rugby Internationals Killed in the Great War* (Barnsley: Pen and Sword Military, 2014)

McKenzie, William J., *The Morayshire Roll of Honour. A biographical record of the men and women connected with the county who took part in the Great War, 1914–1918* (Elgin: 1921, online at https://archive.org/details/morayshirerollof1921mora)

MacLean, Norman, *Life of James Cameron Lees* (Glasgow: Gordon Hill, 1922)

MacMillan, Margaret, *The War That Ended Peace* (London: Profile, 2013).

Morris, Frank, *The First 100: A History of London Scottish Football Club* (Richmond: The London Scottish Football Club, 1978)

Moynihan, Michael (ed.), *Black Bread and Barbed Wire: Prisoners in the First World War* (London: Cooper, 1978)

Nash, Jennifer, *Caledonian Postings* (Edinburgh: Royal Caledonian Education Trust, 2017).

Newcater, John, *Old Caledonian* (Royal Caledonian Schools Trust, March 1914, June 1914, December 1914, December 1915, December 1917, June 1918, December 1919).

Newcater, John, *Report and List of Subscribers* (London: Royal Caledonian Schools, 1922)

Nicholson, G.W.L., *Official History of the Canadian Army in the First World War: Canadian Expeditionary Force 1914–1919* (Government of Canada, 1964)

Nicol, Randall, *Till The Trumpet Sounds Again: The Scots Guards 1914–1919 in Their Own Words* in two volumes (Solihull: Helion & Co Ltd, 2016)

Noble, Malcolm, "Canadian Scottish at the Regina Trench 1918", *The Caledonian* (London: The Caledonian Club, 2014)

Noble, Malcolm, *A National Institution of the Scottish Nation* (Glasgow: Connect Communications, 2015)

Noble, Malcolm, "The NLC during World War 1 (1916)", *National Liberal Club Magazine* (London: National Liberal Club, 2016).

Plaster, John, *History of Sniping and Sharpshooting* (Boulder, Colorado: Paladin Press, 2008)

Regan, D.E., *Local Government and Education* (London: George Allen and Unwin, 1977)

Reid, Col A.K., *Shoulder to Shoulder: the Glasgow Highlanders, 9th Bn. Highland Light Infantry, 1914–1918* (Glasgow: Alex Aiken, 1988)

Ruvigny et Raineval, Melville Henry Massue Marquis de, *De Ruvigny's roll of honour 1914–18: A Biographical Record of Members of His Majesty's Naval and Military Forces Who Fell in The Great War 1914–1918* (Uckfield: Naval & Military Press reprint; 2003)

Sewell, E.H.D., *The Rugby Football Internationals Roll of Honour 1914-1918* (London & Edinburgh, 1919; Uckfield: Naval & Military Press reprint, 2015)

Snape, Michael, "Archbishop Davidson's Visit to the Western Front, May 1916" in M. Barber and S.J.C. Taylor (eds), *From the Reformation to the Permissive Society: A Miscellany in Celebration of the 400th Anniversary of Lambeth Palace Library* (Church of England Record Society, 2010)

Snow, Dan, "Viewpoint: 10 big myths about World War One debunked", *BBC Magazine, 25 February 2014*, (http://www.bbc.co.uk/news/magazine-25776836)

Stewart, Timothy J., *Toronto's Fighting 75th in the Great War 1915–1919 – A Prehistory of the Toronto Scottish Regiment* (Toronto: Wilfred Laurier University Press, 2017)

Taylor, Justine, *A Cup of Kindness* (East Linton: Tuckwell Press, 2003)

Wakefield, W.A., *Rugger* (London: Longmans, Green & Co Ltd, 1928)

Walmsley, David, "1904: Bedell-Sivright pulls no punches", *Daily Telegraph*, (30 June 2005)
War Office, *Soldiers Died in the Great War, 1914–1919*, (London: Naval & Military Press comp, 1998, online version)
White, Jerry, *London in the Twentieth Century: A City and its People* (London: Vintage, 2008)
White, Jerry, *Zeppelin Nights: London in the First World War* (London: Vintage, 2015)
Wilhelm II, Emperor of Germany, trans by Thomas R. Ybarra, *The Kaiser's Memoirs*, (London: N&M Press reprint [original pub 1922])

Online Sources

A History of the Caledonian Society of London via http://www.calsoclondon.org/site_code/pages/history.html
Abercrombie, Wilson and the Battle of Jutland, Phil McGowan, 31 May 2016, https://worldrugby museumblog.wordpress.com/2016/05/31/abercrombie-wilson-and-the-battle-of-jutland-by-phil-mcgowan/
Baker, Chris, *The Long, Long Trail: the British Army in the Great War* website, www.longlongtrail.co.uk
Commonwealth War Graves Commission www.cwgc.org
Forces War Records www.forces-war-records.co.uk
Four Extraordinary Heroes https://sistercelluloid.com/2015/11/05/world-war-i/
Glasgow University *Roll of Honour*, http://www.universitystory.gla.ac.uk/ww1-intro/
Great War Forum http://1914-1918.invisionzone.com
Legg, Joanna, Parker, Graham, and Legg, David, *The Great War 1914–1918*, www.greatwar.co.uk
Library and Archives of Canada, *First World War*, http://www.bac-lac.gc.ca/eng/discover/military-heritage/first-world-war/Pages/introduction.aspx
Local Rolls of Honour online via www.archive.org
McEwen, Alistair, research on all 31 Scottish international rugby players who died in the Great War, http://news.bbc.co.uk/1/shared/bsp/hi/pdfs/18_12_14_rugbywar.pdf
Military History Forum www.militarian.com
Ministry of Defence http://www.army.mod.uk/srmedforcescovenant/education
Oxford Dictionary of National Biography Online via http://www.oxforddnb.com
Rugby from the Front, 1914–1918, Stephen Cooper, 14 July 2015, https://worldrugbymuseumblog.wordpress.com/2015/07/14/rugby-from-the-front-1914-1918/
ScotsCare www.scotscare.com
The Chronicles of the Caledonian Society of London, volumes 1839–1984, via http://www.calsoclondon.org/site_code/pages/history.html
The Gowlland Family http://www.gowlland.me.uk/
The Hollywood Battalion, James Cronan, 7 October 2014, http://blog.nationalarchives.gov.uk/blog/hollywood-battalion/
The Scottish Military Research Group http://warmemscot.s4.bizhat.com
Studies of the 1911 Census and numbers of Scots in London http://www.visionofbritain.org.uk/census/EW1911GEN/8
Historical inflation figures http://inflation.stephenmorley.org/ and http://www.bankofengland.co.uk/education/Pages/resources/inflationtools/calculator/default.aspx

Index

Index of People

Index of Places

Index of Military Units & Formations

Index of Miscellaneous & General Terms